More pre-publication
REVIEWS, COMMENTARIES, EVALUATIONS . . .

This book has something powerful for every social work practitioner—be they in research, education, policy development, or direct services."

Evelyn P. Tomaszewski, ACSW
Director, Pearl Associates
Washington, DC

" **W**hen I started reading the preface to *Building on Women's Strengths,* my immediate response was to wish that I could have been part of the University of Kansas gathering of these 12 strong women as they shared their works-in-progress. However, by publishing and thus making available their works-in-progress from that conference, the authors have given us a real gift, a book to be read and reread, savored and shared with our colleagues, students, and clients. As I read each chapter I became energized, excited, and hopeful by the challenging questions raised; I felt as if I were in the room with them, sharing visions of what we would like the world to be.

The authors' commitment to validating and building on women's strengths, to transforming how we think about reality, and to listening to a diversity of women's voices and stories are underlying themes of each chapter. Perhaps their major contribution is t. it transforming how we view the traditional public/private dichotomy; in doing so, they reconstruct how we think about child welfare, public policies for older women, programs to promote economic self-sufficiency, mental health practice, and the effect of women's employment on the family.

As women have been relegated to the private sphere, their lives have been made invisible and their voices silenced. The book closes with recognition of the interconnection between knowledge and gender, the public discourse and the individual story, the rich history of women in social work as a vision of what women can do, and the ways in which social workers can help restore the lives of women and transform their lives of oppression. In many ways, the whole book is a restoring process—constructing a different reality than that which has been imposed on women and for too long accepted; as such, it offers an agenda for fundamental change."

Nancy R. Hooyman, PhD
Dean and Professor,
University of Washington
School of Social Work

women's true equality, and the importance of the women's liberation movement place these critical issues in a wider social context and highlight the need for social change. The emphasis on women's realities and the ways in which social workers can play an active role in addressing the unfinished women's agenda make this timely book essential reading for all social workers. Practitioners, policy analysts and researchers as well as non-feminists, emerging feminists, and those fully committed to feminism have something to learn from this first-rate volume."

Mimi Abramovitz, DSW
Professor of Social Work,
Hunter College School of Social Work

The Haworth Press, Inc.

NOTES FOR PROFESSIONAL LIBRARIANS AND LIBRARY USERS

This is an original book title published by The Haworth Press, Inc. Unless otherwise noted in specific chapters with attribution, materials in this book have not been previously published elsewhere in any format or language.

CONSERVATION AND PRESERVATION NOTES

All books published by The Haworth Press, Inc. are printed on certified ph neutral, acid free book grade paper. This conforms to recommendations ensuring a book's long life without deterioration.

Building on Women's Strengths

A Social Work Agenda for the Twenty-First Century

HAWORTH Social Work Practice
Carlton E. Munson, DSW, Senior Editor

Building on Women's Strengths

A Social Work Agenda for the Twenty-First Century

Liane V. Davis, PhD
Editor

The Haworth Press
New York • London • Norwood (Australia)

The Haworth Press, Inc., 10 Alice Street, Binghamton, NY 13904-1580

Library of Congress Cataloging-in-Publication Data

Building on women's strengths : a social work agenda for the twenty-first century / Liane V. Davis, editor.
    p.   cm.
Includes bibliographical references and index.
ISBN 1-56024-863-7 (alk. paper).
1. Social work with women–United States. 2. Women–United States–Social conditions. I. Davis, Liane V.
HV1445.B85   1993
362.83'0973–dc20   93-39418
                                                                CIP

In memory of my father, Leon J. Davis, whose commitment to building on women's strengths led to the creation of a powerful and humane labor union. He was a loving and compassionate father who taught me that being out of step with those in power was the only way to assure the empowerment of those who are oppressed.

CONTENTS

ABOUT THE EDITOR

Liane V. Davis, PhD, MSW, is Associate Professor and Associate Dean at the University of Kansas School of Social Welfare. She has written extensively about women's issues, taught courses in social work practice with women, presented at national professional meetings, and been active in promoting women's reproductive rights. Dr. Davis is a past chair of the National Association of Social Workers National Committee on Women's Issues and presently serves on the Board of Directors of the Kansas chapter of the National Association of Social Workers.

CONTRIBUTORS

Brenda Crawley, MSW, PhD, is an Associate Professor at the School of Social Welfare, University of Kansas. Her writings focus on issues affecting women of color and the aging population.

Liane V. Davis, MSW, PhD, Associate Professor and Associate Dean for Academic Programs at the School of Social Welfare, University of Kansas, has published on practice and policy issues affecting women as clients and women in the social work profession.

Edith Freeman, MSW, PhD, Professor at the School of Social Welfare, University of Kansas, has published extensively on issues affecting people of color. Her most recent book, co-authored with Sadye Logan and Ruth McCoy, is *Social Work Practice with Black Families.*

Liz Gowdy, MSW, a doctoral student at the School of Social Welfare, University of Kansas, has recently completed an evaluation of the effectiveness of the Women's Employment Network. She has also written on services for lesbian clients.

Jan L. Hagen, MSW, PhD, Professor at the School of Social Welfare, University of New York at Albany, has published extensively on public welfare issues. She is presently conducting a national implementation study of the JOBS program.

Elizabeth Hutchison, MSW, PhD, Associate Professor at the School of Social Work, Virginia Commonwealth University, has published extensively in the area of child welfare practice and policy.

Joan Laird, MSW, Professor at Smith College School for Social Work, writes in the area of family work. She is the co-author with Ann Hartman of the widely used text, *Family-Centered Social Work Practice.*

Dorothy Miller, MSW, PhD, is Associate Professor in the Center for Women's Studies at Wichita State University. Her most recent publication is *Women and Social Welfare: A Feminist Analysis.*

Sue Pearlmutter, MSW, is a doctoral student at the University of Kansas School of Social Welfare where she is working on various issues relating to Kansas' implementation of the Kanwork program, the state's response to the JOBS legislation.

Barbara Simon, MSW, PhD, Associate Professor at Columbia University School of Social Work, has written on varied issues affecting women and their multiple roles as workers and caregivers.

Ann Weick, MSW, PhD, Dean and Professor at the University of Kansas School of Social Welfare, has written extensively on women's issues as well as on the philosophical underpinnings of the profession.

Janice Wood Wetzel, MSW, PhD, Dean and Professor at Adelphi University School of Social Work, writes in the area of women and mental health.

Preface

This book represents the unique collaboration of 12 strong women. We have a shared commitment to our chosen profession: social work. We have a shared commitment to discover and develop the unique strengths in the women who are and have always been the majority of clients. We also have our differences. Some of us are Caucasians, some of us are women of color. Some of us are heterosexual, some of us are lesbians. We are Catholic, Jewish, Protestant, and atheist. Some of us proudly call ourselves feminists, some of us are uncomfortable with that label.

We all came together for two days at the University of Kansas for a special experience: to engage one another in a dialogue and out of that dialogue to build a social work agenda for women for the twenty-first century. Because we are all academics we had put much thought into the papers we brought to share. But rather than be completed pillars of stone into which we had poured our fragile egos, our papers were works-in-progress. Our instructions were clear: come with an openness to share ideas and hear other voices.

None of us was fully prepared for the impact of those two days. Something different was going on, something few of us had experienced within the context of our academic lives. We knew what was different, but it took a while for us to feel free enough to express it. We were all women. While the conference was open to interested faculty, students, and community professionals, the few who joined us were almost all women. One man, a doctoral student, sat silently through a day of our meeting. He later commented, in private, that he felt he was an intruder, yet he was learning too much to leave. A second man, a faculty member, joined us briefly to hear a former colleague. But mostly we were women. As we sat and talked in the small, homey conference room nestled in the library, we became increasingly aware of our shared gender and the comfort we felt in being able to speak in our own voices without having to explain ourselves to others, without having to worry about hurting others' feelings, and without fearing that we would become invisible or be discounted if we said something too radical or too feminist. We rejoiced in being able to hear the voices of different women and were enriched by our diversity.

Throughout the two days we kept coming back to the uniqueness of the experience. We were engaged in a dialogue. This was why we had come into academia: to think, to be challenged, to expand our own parochial views. Instead, we often found ourselves in settings where people performed and most of us felt obligated to join the game. For once we were in an environment in which we could be ourselves. An important part of being ourselves was letting down the barriers we often erected between our professional, scholarly, and private selves. We talked as women to women.

But lest you get the wrong impression, we were not engaged in male-bashing. To the contrary, we were unapologetically celebrating the strengths of women, without much concern for the other gender. For those two days, some of us implicitly understood the appeal of separatism, although few of us would choose that either for our personal, political, or professional lives.

The papers in this volume were enhanced by this process. We all went home, enriched by the lively discussions, and looked anew at what we had written. In some cases, we made minor changes. In others, we wrote entirely new papers.

The papers address issues we believe central to transforming women's lives as we approach the new century. We could not address everything relevant to improving the lives of women in the twenty-first century. In fact, as we thought about it, there is little that is not revelant to improving the lives of women. In deciding who to invite, more concern was given to *who* the women were than to the specific expertise they brought. We wanted a group of women who were able to have a conversation with one another, a group of women committed to enhancing a woman's agenda rather than their own. We also wanted social workers who could speak to issues of social work practice and social policy and who understood the common ground that lay beneath them.

While many themes frame this book, two interconnected ones are central. Throughout history women have been taught to see the world through the eyes of those who are more powerful (who happen to be men), and to accept that world as *reality*. A major aspect of that world has been the definition of women as incomplete, defective, and weak. There have always been voices to challenge men's hegemony over reality making, but those voices have become louder over the past few decades. If it has achieved nothing else, the women's movement (if we can still call it that) has fueled the construction of alternative, highly credible realities. The newer realities validate the strengths that women have always had, but too often have kept hidden. The first theme of this book then is that any agenda for women must be built on their already present strengths.

Reality making extends beyond women's conception of themselves. It encompasses making sense of the world in which we all live. This dual focus on self and society is the second theme of this book.

Emily Grosholz (1988), in writing about feminist historians, asks: "Why are we feminists?" Her response reflects our hope for this book. We are feminists, she says,

> because we want to change social reality in accord with our perception of certain kinds of inequalities; and part of this change is that women take a broader, more active role in the construction of social reality. We want to criticize the world as its stands, in accord with certain moral principles, and we want people (including ourselves) to act differently in the future. (174)

This book represents our efforts as women and as social workers to actively construct a new agenda for our profession, an agenda whose aim is to redress the continuing inequalities that women face, that is built on the strengths of women, that is firmly grounded in the values of our profession, and that guides us to act differently as we enter a new century.

Liane V. Davis
University of Kansas
School of Social Welfare
Lawrence, Kansas

REFERENCE

Grosholz, E. (1988). Women, history, and practical deliberation. In *Feminist thought and the structure of knowledge,* edited by M. M. Gergen. New York: New York University Press.

Chapter 1

Why We Still Need a Woman's Agenda for Social Work

Liane V. Davis

INTRODUCTION

Social work has a unique perspective on "women's issues." From the beginning, women have been the major players on both sides of the profession: as workers and as clients. (See Vandiver 1980, for a brief "herstory" of women in social work.) We have powerful foremothers, women like Jane Addams, Bertha Reynolds, and Mary Richmond, who, from the earliest days, provided strong leadership in developing strategies to meet the needs of persons who were oppressed, most of whom were women and their children. Today, we have a professional code of ethics that provides us with an ongoing reminder of our commitment to work actively for a society in which all persons, irrespective of personal characteristics, condition, or status, have equal opportunity (NASW 1990).

And yet, despite (or perhaps because of) our roots as a profession primarily of and for women, and despite our historic commitment to equal opportunity for all persons, social work is only now recognizing the pervasiveness and persistence of discrimination against women and the damage done to women (and to society) by their systematic exclusion from society's major institutions.

The authors of this book examine some of the major social issues affecting the lives of women clients and how these issues can be addressed by both policymakers and practitioners. The individual chapters, built on the theme of "building on women's strengths," challenge the readers to look anew at major areas of women's lives and how they, as social workers, can engage in practice that is empowering for women. Understanding where we are to go in the twenty-first century and how we are to get there, however, requires knowing where we have come from. It also requires understanding where we are at present. This first chapter seeks to ground the reader in the immediate past and present of women's struggle to be included as an equal participant in U.S. society.

It begins with a brief history of twentieth-century political changes that were attempted and achieved in the fight to gain equality for women. It concludes with a more troubling discussion of the changes that are still needed if women's voices are to be heard throughout social institutions. The first section of this chapter is a discussion of political battles that touch on deep interpersonal and personal issues. The second section is a discussion of the very foundations of our knowledge and reality-making enterprise. Understanding both is necessary if we, as social workers, are to effectively participate in the future struggles to achieve equality for women.

THE WOMEN'S MOVEMENT AND POLITICAL CHANGE

It is more than a century since women first came together in any mobilized way to fight for women's rights. It took this "first wave" of feminists, as they have since been called, some 40 years to achieve their overarching goal: securing the right to vote. It was to be another 40 or so years before women once again mobilized. This "second wave" of feminists had a far broader goal, the liberation of women. Women's liberation, or "women's lib" as its critics disparagingly called the movement, conjured up, for many, images of combat-boot dykes and bra-burning hippies, as threatening to the social order as the draft card burners of the Vietnam protests. The public perception, or the media-inspired perception, was that these women wanted a social revolution and had little need or tolerance for men in their new society. Needless to say, there was much resistance to what was perceived as a call for radical action.

As with any social movement, there are multiple views of what went right and what went wrong with the women's movement.

Some perceive that women have achieved a tremendous amount since the early 1970s. They talk about the choices now open to young women, the growing numbers of women in schools of law and medicine, and the military, and the increasing involvement of men in arenas traditionally reserved for women, such as child-rearing. Others perceive that little of importance has changed. They talk about the impoverishment of women or the feminization of poverty (see Abramovitz [1991] for a stimulating discussion of how labels affect social workers' perception of issues affecting women), violence against women, single-mother families, and the glass ceiling that prevents women from rising to positions of leadership. Some perceive that feminism is no longer either a necessary or viable political philosophy (see, for example, Davidson 1988); some perceive that feminism is as necessary and as viable today as it was 100 years ago (see, for example, Davis 1991; Hawkesworth 1990).

How there can be such divergent views of where we are and where we are to go is a part of this chapter. There are two major political battles that illustrate these differing perceptions. The first centers around achieving equality under the law; the second centers around reproductive rights.

The Equal Rights Amendment: An Unfinished Story

With much hope and hoopla, both houses of Congress overwhelmingly passed the Equal Rights Amendment (ERA) in 1972 and sent it to the states where its ratification was believed likely. And yet, as we all know, the ERA failed to achieve approval by the 38 states needed for it to be enacted into law. The story of its demise provides an important lesson for future efforts for change in this country's women's agenda. It is fitting that the historical discussion begins here.

What exactly was the Equal Rights Amendment? Although the Equal Rights Amendment was the banner carried by the women's movement of the 1970s, it was not created by the second wave of feminists. It was first proposed in 1923 by the National Women's Party specifically because post-Civil War court decisions continued to hold that sex, unlike race or national origin or religion, was a legitimate basis for discrimination (Freeman 1975). The original amendment first introduced in Congress in 1923, which read: "Men and women shall have equal rights throughout the United States and every place subject to its jurisdiction," was reintroduced in various forms in almost every Congress until its final passage in 1972 (Boles 1979). The Amendment that finally passed was brief. It had three provisions:

> *Section 1.* Equality of rights under the law shall not be denied or abridged by the United States or by any State on account of sex.

> *Section 2.* The Congress shall have the power to enforce, by appropriate legislation, the provisions of this article.

> *Section 3.* This amendment shall take effect two years after the date of ratification.

To its supporters, "the ERA was to be an important but benign implement for removing the legal barriers to female equality" (Boles 1979, 7). To its opponents, it was a tool so powerful that it would undermine family life as we know it, and weaken our nation's ability to defend our country. Its demise is due, in large part, to the success of opponents in convincing state legislators of the truth of their version of the story (Boles 1979; Davis 1991).

As with much legislation, it is difficult to know exactly what its framers intended and impossible to predict how it would have been interpreted subsequently. The evidence suggests, however, that the intent of the ERA was far less revolutionary than portrayed by its opponents.

This amendment to the Constitution was designed to make it illegal to discriminate on the basis of gender just as the 14th Amendment had made it illegal to discriminate on the basis of race. According to contemporary legal scholars, the ERA was expected to affect four major arenas: education, employment, military service, and family law (Boles 1979). It was designed to eliminate all forms of discrimination against women in publicly supported schools. This included eliminating sex-discrimination from admissions and scholarship decisions and from employment policies. It was designed to eliminate gender discrimination from employment, for example, barring policies that forbade women from certain occupations just because of their gender. It was intended to enable women to join the armed forces and to obtain post-service military benefits under the same conditions as their male peers. And it was designed to eliminate gender discrimination from family law. This meant that alimony and child support provisions would be gender-neutral. Such decisions could take into account the circumstances of the individual, but not the gender of the parties (Boles 1979; Davis 1991).

Despite the opponents' claims, the original framers of the amendment did not intend that pregnant women or mothers would be drafted into the armed forces. There have always been exemptions from the draft for specific groups of persons; the ERA would have made such exemptions gender-neutral. For example, all expectant parents or custodial parents of children under the age of two could have been exempted. They did not intend to eliminate gender itself from family law. The intent was to eliminate disparities based on gender. Thus states could prohibit marriages between same sex persons as long as they applied the provisions equally to women and men. There was no intent to bar the separation of persons of different genders *under appropriate circumstances*. For example, it would be all right to have same-sex bathrooms or same-sex dormitories to assure persons the constitutional right to privacy. Nor was the law intended to prevent policies that protected women in employment as long as those policies could also be extended to men (Boles 1979; Davis 1991).

The cause of the failure of the ERA has been widely debated (see, for example, Boles 1979; Conover and Gray 1983; Davidson 1988; Davis 1991; Gelb and Palley 1987). A common belief is that the ERA failed largely because its supporters were white, middle-class, liberal women blinded to the realities of other women's lives. In their blindness they failed to see that their desire to achieve equality in the labor market was not shared by two other significant groups of women: those who enjoyed and wanted to retain their protected status as homemakers and mothers and those who, thrust by necessity into the low-paid labor market, wanted nothing more than the opportunity to come home to care for their children and families. And yet, there is evidence that feminists were not misreading public sentiment. A 1972 Roper poll had found that 49% of men and 48% of women were in favor of efforts to strengthen or change women's status in society. By 1974, 63% of men and 57% of women were in favor of such changes (Boles 1979, 52). Perhaps, the ERA's failure was due less to feminist myopia than to poor timing. Public sentiment had not yet reached the halls of the state houses (Boles, 1979). Or perhaps, while a majority of both women and men favored unspecified changes in the status of women, they were not yet ready for the radical overthrow of traditional societal and family values that the opponents of the ERA kept vividly in public view.

Gelb and Palley (1987) suggest that a major factor in women winning some battles while losing others is whether an issue is seen to produce role equity or role change.

> Role equity issues are those policies which extend rights now enjoyed by other groups (men, other minorities) to women and which appear to be relatively delineated or narrow in their implications. . . . In contrast, role change issues appear to produce change in the dependent female role of wife, mother, and homemaker, holding out the potential of greater sexual freedom and independence in a variety of contexts. (6)

While the intent of the pro-ERA forces was to give equity to women, opponents played into the fear that the entire fabric of society as we know it would be radically transformed. They portrayed a world in which women and men shared the same public restrooms and prisons, pregnant women and mothers were forced to go to war, and homosexuals could marry and adopt children. They played on women's fears that gender-neutral laws would no longer grant them alimony or custody of their children following divorce or that they would be forced to enter the labor market to share the financial burden of caring for their families even if they were married (Davis 1991). (See Crawley, Chapter 7 of this book, for a discussion of how changes in divorce laws have affected older women.) In fighting the ERA, the New Right, as it was soon to be called, developed a "pro-family" agenda that successfully energized those wanting to maintain the status quo (Conover and Gray 1983).

While the commonly held belief is that the ERA was lost by

feminists who failed to take into account the interests of women different from themselves, perhaps this is just another instance of blaming the victim. To assume that feminists lost the fight is to assume they had the power to win it. But, while women, both feminist and nonfeminist, were most audible in defining and lobbying the issues, they were largely absent where it really mattered: in the state legislatures. In the states that failed to ratify the amendment, women legislators were overwhelmingly in favor of its passage; the men were not (Davis 1991). Had women been equitably represented in the legislatures, which they were not, the ERA would have passed. A more credible view, therefore, is that the ERA was not lost by feminists, but was defeated by those who stood most to lose: the white, privileged men who cast the votes in state legislatures across the country.

Piecemeal Change Is Easier than Global Change

The ERA represented the hopes of what were labeled "liberal feminists" (see Jagger and Struhl [1978] for a discussion of the political spectrum of feminists). Liberal feminists wanted to have an equal share of the U.S. pie and believed that the way to obtain their fair share was through federal action. In their idealism, they had hoped that the ERA would lay a foundation for broad social change. But as the death of the ERA taught them, they were going to have to achieve their share of the pie little piece by little piece. And they succeeded to some extent.

Not surprisingly, many of their successes related to equality in the workplace, the most pressing concern to the millions of women who were finding themselves, both by choice and necessity, in the paid labor market. The Civil Rights Act of 1964 was a major vehicle for such change. Title VII, the Equal Employment Opportunity section of the Civil Rights Act, prohibited private employers, as well as state and local governments, from discriminating on the basis of race, color, religion, and national origin. Feminists achieved a surprising victory when gender was added to the list. The Civil Rights Act also created a new federal agency, the Equal Opportunity Employment Commission (EEOC), whose duty it was to interpret and enforce the legislation. In 1980 the EEOC took a major step when it issued guidelines making sexual harassment a form of sex discrimination covered under Title VII of the Civil Rights Act (Hazou 1990).

Other important changes also occurred. Title IX of the Education Amendments Act of 1972 prohibited any school that obtained federal monies from discriminating on the basis of gender (Gelb and Palley 1987). The Pregnancy Discrimination Act of 1978, an amendment to Title VII of the Civil Rights Act, gave guarantees to women that pregnancy would not threaten their employment, while giving them qualified guarantees that they could return to their jobs after a reasonable unpaid maternity leave (Hazou 1990).

Changes that had a profound effect on women's lives occurred in other arenas as well. For example, the Equal Credit Opportunity Act, passed in 1974, made it illegal to discriminate on the basis of gender in the granting of credit (Gelb and Palley 1982). This was vital for the economic well-being of the growing numbers of never-married and no-longer-married women.

By small steps, women were achieving some degree of equality under the law. Many of these successes can be credited to the ongoing battle for the ERA which called attention to the widespread discrimination against women (Davis 1991). As history was to reveal, however, constant vigilance was needed to maintain the successes.

Reproductive Rights: A Major Battle

Nowhere has the need for vigilance been clearer than in the ongoing battle to secure for women the right to control their own reproduction. In 1973, feminists achieved a major victory when the Supreme Court extended the right to privacy to include women's right to decide for themselves whether or not to bear a child. It is important to understand the depth of that victory.

The most unalterable difference between women and men is that women are the bearers of society's children. For society to continue, women, as a group, must continue to fulfill that function. For individual women to achieve equality with men, however, they must have the right to make their own decisions about whether and when they will reproduce and must have access to the safest, most effective, and most affordable means to carry out their decisions. For feminists, women's right to choose abortion (as well as access to safe contraceptives) makes bearing children a choice that each individual woman can make, not a social mandate that she must fulfill. When only one alternative is available and publicly supported, regardless of whether that alternative is pronatal or proabortion, the right of individual women to determine their own lives is sacrificed in the interest of the social good.

When framed in this way, the emotional energy behind the battle to maintain women's reproductive rights becomes understandable. When women are fighting to achieve equality in the classroom, equality in employment, equality under the law, it is deeply threatening to be told that, despite all these achievements, they still cannot make the most personal decision–whether or not to bear a child.

The passions (and inconsistencies) of the antichoice forces are also understandable. While their public rhetoric is about the right of the unborn children, (and while many deeply hold these beliefs), they, too, are energized by the far-reaching implications of giving women the right to control their own reproduction. George Gilder, a conservative author widely cited by the New Right, expressed their fear in his 1973 book:

> When the women demanded "control over our own bodies," they . . . were in fact invoking one of the most extreme claims of the movement. . . . For, in fact, few males have come to psychological terms with the existing birth-control technology; few recognize the extent to which it shifts the balance of sexual power in favor of women. A man quite simply cannot now father a baby unless his wife is fully and deliberately agreeable. There are few social or cultural pressures on her to conceive. (as cited in Davis 1991, 453-454)

Forcing women to bear children not only violates women's right to make their own decisions, it also seriously impedes their ability to compete equally with men in the economic realm. While the bearing, and subsequent rearing, of children is deeply rewarding, it is also very costly, especially to women. For poor women, the birth of children results in their further impoverishment as well as their continued dependence on the highly stigmatizing welfare system

(Hayes 1987). Children can be so detrimental to the career aspirations of more affluent women that one prominent business consultant suggested, in a much-criticized article, that the corporate world needed to develop a "Mommy" track (Schwartz 1989). It is not difficult to see how legislating women's right to make their own decisions keeps women dependent, both on their partners and on the state.

The right to abortion, achieved in *Roe v. Wade* (1973), has been seriously eroded by Congress, the courts, and administrative actions ever since. This has affected poor women the most. Funding for abortions has been seriously curtailed since 1976 when the Hyde Amendment prohibited the use of federal funds for abortions except in cases of rape, incest, or when a woman's life is endangered. In 1981 federal funding was further restricted to cases where the woman's life is endangered. This more restrictive wording has been included in the annual Medicaid appropriations bill ever since (Lieberman and Davis 1992).

Major Supreme Court decisions have so seriously curtailed *Roe v. Wade* that, at the time this is being written, it is unclear whether there will be any federally guaranteed right to abortion after 1993. In *Webster v. Reproductive Health Services* (1989), the Court upheld a Missouri statute prohibiting abortions from being performed in publicly financed facilities, even if paid for privately. In *Rust v. Sullivan* (1991), the Court upheld administrative regulations that bar clinics receiving public funds from Title X of the Public Health Service Act from providing any information about abortion to pregnant women. The Bush administration backed off on this extreme infringement on free speech for physicians, but continued to bar social workers and other health care professionals in these clinics from providing such information to their clients. In the first days of the Clinton administration, and on the twentieth anniversary of *Roe v. Wade*, President Clinton took the first steps to stem this wide-scale erosion of the right to choose. By Executive Order, he lifted what had popularly become known as the "gag rule." While there is strong hope that the new administration will be friendlier to women's right to choose, there is continued evidence that anti-choice forces on the Supreme Court are becoming more firmly entrenched.

The onslaught of government attacks on reproductive freedom during the 1980s, combined with an antichoice movement increasingly engaging in direct actions to prevent women access to clinics where abortions are performed, has resulted in a decrease in the number of physicians able and willing to perform abortions. This is most visible in rural parts of the country where there has been a 51% decline in services since 1977 (Lewin 1990).

While the battle over the ERA divided the country in the 1970s and 1980s, the battle over reproductive rights is dividing the country in the 1990s. The depth of passion on both sides of the battles' lines (and in some cases there are literal battle lines) suggests that these fights are about more than keeping women out of the army or protecting unborn fetuses. It is about continuing to exclude women from equal participation in society.

REALITY: A SOCIAL AND POLITICAL CONSTRUCTION

While political activists were fighting to expand women's rights in the public arena, a potentially more seditious political activity was occurring elsewhere. The very nature of reality was being challenged.

Early feminists had developed an essential political tool: consciousness raising. Women would come together to tell their personal stories, discover the personal/political meaning of their lives, and develop personal/political strategies to transform not only their own lives but society as well. Consciousness raising assumed that reality, or what we had come to think of as reality, "is a political as well as a social construction" (Bricker-Jenkins and Hooyman 1986, 17).

The notion that reality is socially constructed, although adopted by feminists, is not a feminist concept. Berger and Luckmann (1967) deserve credit for introducing the term "the social construction of reality" into the lexicon. Their ideas have been widely accepted by subsequent scholars interested in what is known as epistemology, or the study of knowledge. In their treatise on the sociology of knowledge, Berger and Luckmann observe that it is people who construct and legitimate society and its institutions.

Over time, however, people act as if what has been constructed by previous generations has a life independent of its human creators. Two concepts are essential for understanding social constructionism: reification and legitimation.

> Reification is the apprehension of human phenomena as if they were things, that is, in non-human or possibly suprahuman terms. Another way of saying this is that reification is the apprehension of the products of human activity *as if* they were something else than human products–such as facts of nature, results of cosmic laws, or manifestations of divine will. Reification implies that man [sic] is capable of forgetting his own authorship of the human world, and further, that the dialectic between man, the producer, and his products, is lost to consciousness. (Berger and Luckmann 1967, 89)

> Legitimation is the process of "explaining" and justifying . . . the institutional order by ascribing cognitive validity to its objectivated meanings. Legitimation justifies the institutional order by giving normative dignity to its practical imperatives . . . Legitimation not only tells the individual why he *should* perform one action and not another; it also tells him why things *are* what they are. In other words, "knowledge" precedes "values" in the legitimation of institutions. (Berger and Luckmann 1967, 93-94)

While many versions of reality may be constructed, only a few get reified and legitimated. These are the versions of those who wield the power. Until now, those in power have been a small group of privileged white men who have "generalized from themselves to all, established their sex/gender, their race, their class, as norms and ideals for all, while also maintaining their exclusivity" (Minnich 1990, 68). It is these elitist definitions of society and its institutions, (which includes its theories, its arts and sciences, its forms of governance and economic structures, the roles it assigns to people and the behaviors it expects of them, as well as its ideologies) that become normative standards against which everything and everyone are judged.

What is the effect of one group having exclusive power to define reality?

> Eventually, that one category/kind comes to function almost as if it were the *only* kind, because it occupies the defining center of power, either casting all others outside the circle of the "real" or holding them on the margins, penned into subcategories. . . . There were at the beginning the few, privileged men who generalized from themselves to Man, thus privileging certain of their qualities that, they asserte ' distinguished them from "the horde." From then on the differences from those few were seen as marks of inferiority. Woman was . . . not the equal opposite of man but a failed version of the supposed defining type, higher than animals but lower then men. (Minnich 1990, 53-54)

Thus women (and members of other marginalized groups) are first marked as deficient and then their deficiencies used to justify their exclusion from power. For a long time, women accepted their devalued status, internalizing the belief that they were not good enough to participate in the public arena. Slowly, however, some began to see that it was the normative standards that were deficient, not they.

Some feminists were also coming to understand that it was not only that it was a male-only game, but, more perniciously, it was men who maintained exclusive control over how the game was played. As Belenky et al. (1986), in their book on how women learn, write:

> Men move quickly to impose their own conceptual schemes on the experience of women, says French feminist writer Marguerite Duras. These schemes do not help women make sense of their experience; they extinguish the experience. Women must find their own words to make meaning of their experiences, and this will take time. (202)

Transforming How We Think About Reality: Listening to Women's Voices

Some feminists realized they did not want to join the game already in play; they wanted to develop their own games, ones that validated the ways in which women experience life. In the words of writer Grace Paley (1991):

> Most of the Women's Libbers I knew really didn't want a piece of the men's pie. They thought that pie was kind of poisononous, toxic, really full of weapons, poison gases, all kinds of mean junk we didn't even want a slice of.

What they wanted was to transform the way we thought about people and their values, about the arts and the humanities, about politics and philosophy, about science and the professions (Minnich 1990). Only this time, women (as well as other previously silenced groups) had to become major players in constructing the new realities. Bringing women in, as an afterthought, meant that women and their work were forever compared to the de facto male model and, through such comparisons, time and again, found to be deficient. Bringing women in as an afterthought meant that the models themselves would never be transformed, merely reshaped. Women had to participate in developing versions of reality that more accurately reflected the worlds in which they lived.

One exemplar of a small-scale transformation is Gilligan's (1982) work on moral development. Prior to Gilligan, the most widely accepted model of moral development had been framed around male development and experience (Kohlberg 1976). At Kohlberg's highest level of moral development, people use abstract universal ethical principles of justice and respect for individual rights to resolve moral dilemmas. Women had been found deficient when judged against this supposedly universal, but implicitly male, standard. What Gilligan did was listen to women (and men) talk about moral dilemmas. As women struggled with moral dilemmas, they worried about the human consequences of their choices and were loath to apply abstract principles to human problems. Women spoke of the responsibility to care for others; men spoke of the importance of protecting individual rights. As Gilligan listened, she heard different voices. This allowed her to rethink moral development, taking into account both women's concern for connection and men's concern with separation.

As we have listened for centuries to the voices of men and the theories of development that their experience informs, so we have come more recently to notice not only the silence of women but the difficulty in hearing what they say when they speak. . . . The failure to see the different reality of women's lives and to hear the differences in their voices stems in part from the assumption that there is a single mode of social experience and interpretation. By positing instead two different modes, we arrive at a more complex rendition of human experience . . . (Gilligan 1982, 183-184)

No longer are women judged deficient when they fail to adhere to a singular universal standard. Instead their approach to moral dilemmas is seen as equally viable and essential to social well-being.

If this discussion of transforming knowledge sounds very alien to you, step back for a moment and think. If men have been the ones who have sat in Congress and on the Supreme Court, telling everybody, men as well as women, how they could run their lives, haven't men also done the research and written the books that tell everybody, women as well as men, what is truth, what is right behavior, what is normal? If reality is a political construction, then like other political actions, isn't it those in power who have been the predominant builders?

Feminism Requires a Paradigm Shift

Feminists were not the first to suggest that the ways in which we think about things need to be transformed. There are certainly precedents for such transformations. They are what Kuhn has called "scientific revolutions," when the prevailing "paradigm" is discarded in favor of another (1970, 10). A paradigm "is what the members of a scientific community share, *and*, conversely a scientific community consists of men who share a paradigm." (176, emphasis in original; underlining added).

Paradigm shifts begin to occur, when facts no longer fit the prevailing paradigm *and* when another better paradigm is set forth. Even in the more objective world of science, acceptance of a new paradigm takes time. As Kuhn observes, the Copernican revolution was not complete until almost a century after Copernicus' death and Newtonian theory took almost half a century to be accepted.

Kuhn (1970) quotes Max Planck to explain how paradigm shifts occur. "A new scientific truth does not triumph by convincing its opponents and making them see the light, but rather because its opponents eventually die, and a new generation grows up that is familiar with it" (151). It is not that scientists are incapable of admitting their errors, rather accepting a new paradigm "is a conversion experience that cannot be forced" (Kuhn 1970, 151).

Feminism is just such a conversion experience. Susan Bordo (1990) has called feminism "a cultural moment of revelation and relief" (137). This conversion experience came about for many feminists over the past 20 years as "the category of the 'human'–a standard against which all difference translates to lack, insufficiency–was brought down to earth, given a pair of pants, and reminded that it was not the only player in town." (Bordo, 137)

Conversions are unsettling. The old and familiar world disappears. The taken-for-granted reality is no longer solidly grounded. To turn to Kuhn (1970) once again:

> . . . during revolutions scientists see new and different things when looking with familiar instruments in places they have looked before. It is rather as if the professional community has been suddenly transported to another planet where familiar objects are seen in a different light and are joined by unfamiliar ones as well. (111)

But in the feminist revolution only some people (and only some feminists) have experienced this conversion, only some feminists have accepted the need for a new paradigm. If we are really in the process of a revolution, why are so many people acting as if the old paradigm is still adequate?

As Kuhn's study of the history of science has indicated, one paradigm is rejected only when a better one is available that explains something that previously felt amiss. But, for most, or at least most of those in the scholarly community, nothing is amiss. Their theories of the world continue to give them comfort. Only those whose stories have been silenced feel that something is seriously amiss. The outsiders are developing competing paradigms, while the insiders remain confident of their social construction of reality. Their ways of thinking about and running the world continue to keep them in power and they have, as yet, no need to think any differently.

At this point in time, only a minority are convinced of the need for an alternative paradigm, one that represents the voices of women and other previously silenced groups. For the majority, an alternative paradigm is not only unnecessary, but absurd. And, at the moment, there is little dialogue between the two. Again turning to Kuhn (1970):

> . . . the proponents of competing paradigms practice their trades in different worlds. . . . Practicing in different worlds, the two groups of scientists see different things when they look from the same point in the same direction. . . . That is why a law that cannot even be demonstrated to one group of scientists may occasionally seem intuitively obvious to another. (150)

To understand how people can see such different things when looking at the same phenomenon, one has only to be reminded of the televised confirmation hearings for Supreme Court Justice Clarence Thomas. "They Don't Get It; They Just Don't Get It" was repeated thousands of times as women throughout the country sat glued to the television set, in wide-eyed amazement as Judge Thomas was confirmed to the highest court in the nation.

Standpoint Feminists: Reality Depends on Where You Stand

For those who do get it, the conversion has been a powerful experience. One group who have participated in this conversion are referred to as feminist standpoint theorists (see Alcoff 1988; Hartsock 1990; Stanley and Wise 1990). The concept of standpoint assumes that all knowledge develops from the objective reality of people's lives. As we look out upon the world or turn inward to understand our inner lives, we are all grounded by our place in society. And our place in society has always been and continues to be firmly grounded by our gender. Most of what society deems worthy of study arises from the standpoint of white men. This ignores, trivializes, and denies vast arenas of life, mostly emanating from the more private realm of family and interpersonal relation-ships in which women's lives are embedded. It is the "dailiness of women's lives" (Aptheker 1989, 37), cleaning the toilets and nur-turing the children and men in private and in public, that leads women to a different understanding of the world than men. And yet it is just these activities and experiences that are made invisible.

There are clearly differences among women. Women differ on the basis of race, class, sexual orientation, culture, and religion. Not all women share the same standpoint; not all women have the same experiences; not all women have the same view of reality. Nancy Hartsock (1990) expresses this well when she writes of the:

> need to dissolve the false "we" . . . into its real multiplicity and variety and out of this concrete multiplicity build an ac-count of the world as seen from the margins, an account which can expose the falseness of the view from the top and can transform the margins as well as the center. (171)

But at the same time, women, because of their shared gender, are all oppressed and marginalized. And being on the margins gives one a special perspective.

> Because women are treated as strangers, as aliens–some more so than others–by the dominant social institutions, and con-ceptual schemes, their exclusion alone provides an edge, an advantage. . . . Women's oppression gives them fewer interests in ignorance . . . and fewer reasons to invest in maintaining or justifying the status quo than the dominant groups . . . thus, the perspective from their lives can more easily generate fresh and critical analyses. (Harding 1991, 126)

The oppressed survive only if they understand not only their own world, but that of their oppressor. As a result they have a more complete, although perhaps not more valid, picture of the world. Collins (1989) vividly captures this point in writing about African-American women. "Black women cannot afford to be fools of any type, for their devalued status denies them the protections that white skin, maleness, and wealth confer" (759).

In their eagerness to articulate a way to think about the oppression that *all* women share, some theorists had assumed that all women share the same standpoint. But voices even more marginalized and oppressed than white, middle-class women reminded them of their different experiences, their different visions of reality.

> As new narratives began to be produced, telling the story of the diversity of women's experiences, the chief imperative was to listen, to become more aware of one's own biases, prejudices, and ignorance, to begin to stretch the borders of what Minnie Bruce Pratt calls the "narrow circle of the self." (Bordo 1990, 138)

There was clearly a need to listen to other women's voices, other women's standpoints. But how many different women's standpoints are there? A lesbian woman's standpoint; a black woman's standpoint; a chicana standpoint; a Jewish woman's standpoint? If there are so many diverse standpoints is it even useful to articulate women's standpoints? Is gender itself even a useful construct?

Postmodernists: Is Gender Still a Useful Construct?

For some feminists, the answer is "no." These are the feminists who have turned to postmodernism, a philosophical perspective that holds that there is no truth; that each individual, situated in her own time, her own place in history, in society, constructs her own reality. Not even oppressed persons can step outside of the social constraints of who they are and the conditions under which they live (Flax 1987). Postmodernists hold that there can be no universal claims. In their commitment to pluralism, they seek to obliterate all group distinctions, all metanarratives. By privileging all perspectives, no one perspective can become the absolute standard against which to judge truth and fiction. In their commitment to hearing multiple voices, all categories, including that of women, become fictions, needing to be dismantled, deconstructed (see, for example, Nicholson 1990).

WHY WE STILL NEED A WOMAN'S AGENDA FOR SOCIAL WORK

These are complex philosophical issues. In this brief discussion, only the contours of the arguments have been drawn. And while they may seem far-removed from social work, they are important to setting a future agenda for women. Should we continue to think about women and their issues as separate from a broader social agenda? Or have we entered the postfeminist era, as Betty Friedan has suggested, where we should be focusing on human issues, not women's issues (Friedan, 1986)?

For me the answer is clear. As I look around me and see male privilege and female oppression, I know it is too soon to move on to a society in which gender is no longer a defining variable. I worry along with Christine Di Stefano (1990), who writes:

> In our haste to deconstruct hierarchical distinctions such as gender as harmful illusions we may fail to grasp "their tenacious rootedness in an objective world created over time and deeply resistant to change." (78)

As you read through this book, you will be continually reminded of the tenacious rootedness of the gender hierarchy in the objective world and the deep resistance to change in our society and even in our profession.

Women may not have a privileged perspective, but women do have many strengths that have for too long been denied and suppressed. Women need to have these strengths recognized and applauded. Many of what are now being written of as women's values have arisen in response to their oppression. Some may bring harm to them by keeping them oppressed. While we need to articulate the previously silenced viewpoints of women, and rethink "our ideas about what is humanly excellent, worthy of praise . . . we need to be careful not to assert merely the superiority of the opposite" (Flax 1987, 641). And yet, Linda Alcoff (1988) observes:

> After a decade of hearing liberal feminists advising us to wear business suits and enter the male world, it is a helpful corrective to have cultural feminists argue instead that women's world is full of superior virtues and values, to be credited and learned from rather than despised. (266)

This brings me to a conclusion that can guide us in our work to construct a more equitable world where women's strengths are validated. Alcoff (1988) goes on to write about "identity politics," a concept originally developed by the Combahee River Collective, a black feminist group. Identity politics acknowledges that one's identity is both a social construction and a point from which to act politically. While women differ from one another in many important ways, these differences are not sufficient to override our common interests. As women, we have just begun to claim our own power, to speak in our own voice, to use our identity as women as a point from which to act politically. Nancy Hartsock (1990) has asked a pointed question.

> Why is it that just at the moment when so many of us who have been silenced begin to demand the right to name ourselves, to act as subjects rather than objects of history, that just then the concept of subjecthood becomes problematic? Just when we are forming our own theories about the world, uncertainty emerges about whether the world can be theorized. Just when we are talking about the changes we want, ideas of process and the possibility of systematically and rationally organizing human society become dubious and suspect. (164-165)

Jeffner Allen (1989) has asked:

> Does difference enter the scene only to vanish in a time when women perform two-thirds of the world's work, receive five percent of the world income, own less than one percent of the world land; when in the United States every seven minutes a woman is raped, every eighteen seconds a woman is battered; when women and children in female-headed households are estimated to comprise almost all of the population in poverty by the year 2000? (41)

BUILDING ON WOMEN'S STRENGTHS: A SOCIAL WORK AGENDA FOR THE TWENTY-FIRST CENTURY

In the remainder of this book, you will find thoughtful discussions of many ways in which we, as social workers, can actively work to validate women's strengths in areas which are central to their lives. Throughout we are reminded of the public/private dichotomy that has been imposed by those in power. Women have historically been relegated to the private sphere where their work has been made invisible. At the same time they have been actively excluded from the public one, the only arena which has carried (and continues to carry) economic reward. Miller (Chapter 2) provides us with a way of thinking about women and the overarching policy changes that must occur for their lives to be transformed as we approach the twenty-first century. Central to her analysis is the need to move away from policies centered on outdated notions of "family" and toward policies that promote community interdependency. True gender equality, she writes, requires far-reaching policies that transform women's roles in society. Incremental change, while politically achievable, may have the unanticipated consequence of maintaining the status quo while offering little significant help to the most oppressed women in society.

Many of the struggles that women continue to experience revolve around their desire and their need to find their own balance between their private and public lives. Three of the chapters directly address different aspects of women's entry into the public sphere. Hagen (Chapter 3), and Gowdy and Pearlmutter (Chapter 4) address what is needed for women to successfully move out of poverty and onto the road of economic self-sufficiency. In her chapter, Hagen highlights the strengths our own profession brings to the hard task of changing the lives of poor women and their children. Freeman (Chapter 5) provides a way to reframe the difficulties that are often blamed on women as they enter the labor force as an opportunity for families (and individuals) to grow and transform themselves. As all of these authors recognize, women can only move into the public arena if somebody else is there to provide the care and nurturance that children need. Hutchison (Chapter 6) directly addresses the many ways in which the welfare of children has historically come at considerable cost to the welfare of women (as mothers, as child welfare workers, as daycare providers). She offers far-ranging suggestions to assure that the well-being of women and children in the twenty-first century will not be traded off for one another. At the other end of the age spectrum, Crawley (Chapter 7) provides vivid examples of how women are sacrified in old age because of their earlier commitments to their children and families. She addresses the need to rethink public policies that tie women's economic viability in old age to their paid labor force participation.

Not only have women been relegated to the private sphere, but their lives within that sphere have been made invisible, their voices have been silenced. Laird (Chapter 8) and Weick (Chapter 9) eloquently write about ways in which social workers can help restory the lives of women and transform their lives of oppression. As Laird illustrates so well, it takes tremendous strength to tell a different story, to construct a different reality than the one that has been imposed on women. As social workers, we have the tools to enable women to restory their lives, to engage in change that can emancipate them from oppression. Wetzel (Chapter 10) takes us on a global journey to find the universal strategies for women's empowerment. The power in making women's lives visible is nowhere better illustrated than in Simon's (Chapter 11) history of the women of Henry Street Settlement. In looking back at the amazing work that women have done, she offers a vision of what women can do. It is fitting that a book devoted to building a future agenda for women should conclude with a passionate appraisal of our rich history.

This is not a complete agenda for women's empowerment. What we have set out to do is to emphasize women's strengths, not their deficits. We have brought into clearer focus the ways in which society has oppressed and silenced women. We have offered some strategies for both policymakers and practitioners to build on the personal and collective strength and resilience of people who thrive despite their oppression. As you pursue your chosen profession, remember that your job is not to teach women to be better, but to provide them the opportunity to name, to express, and to celebrate the strengths that they have.

REFERENCES

Abramovitz, M. (1991). Putting an end to doublespeak about race, gender, and poverty: An annotated glossary for social workers. *Social Work, 36*: 380-384.

Alcoff, L. (1988). Cultural feminism versus post-structuralism: The identity crisis in feminist theory. In *Reconstructing the academy: Women's education and women's studies*, edited by E. Minnich, J. O'Barr, and R. Rosenfeld, 257-288. Chicago: University of Chicago Press.

Allen, J. (1989). Women who beget women must thwart major sophisms. In *Women, knowledge, and reality: Explorations in feminist philosophy*, edited by A. Garry and M. Pearsall, 37-46. Boston: Unwin Hyman.

Aptheker, B. (1989). *Tapestries of life: Women's work, women's consciousness, and the meaning of daily life*. Amherst, MA: University of Massachusetts Press.

Belenky, M.F., B.M. Clinchy, N.R. Goldberger, and J.M. Tarule. (1986). *Women's ways of knowing: The development of self, voice, and mind*. New York: Basic Books.

Berger, P. L., and T. Luckmann. (1967). *The social construction of reality: A treatise in the sociology of knowledge*. New York: Anchor Books.

Boles, J.K. (1979). *The politics of the Equal Rights Amendment: Conflict and decision process*. New York: Longman.

Bordo, S. (1990). Feminism, postmodernism, and gender-scepticism. In *Feminism/postmodernism*, edited by L.J. Nicholson, 133-156. New York: Routledge, Chapman, and Hall.

Bricker-Jenkins, M., and N.R. Hooyman. (1986). A feminist world view: Ideological themes from the feminist movement. In *Not for women only: Social work practice for a feminist future*, edited by M. Bricker-Jenkins and N.R. Hooymans. Silver Spring, MD: National Association of Social Workers.

Collins, P. H. (1989). The social construction of Black feminist thought. *Signs, 14*: 745-773.

Conover, P.J., and V. Gray. (1983). *Feminism and the new right: Conflict over the American family*. New York: Praeger.

Davidson, N. (1988). *The failure of feminism*. Buffalo, NY: Prometheus Books.

Davis, F. (1991). *Moving the mountain: The women's movement in America since 1960*. New York: Simon and Schuster.

Di Stefano, C. (1990). Dilemmas of difference: Feminism, modernity, and postmodernism. In *Feminism/postmodernism*, edited by L.J. Nicholson, 63-82. New York: Routledge, Chapman, and Hall.

Flax, J. (1987). Postmodernism and gender relations in feminist theory. *Signs, 12*: 621-643.

Freeman, J. (1975). *The politics of women's liberation. A case study of an emerging social movement and its relation to the policy process*. New York: David McKay Co.

Friedan, B. (1986). *The second stage*. Revised edition. New York: Summit Books.

Gelb, J., and M.L. Palley. (1987). *Women and public policies*. Princeton, NJ: Princeton University Press.

Gilligan, C. (1982). *In a different voice: Psychological theory and women's development*. Cambridge: Harvard University Press.

Harding, S. (1991). *Whose science? Whose knowledge?: Thinking from women's lives*. Ithaca, NY: Cornell University Press.

Hartsock, N. (1990). Foucault on power: A theory for women? In *Feminism/post-*

modernism, edited by L.J. Nicholson, 157-175. New York: Routledge, Chapman, and Hall.

Hawkesworth, M.E. (1990). *Beyond oppression: Feminist theory and political strategy.* New York: Continuum.

Hayes, C. (Ed.). (1987). *Risking the future*, vol. 1. Washington, DC: National Academy Press.

Hazou, W. (1990). *The social and legal status of women: A global perspective.* New York: Praeger Publishers.

Jagger, A., and P. Struhl. (1978). *Feminist frameworks: Alternative theoretical accounts of the relation between women and men.* New York: McGraw Hill.

Kohlberg, L. (1976). Moral stages and moralization: The cognitive-developmental approach. In *Moral development and behavior: Theory, research, and social issues*, edited by T. Likona. New York: Holt, Rinehart, and Winston.

Kuhn, T. S. (1970). *The structure of scientific revolutions.* 2nd edition. Chicago: University of Chicago Press.

Lewin, T. (1990, June 28). Abortions harder to get in rural areas of nation. *New York Times (National)*: 9.

Lieberman, A., and L.V. Davis. (1992). The role of social work in the defense of reproductive rights. *Social Work, 37*: 365-371.

Minnich, E. K. (1990). *Transforming knowledge.* Philadelphia: Temple University Press.

National Association of Social Workers. (1990). *Code of ethics of the National Association of Social Workers.* Washington, DC: NASW Press.

Nicholson, L. (1990). Introduction. In *Feminism/postmodernism*, edited by L.J. Nicholson, 1-16. New York: Routledge, Chapman, and Hall.

Paley, G. (1991). Conversations. In *Long Walks and Intimate Talks*, edited by G. Paley. New York: The Feminist Press.

Roe v. Wade 410 U.S. 113. (1973).

Rust v. Sullivan, Nos. 89-1391, 89-1392, Slip opinion. U.S. (1991).

Schwartz, F. N. (1989). Management women and the new facts of life. *Harvard Business Review, 67*: 65-76.

Stanley, L., and S. Wise. (1990). Method, methodology, and epistemology in feminist research processes. In *Feminist praxis: Research, theory and epistemology in feminist sociology*, edited by L. Stanley, 20-60. New York: Routledge.

Vandiver, S. T. (1980). A herstory of women in social work. In *Women issues and social work practice*, edited by E. Norman and A. Mancuso, 21-38. Itasca, IL: Peacock Pub.

Webster v. Reproductive Health Services 492, U.S. 109 S.Ct., 3040, 106 L.Ed. 2d 410 (1989).

Chapter 2

What Is Needed for True Equality: An Overview of Policy Issues for Women

Dorothy C. Miller

INTRODUCTION

The National Organization for Women (NOW) remains the largest feminist organization in the U.S. today, and while some feminists consider it to be too mainstream, it represents a sort of common denominator of feminist thinking, working as it does for gender equality in society and at home. In 1966, NOW's "Statement of Purpose" called for an end to discrimination against women in the legal system, employment, and education and "a true partnership between the sexes," including a "different concept of marriage, an equitable sharing of the responsibilities of home and children and of the economic burdens of their support" (Harrison 1988, 56). Looking back, it is instructive to notice that modern feminist leaders recognized from that beginning that for true equality between men and women to exist, men had to accept a central role in caring for children and women had to play a central role in providing for their upkeep. It is striking that, more than 20 years later, we have fallen quite short in achieving that goal.

Gelb and Palley (1987) submit that policy proposals that imply "role equity" are more likely to be politically acceptable than those that are thought to promote "role change." Thus, "equal pay for equal work," a role equity issue, makes sense to our democratic society's notion of fairness. Affordable and accessible child care, on the other hand, may be seen as promoting unwanted role changes among women (Gelb and Palley 1987). From this perspective, feminist social workers and policy analysts face a dilemma as they look to achieve equality-based policy changes. Policies that would ensure true equality for women often suggest changes in women's and men's roles and are consequently threatening to society. Gelb and Palley have described how feminist advocates have downplayed the role change aspects of policies in order to achieve political acceptance. Indeed, the changes that have been achieved, at least on paper, tend to promote role equity. The more difficult role change issues, centered on family issues, have been stalled. As society becomes more sensitive to feminist concerns, it will be increasingly difficult to obscure the role change implications of needed policies. Instead, feminists will have to bear the burden of proof that role change policies would in fact be beneficial also to men and children and would build a better society.

There is a large literature that explicates proposed social and regulatory policies that would be of tremendous help to the lives of women and men today and well into the twenty-first century. I would suspect there is a strong likelihood of consensus among feminist social workers in favor of most of the following proposals.

1. Affordable, quality child care, subsidized by government and employers, and monitored for minimum standards, would accommodate parents and improve the quality of life for children (Kahn and Kamerman 1987).

2. Better work and family coordination, brought about through a combination of parental leave policies and flextime or through shorter work days and/or shorter work weeks for everyone would enhance family life (Stoper 1988; Hartmann and Spalter-Roth 1989).

3. Pay equity, soundly enforced affirmative action, and policies to encourage more young women to enter nontraditional occupations would increase women's vocational choices and economic well-being (Bergmann 1986).

4. Antipoverty strategies that would, at best, do away with poverty altogether or, at least, alleviate its worst forms are within our reach. These could include children's allowances; increasing and broadening the Earned Income Tax Credit for families; housing subsidies that guarantee housing to all; better job training and better linkages to jobs for low income young women and men; and in-

creasing public assistance amounts (Miller 1990; Ellwood 1988; Rodgers 1988, 1986; Sidel 1986).

5. Real enforcement of child support laws and increases in the amounts of the awards would help many women raise their children in more adequate financial circumstances. The enforcement of child support laws has increased a great deal in recent years but the low award amounts per child have limited the antipoverty effects of the payments. There is evidence that among divorced and separated couples, the fathers have the financial capacity to pay more than the current average award of $2063 per year. Less is known about unmarried parents (House of Representatives 1991; Miller 1990; Kahn & Kamerman 1988; Schafran 1988; Weitzman 1985).

6. The U.S. needs some form of national health insurance to guarantee health care for all. This can be accomplished through government health insurance or a combined government/private employer plan that would cover everyone. We also need government policies that ensure adequate professional services and treatment for children and adults for substance abuse, relationship problems, and other psychological difficulties (Starr 1986).

7. Changes in Social Security and private pension regulations are needed to ensure that elderly women can count on economic security upon retirement, even when their spouses have died (Miller 1990; Holden 1989; Fierst and Campbell 1988; Rix 1984). (See also, Crawley, Chapter 7.)

8. Finally, antidiscrimination laws with teeth, geared to eliminating discrimination based on race, ethnicity, sexual orientation, marital status, age, and physical appearance and abilities, are essential to a free and fair society.

These proposed policies taken together have the potential to transform women's roles in society. Because they are so far-reaching, in many cases expensive, and have the potential of institutionalizing fundamental gender role changes, most are politically difficult. To achieve partial change, many policy analysts have narrowed their horizons to concentrate on obtaining incremental gains.

Considering the condition of U.S. social policy today, prioritizing what can be done over what should be done is compelling. On the other hand, incrementalism, by its very nature, effects change in such small doses that the status quo is not threatened, or at least not threatened enough to obstruct the desired change. There is always a danger, however, that incremental change will have the unanticipated consequence of perpetuating the status quo rather than extending the boundaries of social provision and opportunity. Feminist social workers must consider such a possibility.

In this chapter, I address several fundamental issues that cut across a great number of policy initiatives that have been implemented or recently proposed. These issues are often ignored or denied because they threaten mainstream ideology and may stymie incremental gains. I suggest that we must include them in our discourse in order to better understand the opposition to policy proposals that suggest gender role changes and to better examine the values that inform our policy choices. Clarity about what is ultimately desirable and what is an acceptable but limited incremental change is essential to a vision for the future. While immediate revolutionary change is unlikely and perhaps undesirable, the vision of a world as we would like it to be is essential to progress toward that world. As bell hooks says, "What we can't imagine, we can't come to be." (hooks 1989, 176)

FAMILY:
THE BASIS OF SOCIAL POLICY

Many current and proposed social policies consider "family" needs as their base. This is understandable since most people live in families and define their fundamental loyalties within families. Yet existing public policies and reform proposals continue to use the traditional nuclear family as the basic unit of concern.

The need for two-parent families is a constant theme among policy analysts and in the popular press. The Social Security system is heavily invested in the traditional family structure, and reforms proposed that would benefit women tend to further encode traditional family systems and women's roles. Similarly, "permanency planning" in child welfare policies is geared to deciding to whom the child should belong rather than providing for shared caring according to caretaker capacity.

Shaping social policies with the "family" as centerpiece places constraints on people's behavior toward and expectations of each other and encodes the primacy of family caregiving in women's lives. A truly inclusive framework for public policy would acknowledge and encourage caregiving behavior among all persons regardless of family ties. For example, child and elder care provided by friends could be recognized in the tax system. Social Security could benefit persons who leave the labor force to care for other people's children, ailing relatives, or young people dying of AIDS. Such policies would encourage all adults in society to participate in child rearing, and well elderly friends to help care for ill elderly. The new policies would promote community interdependency among persons, groups, and extended families.

A Conservative Concept

Family is a conservative concept, however much liberals try to take it on as their own. So-called "family values" are usually not feminist values. For example, consider the following nostalgic view of the family that appeared recently in a syndicated Knight-Ridder column, written by Charles Whited of the Miami Herald.

> When I was a young married man, wives for the most part did not go out to work but worked at home; husbands fulfilled their responsibilities, or tried to, as breadwinners and providers. It seemed a happy arrangement, and I think the typical American woman, if there is such a person, found fulfillment in it. There is dignity to child-rearing and homemaking; not every woman has to seek self-worth by being a brain surgeon. . . . There was pride to being breadwinner and provider. There was respect for the man who stuck loyally to his family and his job, no matter how humdrum the work or how much he hated it. And that respect came home with him. A man who did his day's work, stayed reasonably sober, paid the bills as best he could and looked after his family, and was there–loyal and unshakable–in sickness, health and hard times, had a special place in the house. . . . If he chose to take a nap in the evening after supper, while his wife and kids did the

dishes, so be it; because on the weekend, likely as not he'd be out mowing weeds in the back lot. . . . It was a sharing, a distinct division of roles. And somehow it worked. . . . It isn't working anymore. . . . We've lost something between the sexes that used to be near and dear, that bonded, strengthened and made life worth living. I'm not sure that we can afford the loss. (Whited 1990, 7A)

What's wrong with this picture? Whited is mistaken about a lot of things. He patronizingly discounts women's need for a variety of work and ignores the fact that men's share of housework and child care was then (and is now) proportionately nil when compared with women's (Hochschild 1989). He ignores the large number of working-class families, white and minority, who could not afford to have just one earner in the family, not to mention single parent families. He neglects to mention that men had total control over the household money and literally all household decision making. They were also free to abuse and rape their wives and their children without fear of consequences. Men's total control was upheld by literally all legal and religious institutions, even when their abuse of family members was apparent. Women were not only less free to go out and earn a living for themselves, but they had few choices about major aspects of their lives, including their childbearing, their geographic location, and their life's work. This type of article appears regularly in the media and is accepted by a large proportion of the American people. It represents not only a dangerous distortion of the past, but also the danger of focusing on the concept of "family" or "marriage" without considering the roles and constraints upon the individuals in those institutional arrangements.

When Is a Family Not a Family?
The Assault on Single Parents

A great deal of social concern has been concentrated on single woman-headed families in the past decade. Charles Murray (1984), for example, in his widely hailed book, *Losing Ground: American Social Policy 1950-1980*, blames poor single women for having children they cannot afford. He blames the welfare system for providing a way for single women to have children and married women to leave their husbands. He appears more concerned with single parenthood than he is with poverty. The only solution to women's poverty he proposes is changing the welfare system to eliminate what he perceives as disincentives to marriage.

Murray is avowedly conservative, but analysts who are more likely to be associated with liberal ideas have similar concerns about single parents. University of Chicago sociologist and self-proclaimed "social democrat" William Julius Wilson (1987), for example, suggests that joblessness among young African-American men prevents the same marriage rates as those among young white men. While he does recommend increased employment opportunities for both black men and women, he concentrates almost exclusively on the unemployment problems of men and defines female-headed families as a social problem akin to crime and drug addiction.

Likewise, Irwin Garfinkel and Sara McLanahan (1986) posit a "new American dilemma." The dilemma focuses squarely on the viability and advisability of single-parent families. They ask whether policymakers should "give priority to reducing the economic insecurity of mother-only families or to reducing their prevalence and dependence"(2). Unlike Murray, they want to help single-parent families, but they don't want this help to be an incentive to this abhorrent family structure. It is not surprising that Garfinkel and McLanahan, who indeed suggest various income maintenance reforms to alleviate poverty, do not suggest labor force reforms for women. Their solutions perpetuate the patriarchal dictates of women's economic dependence upon men.

Meanwhile husbands who abandon their families to form other families are not blamed for having unaffordable children. In fact policy analysts are constructing child support policies that accommodate men's new families (Kahn and Kamerman 1988). In Kansas, for example, new child support guidelines reduce a noncustodial parent's obligation when he (usually the father) has additional children in a new family.

In patriarchal society, families are formed through men's initiatives and family members take men's names. Children born outside of the patriarchal structure are "illegitimate." Men "head" their households. While many of the family-related trappings of patriar-

chy, such as barring married women from owning property or sign-
ing contracts, have been successfully defeated by the women's
movement, some cultural assumptions remain. Thus the term "female-headed family" is recognizable as describing a family without
a man in it. "Male-headed family" is a redundancy. We continue to
accept men's right to form families and their need to have their
"own" children with the women they marry. Yet there is a clear
distinction between rights and responsibilities.

In 1987, 9.4 million women had children under 21 from an absent father, but 41% of these women did not have child support
orders. About half of the 4.8 million women who were owed child
support payments received the full amount, one-quarter received
partial payments, and one-quarter received nothing. Women who
received payments in 1987 received an average of $2710, about
19% of their average total incomes (House of Representatives 1991,
666). A recent report from the state of Wisconsin indicated that
70% of absent parents became delinquent in their payments within
three years (Garfinkel 1988).

In spite of the popular belief that court child support awards are
exorbitant, research indicates that most men can comfortably afford
to pay the mandated awards. Haskins reports that "nearly all America's absent fathers, even those whose children are on welfare, earn
enough to be capable of contributing a significant amount toward
supporting their children" (Haskins 1988, 306). Weitzman points
out that the average award is less than the level of welfare, and that,
except for the lowest income levels, it is unusual for a court to order
more than a quarter of a man's income in child support or more than
one-third for child support and alimony combined (Weitzman
1985). (Most women, of course, are not awarded alimony. Note that
just 19% of women divorced before 1970 and 13% of women
divorced after 1980 had alimony agreements or awards, and their
record of actually receiving the amounts due is about the same as
for child support [Schafran 1988].) Furthermore, negligence in paying child support spans all income levels (Weitzman 1985).

In spite of the fact that absent fathers tend to shirk their financial and
social responsibilities, single-parent families are said to be deficient because of the absence of the stabilizing influence of a husband
and father. At best, woman-headed families are tolerated as stemming

from an unfortunate happenstance that must be set right. While some families may feel this way about themselves, it hardly helps children's self-esteem to see themselves constantly depicted as hopelessly lost without fathers. It can also serve as a self-fulfilling prophecy. Note that in the face of violence and drug abuse among poor teenage boys, one hears literally nothing among professionals or the media about encouraging these boys to listen to their mothers. Social critics lament the existence of so many teen boys without fathers at the same time sending a strong message that their mothers are incapable of disciplining them adequately. It is no wonder that we observe that boys in fatherless homes become unmanageable.

A recent article in the *Atlantic* by Karl Zinsmeister, a scholar from the American Enterprise Institute, conveys this theme. Discussing crime in inner city neighborhoods, he essentially puts all the blame on single-parent families and recommends public policies that give even more special breaks to "intact" families.

> The most important source of violence by and among children is family break-down. . . . The point is, having only one parent's time, energy, and earning and teaching power is a serious blow from which a child recovers only with effort. Lack of male direction is an additional problem for many such children. . . . A broad public effort to document the human damage that results from widespread family meltdown, and [encouraging] marriage as the appropriate locus of childbearing, could eventually help curb family abandonment and neglect. . . . The typical single mother on public assistance lives in stark withdrawal–closeted in an apartment to avoid the dangers beyond, doing no outside work, having no civic attachments or other means of integration into the larger world. . . . A check slips through her mail slot every two weeks. (1990, 54).

Zinsmeister's words echo those of noted African-American psychiatrist Alvin Pouissant, who is Associate Professor of Psychiatry and Associate Dean for Student Affairs at the Harvard Medical School. Pouissant, in a 1989 letter to *The New York Times*, wrote:

> One problem, which deserves further study, is that many single black mothers are angry with black men, sometimes

with justification. When they talk among themselves, these women commonly disparage men. Their conversations symbolize the negative atmosphere in which many black boys are being raised. . . . These boys often grow up feeling ill-equipped to become competent members of society. . . . A significant number of black men in prison have themselves been victims of neglect and child abuse and, in turn, they assault and murder one another at alarming rates. (26A)

Overlooking poverty, racism, and international drug trafficking (to name a few alternative explanations to their discussions of children and crime), these writers place blame for children's violence squarely on their mothers. This is an example of how patriarchy can completely turn reality upside down. While women are, of course, capable of a great deal of violence, most violent acts are perpetrated by men. Among female murder victims in 1990, 30% were slain by husbands or boyfriends. Four percent of the male victims were killed by wives or girlfriends. In 1990, 88.7% of those arrested for violent crimes (murder, forcible rape, robbery and aggravated assault) were men (Federal Bureau of Investigation 1991). Yet a chorus of citizens, media, *and* policy analysts is saying that boys need fathers to make them law-abiding and nonviolent. This assertion would be amusing if it were not so outrageous.

Denigrating mother-only families is a variation on the theme of illegitimacy. What makes a child illegitimate is the lack of a father. Now some families are more legitimate than others.

Current "Family" Policies

The National Association of Social Workers (NASW) inaugurated a two-year public service campaign "focused on strengthening the American family, adopting the phrase 'Family Ties' as its motto." They define family broadly as "two or more individuals who consider themselves family and who assume typical family obligations" (Hartman 1990, 195). From a policy perspective, however, it is not apparent that the government is moving to a broader definition of family. On the contrary, examples abound of our tenacious hold on traditional notions of families.

With the notable exception of the food stamp program, the availability of assistance to a person in need depends upon the structure of the person's family, the person's age, his or her physical condition, and the history and current labor force attachment of a family member. For example, children of deceased fathers who were gainfully employed receive Social Security Survivor's benefits. (This policy is "gender neutral" in that it applies as well to children of deceased mothers. However, in reality, most beneficiaries are women and children.) These benefits are much more generous than those provided by Aid to Families with Dependent Children (AFDC), available to poor children whose fathers are living but absent, unemployed (AFDC-UP), or who died without having been covered by Social Security. I know of a woman who received AFDC for herself and her children. Her ex-husband died, making them eligible for Social Security benefits, and their income doubled overnight. The same family, with the same needs, received different benefits based solely on the father's circumstances. Children in families with unemployed fathers may or may not be helped by AFDC, since the requirements are more stringent than they are for single parent families. Furthermore, states can choose to provide AFDC-UP benefits in only six out of 12 months. Thus, the family in which a needy child resides can determine the adequacy of the benefit she or he receives.

The Social Security system is perhaps the social welfare program most heavily invested in the traditional family structure. For dependents' benefits, only spouses and children need apply. The system favors one-earner families who correspond with the white nuclear model of male breadwinner and female housewife. Yet women's work at home is not valued. Homemakers cannot receive disability benefits. Women who take time out of the labor force to care for children and/or elderly relatives are penalized because the system favors workers whose lifetime work patterns resemble those of white males (Miller 1990).

To reform the gender-related anomalies in the Social Security system, a "Modified Earnings Sharing Plan" was devised by the Technical Committee on Earnings Sharing, a Washington-based feminist group. Their comprehensive reform treats marriage as an economic partnership, acknowledging that women's work at home is work. It divides Social Security credits equally between spouses based on their combined total incomes. The plan also includes a 24-month survivor's "adjustment benefit" for widow(er)s; provisions for adequate disability benefits for both spouses, including homemakers; caretaker benefits not only for survivors caring for children but for spouses caring for their disabled spouses; and child caring credits for very low earners (Fierst and Campbell 1988). Their reform, while not likely to be taken seriously on Capitol Hill at the moment, has been hailed by feminists as a positive step toward equality for women.

The Technical Committee's plan would be very helpful to white women. It also enshrines and further institutionalizes conventional marriage and women's roles within it. In spite of the gender neutral aspects of the provisions, we know from European experience (Stoiber 1989), and the experiences of all we see around us, that it is women who are now and will be the caretakers of the children and elderly; it is women who will be further encouraged to fulfill their social role as mothers and stigmatized if they do not. It is women whose opportunities would be restricted even as they receive better compensation for their roles. The proposal ignores the large numbers of never-married women in African-American communities. The reform also might make life harder for women who choose not to be caretakers. Thus, women who do not wish to stay home with their young children or personally care for their ailing husbands, even in the face of social provision, will potentially be viewed as unwomanly and/or selfish. Such a system would institutionalize a woman's role as a caretaker as the best (and perhaps only) way of providing for the care of family members, and would leave differently structured families out in the cold.

The dilemma I pose is, in a sense, the reverse of that suggested by Garfinkel and McLanahan. They wish to help single women who are parents without institutionalizing that family form. I wish to help women in traditional families without perpetuating traditional gender roles, discouraging other family forms, or excluding the increasing numbers of women and men who are forming nonnuclear and nontraditional "family" ties. One solution to my dilemma would be to expand the Social Security caretaker provisions beyond the traditional nuclear family.

New Directions: Policies for Families, Lovers, Friends, and Children

Consider the people who are living with AIDS and being cared for by partners and friends. In African-American communities, extended family as well as "fictive kin," persons considered family but who are not related by blood, have always been important to family care and household tasks (Amott and Matthaei 1991; National Research Council 1990; Joseph and Lewis 1981; McAdoo 1980; Stack 1974). Where are the Social Security caregiver provisions for these people? Extended families, gay men and lesbians, nonmarried heterosexual couples, and friends who care for and about each other are invisible to the social welfare system. The only group that has a choice about their status consists of heterosexual couples for whom there are enormous material and social incentives for joining the ranks of the "married with children." The others may consider themselves "family," but to society and in public policy their roles are narrowly interpreted and unsupported.

I remember the group of women senior citizens to which my mother belonged. A continuous theme among them was the proximity of their grown children and how much–or how little–the women's children (particularly their daughters) did for them. When someone was in need and her daughter neglected to help–or to help enough–the women reacted with a combination of judgment and sympathy. There were clear boundaries, though, on what they would do for each other. Their mutual aid was limited to the things that "friends" do, such as sharing food sometimes and giving each other rides to events. Other areas of help, more commonly addressed by families, were off limits. They did not stay over at each other's houses when illness struck, for example, even if a sick friend had no family nearby to help. The women were restrained by unwritten rules about what friends and family should do. The rules were taken for granted. More expansive helping behaviors appeared to be so outside of expected norms that they never occurred to anyone.

President Bush's concept of the "thousand points of light" was supposed to emphasize voluntary help from people to people–but no public policies supported this. Public policies only recognize nuclear family help and support. They ignore the help that extended families and friends give to each other and discourage those (especially those in white society) who might help but see such help as socially unacceptable. We not only assign caretaking responsibilities to women but we want them to carry out these responsibilities in conventional family systems.

Policies that would encourage all adults in society to participate in child care and child rearing are non-existent, placing the full responsibility (and burden) on the nuclear family. Permanency planning, while beneficial to alleviating the uncertainty that foster children experience, is geared to deciding once and for all who the child belongs to rather than, for example, providing for shared caring according to caretaker capacity. An alternative to the construction of foster care as a " 'pretend' natural family home" has been conceptualized by Carol Meyer (1985), who suggests that foster parents need not be mothers but can be staff members in placements in neighborhoods where the children live, allowing free visiting with their mothers, family, and friends, avoiding the traumatic separations from home, school, and all things familiar. This would replace the common practice of removing children from their poor urban neighborhoods and placing them in middle-class suburban homes, a classist rescue operation that makes it even harder to return the children to their families. (See Hutchison, Chapter 6, for a further discussion of child welfare.)

The adoption system continues to be weighted in the direction of rewarding the parents rather than providing for the children. Young, white, married couples with good incomes have the best opportunity to adopt the few healthy white babies available today. Single persons, who have only recently been allowed to adopt at all, are now allowed to adopt "special needs" children–those over the age of two, of mixed race, or with handicapping conditions (Wolins 1983). Thus, the children most in need go to single adults who must be mother and father to the children and are in the labor force most of the week. If the adoption system were really devoted to helping the children, surely the children most in need would go to the families considered best equipped to help them–families with resources such as a full-time mother and a comfortable income. Paradoxically, patriarchy is upheld through the reward system of giving infants only to families with acceptable structures. The needs of children are subsumed in the interests of institutionalized family arrangements, precluding more creative conceptualizations.

Day care's impact on children is also a threat to traditional notions of family and motherhood. Meyer suggests that day care introduces to children a more expanded sense of socialization and sharing, acceptance of the "population mix of their society," and a different understanding of care and protection. "It is the feminist perspective that allows for a different kind of understanding of day care through its redefinition of the rigid and stereotyped boundaries of the idea of parenting or mothering" (Meyer 1985, 253-254). Children growing up in day care might come to accept as commonplace the notion that a variety of persons can offer love, protection, and educational experiences to children.

If one considers that day care might usher in a new conception of what it means to be a mother, it is not surprising that a great deal of the research on day care has focused on whether it causes damage to the mother-child bond. In fact, research has shown that children's bonds with their parents are not disturbed by day care and day care need not be deleterious to children's growth and development, depending on the quality of the specific care provided (Rutter 1982).

The lack of alternatives to women's care of children within the traditional nuclear family structure forces women to make choices that involve a competition between their own and their children's well-being. Children are hostages to women's achievement of equality. Society is essentially saying "OK, if you want equality, you will have to destroy your children's lives. Do you really want that?" Formulating children's policies in the context of family policies perpetuates and exacerbates this dilemma for women because it continues to place on mothers primary and almost exclusive responsibility for children's well-being.

VIOLENCE AGAINST WOMEN

Sheffield has coined the term "sexual terrorism" to mean "a system by which males frighten and, by frightening, control and dominate females" (Sheffield 1989, 3). She compares it to political terrorism in that it is supported by ideology and propaganda, is indiscriminate and unpredictable, and relies on "voluntary compliance," that is, numbers of men who are socialized to maintain the fear, and numbers of women who are socialized to be victims. The only difference between political terrorism and sexual terrorism is that we sympathize with the victims of political terrorism and the perpetrators of sexual terrorism (Sheffield 1989).

The societal presence of sexual terrorism, which includes rape, wife battering, sexual harassment, and childhood sexual abuse, informs almost every aspect of women's lives, whether these things happen to us as individuals or not. Sexual terrorism dictates to some extent how women dress, how we walk down the street, how we look at men we see on the street, and how we behave toward men we know casually–the guy in the next office, the workman, the janitor. Young women are cautioned about blind dates–or any date. Sexual terrorism dictates where women go at night and what time to go–where to park and when to get home. Sexual terrorism dictates whether we travel alone or not and if so, what precautions we take–what protection to carry, where to stop to eat or sleep. Even two women traveling together on a camping trip on the Appalachian Trail in 1988 were stalked and shot (Zia 1990). Sexual terrorism makes us restrict our daughters' activities, but not our sons. While we protect our daughters, we also socialize them into forming identities as victims.

The point of sexual terrorism is that women are always potential victims and never safe. If the "safety rules" held and women obeyed them, they would be prisoners, but at least could know they would not be attacked. However, it doesn't work that way. Attacks are perpetrated on women of all ages, at all times of day and night, however they behave and however they are dressed. Sexual terrorism has the effect of keeping women in their place and keeping them on guard at all times. Sexual terrorism functions, therefore, as an incredible waste of women's energy and human potential. In addition, sexual terrorism is what Griffin has termed a "protection racket," because women look to men to protect them from other men (Griffin 1989). All men benefit from sexual terrorism because it gives them dominance and control over the women in their lives–in the form of "protection." But of course "protectors" sometimes beat and abuse their wives and children. These crimes against women are the least prosecuted and when prosecuted obtain the fewest convictions (Sheffield 1989). Society does not take them seriously.

Every six minutes a woman is raped in the United States and every 18 seconds a woman is battered by a husband or boyfriend (Wichita Area Sexual Assault Center 1990a). Research with convicted rapists indicates that most rapes are planned (cited in Brownmiller 1975) and committed by men known to their victims. Anecdotal evidence gleaned through interviews with rapists also supports this conclusion (Skipper and McWhorter 1989). Most rapists are not crazy–they are indistinguishable from "ordinary" men except for a higher measure of anger, only detectable after the fact (Griffin 1989). This should not be surprising since more than 50% of high school boys and 42% of high school girls believe there are times when it is acceptable for a male to hold a female down and physically force her to engage in intercourse. One out of eight Hollywood movies depicts a rape theme, and by age 18, the average American will have seen 250,000 acts of violence and 40,000 attempted murders on television (cited by Wichita Area Sexual Assault Center 1990b).

Rape is not only a crime of violence but a crime of control and dominance. It is similar to wife battering in that regard. Each year about 1,500 women are killed by husbands or boyfriends, most after they have left the situation. Many are stalked by their ex-mates and killed years later (Polman 1989).

Sexual harassment on the job, perpetrated by bosses and coworkers, is another form of everyday violence against women. There are two types of sexual harassment: *quid pro quo*, which suggests the exchange of sexual favors as a condition of employment or promotion; and a hostile work environment, in which a woman is made uncomfortable by comments, actions, pictures, etc. One study indicated that sexual harassment from coworkers is more likely to happen to women in nontraditional occupations; the message from their coworkers is "You don't belong here." Bosses, on the other hand, use it to keep women in their subordinate positions. Most women either tolerate sexual harassment or quit their jobs in the face of it.

Those who do complain often feel worse off than before (Martin 1989).

Policy issues dealing with everyday terrorism and violence against women should take top priority in the twenty-first century. We must promote public policies that enforce existing laws against violence and move society to nonviolence. Instead of trying to pick and choose what violent acts are acceptable and which are not, let's oppose them all. Promoting new ways of socializing children, particularly boys, to nonviolence, and socializing girls to be assertive would help to reduce and prevent sexual terrorism and wife battering. Instead of keeping our daughters behind closed doors at night, let's teach them how to assert and protect themselves. Fewer men would attempt violent acts against women if they knew that most women had learned self-defense from an early age. Empowered to use their energies proactively, women would not identify as victims. Loving, concerned men would be relieved since they cannot always be there to protect the women they love, however sincere their intentions.

The far-reaching implications of these changes, however, are profound changes in women's roles. Women, not bothered by sexual terrorism, would likely have more time and energy to devote to their lives, would be less likely to identify as victims, and be more self-confident. I suggest that the role change nature of effective strategies to end sexual terrorism and violence against women blocks efforts to solve the problem.

WOMEN'S EMPLOYMENT AND ECONOMIC WELL-BEING

Women's economic well-being in the United States can best be described as precarious. Women are at a higher risk of poverty than men because they make less money than men and because they are primarily responsible for the care of their children. Most poor people in the United States are women and children in single-parent families. White, black, and Hispanic mother-only families have poverty rates of 38%, 56%, and 59%, respectively. One in five children in the United States is living in a poverty household. Forty-four percent of African-American children and 36% of Hispanic children were poor in 1989, compared to 15% of white children (House of Representatives 1991). The poverty rate for children in the United States is more than twice that for children in Australia, Canada, West Germany, Sweden, the United Kingdom, the Netherlands, and France (House of Representatives 1991). Yet we are doing little in the United States to alleviate this condition.

Aid to Families with Dependent Children (AFDC) is the major cash assistance (welfare) program in the United States for families with children. It is administered by the states under federal guidelines and funded with state and federal revenues. About 90% of AFDC recipients are single mothers and their children. While the average amount of time a family spends on AFDC is two to three years, many people who escape welfare do not escape poverty. About 40% of families that go off welfare remain poor (House of Representatives 1991).

AFDC payment levels are set by the state legislatures and vary considerably. In January, 1991, monthly state payments for a family of three with no other income ranged from $120 a month in Mississippi to $891 in Alaska. AFDC payments nationally are more than 40% lower today than they were in 1970, taking inflation into account (House of Representatives 1991). AFDC provides much less per person than welfare programs for the poor elderly and disabled. Unemployment insurance and Social Security payments are also much higher. These other programs also include automatic benefit increases to keep up with the cost of living.

The latest federal endeavor supposedly geared to alleviating poverty among women and children was encoded into the Family Support Act of 1988. Billed as the expression of a "new consensus" in the *New York Times* (Stevens 1988), it adds significantly more work-related requirements to the AFDC program. It exemplifies the degree to which the American people can accept a philosophy which bears no relation to reality. This legislation was the result of several years' debates about welfare reform that commenced with the election of Ronald Reagan. It was based on the view, characterized by Lawrence Mead's (1986) *Beyond Entitlement: The Social Obligations of Citizenship*, that welfare benefits should not simply be a hand-out but should be given as one side of a "social contract," whereby the government expects work efforts in exchange for benefits. Such sentiment was supposedly behind the Reagan Administrations's encouragement in the early 1980s of demonstration projects in which women on AFDC were required to participate in job search, training, or education programs in exchange for their welfare checks. When the demonstration projects "worked," their best elements were subsumed into the Family Support Act. Title II of the Act, the Job Opportunities and Basic Skills (JOBS) Training Program, consolidates the various existing work and job search programs into a new Title IV-F of the Social Security Act.

A great deal of research was conducted on the experimental programs that preceded the passage of the JOBS program (Gueron 1986; 1987; Porter 1990; General Accounting Office [GAO] 1987; 1988). Findings indicate that the programs succeeded in producing welfare savings, but for the most part failed to help women achieve earned income above poverty level. While the JOBS program is still new, there is evidence that its accomplishments are similar to those achieved by the demonstration projects that preceded it (Commonwealth of Massachusetts 1986; Snyder 1991). For example, in a recent evaluation of KANWORK, the Kansas version of JOBS, a list of the 22 most frequent job titles held by participants who got jobs included housekeeping worker, cook, waitress, day-care helper, food service worker, office assistant, cashier, and hair care specialist. Of the 22, at least 12 jobs are commonly associated with low pay, part-time, or temporary work. About 20% of the sample earned minimum wage and only 10% earned more than $7 per hour (Snyder 1991). From a philosophical standpoint, Mead and many policy analysts and politicians err in singling out just one population that receives social benefits (persons on welfare, particularly AFDC recipients), ignoring all of this population's work efforts as well as the barriers to job attainment, and assuming that job turnover is always the fault of the employees. From a practical standpoint, his "error," and the fatal flaw in the Family Support Act, is the assumption that families can be supported by women's wages. Indeed, the welfare reform debate has been remarkable in its ignorance of women's experiences in the labor force. (See Hagen, Chapter 3, for a further discussion of the Family Support Act.)

A strong case can be made, of course, that welfare reform was never about bringing women and their children out of poverty.

Instead it is geared to welfare savings, maintaining a cheap pool of labor, and the social control of women (Miller 1990; Abramovitz 1988). Mead epitomizes this thesis in that while claiming to favor work in exchange for wages or benefits, he prefers workfare to Public Service Employment (a program that has been eliminated), which was, after all, a real job with real wages (Mead 1986). This is all the more reason why feminist policy analysts and social workers must make the connections between women's poverty, their family roles, and labor force discrimination. The JOBS program is entirely focused on the individual, ignoring the fact that the jobs out there for women will not offer them subsistence.

The pay gap between men's and women's wages is still quite real and not narrowing rapidly. In 1989, women working full-time earned just 70% of what men earned (Women's Bureau 1990a). That appears to be progress, since in the 1970s the proportion was 59%. Yet college-educated women employed full-time, year round, still earn only 59 cents for every dollar earned by college-educated men (Harrison 1988). Moreover, women's choices of work are severely limited. In 1989, one-third of women were employed in only six occupations: secretaries, school teachers (except for higher education), semiskilled machine operators, managers and administrators, personal sales workers, and bookkeepers and accounting clerks (Women's Bureau 1990b). They are in job ghettos consisting mostly of low-paid service occupations. This gendered segregation of labor is very effective in maintaining women's low wages. The lack of women in nontraditional jobs is related to the wage gap. Not only are women not receiving equal pay for equal work, the fact that men and women have different jobs exacerbates their difficulties. Traditionally "women's jobs" pay less, even when they require more education and entail more responsibility.

Although they pay 20-30% more than traditional jobs, blue collar jobs that are "nontraditional" for women have been especially difficult for women to obtain. The percentage of women in the construction trades, for example, was 1.7 in 1970 and rose to 2.1 in 1980. Between 1983 and 1988, the number of women in nontraditional jobs remained unchanged at 4% of the total work force. Just 9% of all working women in 1988 were employed in nontraditional occupations (National Commission on Working Women, 1990). On the other end, few college women are in engineering, math, and science. It is particularly discouraging that the new field of computer science is already dominated by men.

Another cause for concern is that women in management positions and women in the professions are relegated to lower-paying specialties and prevented from advancing, hitting the "glass ceiling" earlier than men do. One 1984 estimate calculated that 49,000 men and 1,000 women were in major policymaking jobs in U.S. corporations (Dipboye 1989).

Part-time work is a growing sector of the economy. One-third of new jobs in 1985 were part-time, and temporary help was one of the fastest growing industries in 1984 (Pearce 1987). In 1987, 50% of women workers worked part-time or part-year or both (Census Bureau 1989). (Another way of putting it is the fact that while about two-thirds of women workers work full-time, just 50% work year-round full-time.) Many part-time jobs have presumably been designed to give women an opportunity to fulfill home responsibilities and participate in wage work as well. Many women, however, have no alternative. The Department of Labor says that most women working part-time choose to do so, but in fact one-quarter of white women and one-half of black women work part-time because they cannot find full-time work or their employers have cut back on their schedules (Pearce 1987).

Some researchers have found that, for men's jobs, employers who need a flexible work force use temporary work contracts (for six to 12 months, for example) or provide overtime opportunities for existing full-time employees. For women's jobs, they create part-time work (Beechey, 1988). The economic advantages to the employer translate into numerous disadvantages to the workers. Part-time work often provides no or few benefits; less pay proportionate to full-time work; little or no chance for advancement; little job security; and no covered pension plan coverage (Pearce 1987).

Felice Schwartz's proposal for the "mommy track," that would supposedly accommodate women executives who put their families first, caused a stir when it first appeared in the *Harvard Business Review*. A close look at her idea reveals that it is essentially a glorified management version of part-time work. She suggests job sharing, with coordination of the job tasks undertaken by the two people *on their own time*, and pay grades that are not proportional to full-time workers (Schwartz 1989). Home work, currently employing large numbers of low-wage workers, as well as increasing numbers of clerical workers, holds similar disadvantages for women (Costello 1989).

Contrary to Schwartz's claim that it is more expensive for companies to employ women than men, in reality the economy *benefits* from defining women as mothers and delegating exclusive child-caring responsibilities to them. If women are primarily mothers, employers can use this excuse to pay them less and keep them in subordinate positions. Men thus have less competition for better jobs and are freed from the distractions of child care and household responsibilities. Faced with women's lower wages and men's greater opportunities in the work world, it makes economic sense for married couples to assign more housekeeping and caretaking responsibilities to the wife. (Single women, by the way, suffer as a result of this behavior, because they compete in the work force against men who have wives to do for them what the single women must do for themselves.) The expectation that women are primarily responsible for the maintenance of home and children reflects reality (Hochschild 1989) and further reinforces employers' channeling women into low-paying dead-end jobs, completing a cycle of discrimination, low expectations, and solidified traditional gender roles. This pattern perpetuates the status quo for married couples and places a great strain on single women parents who also experience the discrimination but lack the economic security of a higher paid partner.

For true reform to be initiated, jobs that will bring all persons into the mainstream of American life should be the first consideration. In this regard, it is important that our confusion and ambivalence about maternal employment be resolved. It is a fact of life that, even in married-couple families, women must be in the labor force for most to attain middle-class status. We also know that quality child care is not harmful to children nor does it interfere with the parent/child bond. It would help enormously if the nation acknowledged these facts and helped to create a society in which women can work and families can experience a quality family life.

The immediate solutions to women's work issues involve policies such as affirmative action, nondiscrimination, and better laws regarding the rights of part-time workers. Pay equity would ensure that women are provided equal pay for jobs of comparable worth and thus mitigate against the wage differentials between "men's" and "women's" jobs. Job requirements, such as skills, education, experience, degree of responsibility and autonomy, and risk would be compared among jobs and prevent instances in which male-dominated job categories, such as truck drivers, are paid more than those dominated by women, such as nurses. By 1987, 20 states were implementing pay equity plans. Just one state, Minnesota, had achieved equitable wage scales for its state employees (Mezey 1992).

The community can work with schools and employers to increase employment, education and training opportunities for young women and men, especially minority youth. Businesses, churches, and community groups can establish and support nonprofit affordable quality child care for low-income parents. Also, paid parental leave for parents of newborn and ill children would help bridge the gap between work and family responsibilities. All of the European countries have mandated maternity or parental leave with full or partial pay (Stoiber 1989). It can be done, and states need not wait for the federal government to mandate it. Financial incentives to businesses to provide such leaves can be established locally and statewide.

Increased opportunities for women to enter nontraditional fields are needed as well. These reforms are more difficult to obtain because they are more likely to bring women equal access to money, power, and status in the work world, thereby effecting gender role changes. Solutions that make women's work and family roles more compatible–flextime, job sharing, on-site child care, home work, and part-time work–are less threatening to society because they uphold capitalist and patriarchal norms. These alternative work arrangements institutionalize women's second-class status in society and enshrine their primary roles as *both* wives and mothers.

States can also expand their JOBS programs to include more participants and to build a more comprehensive program of training and education. This would help the business community in its need for skilled workers as well as the participants, who would be prepared for higher-paying jobs. States can also raise AFDC payment levels to allow welfare children to grow and thrive while their parents participate in education and job-training programs. This increase would help families to live with less stress and deprivation, boost children's sense of well-being, and decrease the incentive to obtain money through illegal activities.

It is commonly suggested that a welfare mother take any job, just to "start somewhere" and get off of welfare. In considering this option she has to think beyond paying the rent, to child care arrangements and medical insurance. How many middle- and upper-class parents would risk depriving their children of medical insurance? On the state level, advocates can promote a health insurance plan funded by business and government to ensure that all persons in the state are covered adequately.

On the national level, advocates can promote an equitable national health insurance plan and the federalization of AFDC with higher, uniform payments. Federalizing AFDC would complete the federalization of welfare that began in 1984 with welfare payments for the poor elderly and disabled. It would eliminate the need for such a large state welfare bureaucracy, be more equitable to clients from state to state, and free the states to administer needed social services and jobs programs that are best designed at the local level.

There are alternatives to maintaining such a large welfare system, however. The United States is the only Western industrialized country that does not have a system of Children's Allowances, payments to families to help defray the cost of child rearing. What we do have is the personal income tax exemption for children. The value of this exemption has eroded considerably since its inception. Furthermore it is not at all helpful to low-income families with little or no tax liability. The National Commission on Children (1991) recommends that we replace the deduction with a new refundable child tax credit of $1,000 per child. With this credit all families would be better off and low-income families would be helped considerably.

Achieving women's equality and assuring adequate household and child-care arrangements requires changes in the work world. The struggles around work and family will not be solved simply through an equalization of household chores between husbands and wives. Because of the demands of the work world, the stress on family life in the absence of change is inevitable (Pleck 1977). Alternative solutions to this problem might involve shortening every worker's day, for example. In considering alternatives, policy analysts must consider the relative importance of women's full participation in the work force (and society), and the implications for changes in men's and women's roles. At the moment, even liberal policy proposals do not change women's roles as much as we would like to think. They just make them a little easier.

CONCLUSION

All social policies have an impact upon women in one way or another. It is important to identify the ways in which they do without apology. At this writing, a societal backlash that blames the women's movement for a variety of social ills is in full force, making it more difficult for women to identify their actual needs and concerns (Faludi 1991). A decade ago Ellen Goodman said, "All I know is I am in the same movement for the second time in my life and I'm not even forty" (cited in Taylor 1986). One of the frustrations of the fight is that some gains, such as reproductive rights, are threatened. (See Davis, Chapter 1, for a further discussion of reproductive rights.) Much work is needed to support and improve women's lives in the twenty-first century.

True equality involves fundamental gender-role changes. Fighting for policies that would facilitate these role changes is difficult, painful, and disruptive. We are not near to this goal. Many proposed policies would be helpful to some women while perpetuating their subordination. Most of these would make it easier for white, married women to "juggle home and family" better, offering little significant help to single parents and women of color. They tend to preserve white-supremacist, capitalist, patriarchal society. Incremental gains are terribly appealing but must not be mistaken for fundamental change.

REFERENCES

Abramovitz, M. (1988). *Regulating the lives of women: Social welfare policy from colonial times to the present*. Boston, MA: South End Press.
Amott, T. L., and J.A. Matthaei. (1991). *Race, gender and work*. Boston, MA: South End Press.

Beechey, V. (1988). Rethinking the definition of work. In *Feminization of the work force: Paradoxes and promises*, edited by J. Jenson, E. Hagen, and Reddy, 45-62. New York: Oxford University Press.

Bergmann, B. (1986). *The economic emergence of women.* New York: Basic Books.

Brownmiller, S. (1975). *Against our will: Men, women and rape.* New York: Simon and Schuster.

Census Bureau. (1989). *Money income of households, families and persons in the United States: 1987,* pp. 167-170. Current Population Reports, Series P-60, No. 162. Washington, DC: U.S. Government Printing Office.

Commonwealth of Massachusetts. (1986, August). *An analysis of the first 25,000 ET placements.* Department of Public Welfare.

Costello, C. B. (1989). *Home-based employment.* Washington, DC: Women's Research and Education Institute.

Dipboye, R. L. (1989). Problems and progress of women in management. In *Working women: Past, present, future*, edited by K.S. Koziara, M.H. Moskow, and L.D. Tanner, 118-153. Washington, DC: Bureau of National Affairs.

Ellwood, D. P. (1988). *Poor support: Poverty in the American family.* New York: Basic Books.

Faludi, S. (1991). *Backlash: The undeclared war against American women.* New York: Crown Publishers.

Federal Bureau of Investigation. (1991). *Uniform crime reports: 1990.* Washington, DC: U.S. Government Printing Office.

Fierst, E. U., and N.D. Campbell, eds. (1988). *Earnings sharing in social security: A model for reform: Report of the Technical Committee on Earnings Sharing.* Washington, DC: Center for Women Policy Studies.

Garfinkel, I. (1988, Spring). The evolution of child support policy, *Focus:* 14.

Garfinkel, I., and S. McLanahan. (1986). *Single mothers and their children: A new American dilemma.* Washington, DC: The Urban Institute Press.

Gelb, J., and M.L. Palley. (1987). *Women and public policies.* 2nd ed. Princeton, NJ: Princeton University Press.

General Accounting Office. (1987). *Work and welfare: Current AFDC work programs and implications for federal policy.* Washington, DC: General Accounting Office.

General Accounting Office. (1988). *Work and welfare: Analysis of AFDC employment programs in four states.* Washington, DC: General Accounting Office.

Griffin, S. (1989). Rape: The All-American crime. In *Feminist frontiers: Rethinking sex, gender, and society*, edited by L. Richardson and V. Taylor. New York: Random House.

Gueron, J. (1986). *Work initiatives for welfare recipients.* New York: Manpower Demonstration Research Corporation.

Gueron, J. (1987). *Reforming welfare with work.* Occasional Paper No. 2. Ford Foundation Project on Social Welfare and the American Future. New York: Ford Foundation.

Harrison, C. (1988). A richer life: A reflection on the women's movement. In *The*

American woman: 1988-89, a status report, edited by S. E. Rix. New York: WW Norton.

Hartman, A. (1990). Family ties. *Social Work, 35*: 195-196.

Hartmann, H. I., and R.M. Spalter-Roth. (1989). *Family and medical leave: Who pays for the lack of it?* Washington, DC: Women's Research and Education Institute.

Haskins, R. (1988). Child support: A father's view. In *Child support: From debt collection to social policy*, edited by A.J. Kahn and S.B. Kamerman, 306-327. Newbury Park, CA: Sage Publications.

Hochschild, A. (1989). *The second shift: Working parents and the revolution at home.* New York: Viking.

Holden, K. C. (1989). Women's economic status in old age and widowhood. In *Women's life cycle and economic insecurity*, edited by M. N. Ozawa, 143-169. New York: Greenwood Press.

hooks, b. (1989). *Talking back: Thinking feminist, thinking black.* Boston, MA: South End Press.

House of Representatives, Committee on Ways and Means. (1991). *1991 Green Book: Overview of entitlement programs: Background material and data on programs within the jurisdiction of the Committee on Ways and Means.* Washington, DC: U.S. Government Printing Office.

Joseph, G. I., and J. Lewis. (1981). *Common differences: Conflicts in black and white feminist perspectives.* Boston, MA: South End Press.

Kahn, A. J., and S.B. Kamerman. (1987). *Child care: Facing the hard choices.* Dover, MA: Auburn House Publishing Company.

Kahn, A. J., and S.B. Kamerman, eds. (1988). *Child support: From debt collection to social policy.* Newbury Park, CA: Sage Publications.

Martin, S. E. (1989). Sexual harassment: The link joining gender stratification, sexuality, and women's economic status. In *Women: A feminist perspective*, edited by J. Freeman, 57-75. Mountain View, CA: Mayfield Publishing Company.

McAdoo, H. P. (1980). Black mothers and the extended family support network. In *The black woman*, edited by L. Rodgers-Rose. Newbury Park, CA: Sage Publications.

Mead, L. (1986). *Beyond entitlement: The social obligations of citizenship.* New York: The Free Press.

Meyer, C. H. (1985). A feminist perspective on foster family care: A redefinition of the categories. *Child Welfare, 64*: 249-258.

Mezey, S. G. (1992). *In pursuit of equality: Women, public policy, and the federal courts.* New York: St. Martin's Press.

Miller, D. C. (1990). *Women and social welfare: A feminist analysis.* New York: Praeger.

Murray, C. (1984). *Losing ground: American social policy 1950-1980.* New York: Basic Books.

National Commission on Children. (1991). *Beyond rhetoric: A new American* agenda for children and families: Final report of the National Commission on Children. Washington, DC: Author.

National Commission on Working Women. (1990). *Women and non-traditional work*. Washington, DC: Wider Opportunities for Women.

National Research Council Committee on the Status of Black Americans. (1990). *A common destiny: Blacks and American society*. Washington, DC: National Academy Press.

Pearce, D. M. (1987). On the edge: Marginal women workers and employment policy. In *Ingredients for women's employment policy*, edited by C. Basse & G. Spitze, 197-210. Albany, NY: SUNY Press.

Pleck, J. (1977). The work-family role system. *Social Problems, 24*: 417-27.

Polman, D. (1989, April 9). In the shadow of violence. *The Philadelphia Inquirer*.

Porter, K. H. (1990). *Making JOBS work*. Washington, DC: Center on Budget and Policy Priorities.

Pouissant, A. (1989, April 19). Letter to the editor. *New York Times*; 26A.

Rix, S. E. (1984). *Older women: The economics of aging*. Washington, DC: Women's Research and Education Institute.

Rodgers, H. (1986). *Poor women, poor families: The economic plight of America's female-headed households*. Armonk, NY: M.E. Sharpe, Inc.

Rodgers, H., ed. (1988). *Beyond welfare: New approaches to the problem of poverty in America*. Armonk, NY: M. E. Sharpe, Inc.

Rutter, M. (1982). Social emotional consequences of day care for preschool children. In *Day care: Scientific and social policy issues*, edited by E. F. Zigler & E. W. Gordon, 3-32. Dover, MA: Auburn House Publishing Company.

Schafran, L. H. (1988). Gender bias in the courts. In *Women as single parents: Confronting the institutional barriers in the courts, the workplace, and the housing market*, edited by E.A. Mulroy, 39-72. Dover, MA: Auburn House Publishing Company.

Schwartz, F. N. (1989). Management women and the new facts of life. *Harvard Business Review, 67*: 65-76.

Sheffield, C. J. (1989). Sexual terrorism. In *Women: A feminist perspective*, edited by J. Freeman, 3-19. Mountain View, CA: Mayfield Publishing Company.

Sidel, R. (1986). *Women and children last: The plight of poor women in affluent America*. New York: Penguin Books.

Skipper, J. K. and W.L. McWhorter. (1989). A rapist gets caught in the act. In *Feminist frontiers: Rethinking sex, gender, and society*, edited by L. Richardson and V. Taylor, 399-401. New York: Random House.

Snyder, N.M. (1991). *KANWORK Evaluation: Final report*. Wichita, KS: Wichita State University, Hugo Wall Center for Urban Studies.

Stack, C. (1974). *All our kin: Strategies for survival in a black community*. New York: Harper and Row.

Starr, P. (1986). Health care for the poor: The past twenty years. In *Fighting poverty: What works and what doesn't*, edited by S. Danziger and D. H. Weinberg, 106-132. Cambridge, MA: Harvard University Press.

Stevens, W. K. (1988, June 22). The welfare consensus. *New York Times*.

Stoiber, S. A. (1989). *Parental leave and 'woman's place': The implications and impact of three European approaches to family leave policy.* Washington, DC: Women's Research and Education Institute.

Stoper, E. (1988). Alternative work patterns and the double life. In *Women, power and policy: Toward the year 2000.* 2nd ed., edited by E. Boneparth and E. Stoper, 93-112. New York: Pergamon Press.

Taylor, V. (1986). The future of feminism: A social movement analysis. In *Feminist frontiers II: Rethinking sex, gender, and society,* edited by L. Richardson and V. Taylor, 473-490. New York: Random House.

Weitzman, L. (1985). *The divorce revolution: The unexpected social and economic consequences for women and children in America.* New York: The Free Press.

Whited, C. (1990, May 2). Widening rift between the sexes leaves us increasing sense of loss. *The Wichita Eagle*: 7A.

Wichita Area Sexual Assault Center. (1990a). Ten facts about violence against women. Wichita, KS: Author.

Wichita Area Sexual Assault Center. (1990b) Newsletter. Wichita, KS: Author.

Wilson, W. J. (1987). *The truly disadvantaged: The inner city, the underclass, and public policy.* Chicago: University of Chicago Press.

Wolins, M. (1983). The gender dilemma in social welfare: Who cares for the children? In *Fatherhood and family policy,* edited by M. E. Lamb and A. Sagi. Hillsdale, NJ: Lawrence Erlbaum.

Women's Bureau. (1990a). *Facts on working women.* (No. 90-2). Washington, DC: Department of Labor.

Women's Bureau. (1990b). Earnings differences between women and men. *Facts on Working Women* (No. 90-3). Washington, DC: Department of Labor.

Zia, H. (1990, Sept.-Oct.). Fighting straight hate. *MS*: 47.

Zinsmeister, K. (1990, June). Growing up scared. *The Atlantic*: 51, 52, 54.

Chapter 3

Public Welfare and Social Work: New Opportunities

Jan Hagen

INTRODUCTION

The feminization of poverty has been widely documented and discussed over the past 25 years (e.g., Pearce 1978; Rodgers 1986; Sidel 1986). Recent statistics highlight the magnitude of the issue: one out of three female-headed households is poor; for blacks and Hispanics, the ratio is one out of two. And among the elderly, women are twice as likely to be poor.

Several feminist scholars (e.g., Boneparth 1988) have called for a focus on poverty issues as part of the redirection of the women's movement, and feminist social workers (Kopacsi and Faulkner 1988) have specifically identified Aid to Families with Dependent Children (AFDC) as part of an agenda to unite black and white feminists within the profession. Except for the work of a few social workers such as Abramovitz (1988a), Miller (1989, 1990), and Ozawa (1982, 1986, 1989), however, social work scholars and practitioners have demonstrated a diminished interest in poverty issues as well as in work with poor families and individuals for the greater part of the past two decades.

Explaining this ebbing interest on the part of social work practitioners requires consideration of both societal and professional developments. One of the reasons for social workers' reluctance to work with the poor has, like the poor, always been with us—working with poor people does nothing to enhance the professional's status. The quest for professional status through social work began early in this century and continues unabated today, as reflected in the continual struggle for increased credentials and in the growing number of social workers who identify themselves as therapists.

Developments in public policy and in policymakers' regard for social work also explain the withdrawal of social work from public welfare, particularly the profession's association with public assistance. One critical development was the perception that social work failed in the 1960s to deliver on its promise to reduce AFDC caseloads through the provision of casework services. Another factor was the federal requirement in the 1970s for public welfare to separate income maintenance functions from social services. This opened the door for the declassification of many positions in public welfare that once had been identified as professional social work positions. Other factors included the withdrawal of training and education monies for social workers and the removal of social workers from policymaking positions in public welfare at all levels of government.

Is there a role today for social work practitioners and for the profession of social work in public assistance policy and programs? Do we as a profession have a responsibility to reinvest and recommit our resources and our expertise in working with public assistance recipients? As a profession, social work has always accepted responsibility for being an advocate for the poor. But beyond the profession's call for addressing poverty issues and the policy analyses of a few social work scholars, what is the fit for social work in today's public welfare environment?

Today's public welfare environment is being driven by the nation's most recent variation on "welfare reform" as embodied in the Family Support Act of 1988. The purpose of this chapter is to review briefly the political and historical background of the Family Support Act, outline its key components, and critique the central issues and challenges posed by the act. I then will consider the implications of this new legislation for the role of social work in public welfare.

THE BACKGROUND

Building on the states' experiences with Mothers' Aid, the Social Security Act of 1935 authorized a public assistance program aiding dependent children. Designed with widows and their children in mind, the original architects of the program envisioned the program's fading away as the social insurance system matured and extended its coverage. By the 1960s, however, the composition of those receiving AFDC had changed. Few recipients were widows with dependent children; social security was, indeed, providing coverage to many in this group. Increasingly, the AFDC population was represented by deserted, divorced, separated, and never-married mothers with their dependent children. This change in demographics was coupled with a dramatic increase in the number of recipients. The increase in and changing composition of able-bodied women receiving public assistance led to outcries for welfare reform, which has been pursued by every presidential administration since Lyndon Johnson's.

Work Incentive Program (WIN)

Following the War on Poverty of the 1960s, efforts at welfare reform focused on strategies to replace welfare with work. The nation has been through a whole series of variations on WIN, a program initially designed to provide welfare recipients with employment, job training, remedial education, job placement, and such supportive social services as child care and transportation. Enacted in 1967, WIN established work requirements for AFDC mothers for the first time. (Work requirements for unemployed male parents in AFDC-UP [Unemployed Parent] households were legislated in 1962.) By 1971, with the passage of the Talmadge Amendments, program priorities shifted from an emphasis on developing human capital to an emphasis on direct job placement (Ehrenberg and Hewlett 1976). In addition to services, WIN created financial incentives for AFDC recipients to work by incorporating the "30 and 1/3 disregard." This allowed employed recipients to keep the first $30 earned and to disregard one-third of remaining earnings from AFDC benefit calculations.

In general, WIN is regarded as a failure. Early concerns about the program included the issue of "creaming"–targeting its efforts on unemployed men with work experience and those AFDC mothers with no or few barriers to employment. Rein (1982) attributes its failure, in part, to a Congress ambivalent about imposing work requirements on mothers and to the ideological opposition to work requirements for mothers by those welfare professionals responsible for implementing WIN, many of whom were social workers.

But the major reason for the failure of WIN was the lack of sufficient funding for meaningful implementation. Peak funding of $395 million occurred in fiscal 1980. This provided an average of $250 for each potential WIN registrant. By 1986, this amount had declined to $227 million, or $140 for each potential registrant (Nightingale and Burbridge 1987, 23). As a result of inadequate funding, WIN was reduced to basically a program in which people registered rather than a program requiring people to work or to participate in related education and training activities.

Omnibus Budget Reconciliation Act (OBRA)

During the Reagan administration, programs aiding the poor came under severe and continual attack. Numerous programs affecting women and their dependents were dramatically reduced and AFDC was particularly hard hit. The changes in AFDC were first introduced through OBRA in 1981. OBRA tightened the eligibility requirements for AFDC by: (1) limiting to $75 a month the amount of work-related expenses that could be deducted from earnings in calculating benefits; (2) restricting the child care exemption to $160 per month per child; (3) limiting the $30 and a third disregard to four months; and (4) applying the earned income disregard to net rather than gross earnings.

As a result of these and related changes, it is estimated that 11% of the AFDC caseload, or 500,000 families, became ineligible and an additional 300,000 families had their benefits reduced (Rein 1982, 223). These changes, combined with the declining real value of AFDC benefits, resulted in a decline in those covered by AFDC. The percentage of poor families covered by AFDC declined from 83% to 63%; for poor children, from 75% to 53% (Rodgers 1986, 75).

OBRA also introduced some significant changes in the work requirements of AFDC, giving states new options that laid the groundwork for the Family Support Act. OBRA allowed states to establish mandatory workfare programs, to develop on-the-job training programs in conjunction with employers for which the AFDC grant could be used to supplement the client's wages (Work Supplementation Program), and to implement WIN demonstration programs. This latter option freed states to establish the welfare department as the provider of various employment and training programs separate from the Department of Labor. In keeping with the New Federalism, states were given a great deal of latitude in designing welfare employment programs. Under these provisions of OBRA the states began to experiment, producing such initiatives as Massachusetts' Employment and Training (ET) Choices Program and California's Greater Avenues for Independence Program (GAIN). The federal monies for these new work programs came from the WIN dollars, a funding source that declined by 70% between 1981 and 1987, "which gives some indication of the federal government's commitment to these programs" (Miller 1989, 10).

Evaluating the New Programs

Major evaluations of the states' new welfare-to-work programs were undertaken by the Government Accounting Office, the Urban Institute, and others (e.g., General Accounting Office 1987, 1988; Nightingale and Burbridge 1987). The most significant of these were the studies conducted by the Manpower Demonstration Research Corporation (MDRC) using experimental designs (see Gueron 1987). The findings from MDRC's studies played a key role in generating congressional support for the Family Support Act. The general conclusions drawn from the MDRC studies were that the welfare employment initiatives did produce positive employment gains for AFDC mothers and that the programs led to welfare savings (Gueron 1987).

However, Gueron (1987, 22) acknowledges that MDRC's findings can be compared to a half-filled glass: is it half-full or half-empty? For example, Gueron (1986, 19) notes an average AFDC participant in an experimental program obtained an $800 net benefit over five years. Miller (1989, 13) calculates this to be $13.33 per month and points out that: "Surely, the 'cost' to the women was more than monetary and should be compared with that $13.33 a month!"

Both Miller and Gueron would seem to agree that the demand side of the labor market, not just the supply side of welfare employment programs, must be taken into account (Gueron 1987, 23; Miller 1989, 17-20). Clearly, today's welfare employment programs will not substantially contribute to a reduction in women's poverty without the addition of other fundamental reforms such as pay equity for comparable work, subsidized dependent care, and occupational sex desegregation.

In addition to the evaluations of the welfare employment programs, Congress had access to information about the dynamics of poverty and the characteristics of the AFDC caseload. Longitudinal in design, these studies highlighted the transitional nature of welfare support for most AFDC families—more than 50% of single mothers leave AFDC within two years (Bane and Ellwood 1983). The work of Bane and Ellwood (1983), along with other longitudinal studies, contributed to the increasing ability of researchers and policymakers to differentiate the various subgroups within the adult AFDC population. For example, those who left welfare because of increased earnings were characterized by education levels of high school or higher and previous work experience (Bane and Ellwood 1983). Those who remained on welfare for eight or more years were more likely to have less than a high school education and no earnings in the year prior to receiving AFDC benefits. This group, which represented 17% of the AFDC caseload, accounted for most of the AFDC expenditures (Bane and Ellwood 1983).

FAMILY SUPPORT ACT (FSA)

Passed in October 1988, the Family Support Act was hailed by liberals and conservatives as a "new consensus" on welfare reform and as the most sweeping revision in the nation's welfare system in the past 50 years. Further, the Act was viewed as part of redefining the social contract between the state and welfare recipients:

> The state has obligations to meet the needs of poor families. But in exchange for income support and a range of mandated employment and support services, the dependent poor can be

expected to make efforts on their own behalf. They can be expected to search for employment, and/or to invest in their own employability through training, education or work experience. Unwillingnesss to meet these expectations when ample support is available constitutes grounds to nullify the contract. (Lurie and Sanger 1990, 1)

The Act was, in fact, passed by Congress with overwhelming bipartisan support but only after two years of intensive Congressional hearings and debates. The strong bipartisan support is more accurately a reflection of skillful political compromise between liberals and conservatives than a "new consensus" on welfare. Any "new consensus" has not been replicated as state legislatures struggled to pass the required enabling legislation for states to participate in the FSA (see Lurie and Sanger 1990).

Nor is the Act a radical departure from previous AFDC legislation; rather, it extends and builds on earlier legislation providing for child support enforcement and work/welfare initiatives for which the nation now has a 25-year history, excluding the work programs operated during the Great Depression. Once again, the legislation emphasizes the short-term, temporary nature of public assistance. And the latitude given to states in work/welfare programs begun under OBRA and the New Federalism is maintained by reserving to state discretion the actual composition of program components and the method of service delivery.

What is new is a recognition that all parents, regardless of income, have an obligation to financially support their children. For AFDC mothers, the legislation sends a clear message that all mothers, even those with preschool children, are expected to work if child care is available. This new legislation also introduces a clear focus on reducing welfare dependency; the targeting of services to those at high risk for long-term welfare dependency; the provision of funds for education in a welfare employment program; and the provision of supportive health and child care benefits during the transition from welfare use to financial independence through work.

The stated purpose of the Act is:

To revise the AFDC program to emphasize work, child support, and family benefits, to amend title IV of the Social Secu-

rity Act to encourage and assist needy children and parents
under the new program to obtain the education, training, and
employment needed to avoid long-term dependence . . . (Public Law 100-485, October 13, 1988; 102 STAT 2343)

FSA's major provisions are to (1) further the enforcement of
child support and the establishment of paternity; (2) operate Aid to
Families with Dependent Children-Unemployed Parent (AFDC-
UP) programs in all states; (3) provide transitional child care and
Medicaid benefits for 12 months to those families who become
ineligible for AFDC as a result of increased earnings or loss of
disregards; and (4) establish job opportunities and basic skills training programs (JOBS) that provide education, training, and employment to AFDC recipients.

The new child support enforcement provisions extend previous
legislation by mandating immediate wage withholding for all cases
served by the Office of Child Support Enforcement. However, beginning in 1994, immediate wage withholding will be required for
all support orders, whether or not the Office of Child Support Enforcement is involved. Thus, automatic wage withholding will become universal for all court-ordered child support. Further, guidelines previously established by the states for child support awards
will now become presumptive.

This provision of the FSA should have some advantages for
many women who retain custody of their children following divorce. The economic consequences of divorce on women and their
children have been well documented (e.g., Duncan and Morgan
1979; Weitzman 1981), and the lack of adequate child support
payments is one of the critical factors contributing to the poor
economic status of divorced mothers and their children (Garfinkel
and McLanahan 1986). Using guidelines of 17% of the noncustodial parent's income for child support for one child, Oellerich and
Garfinkel (1983) estimate that the poverty gap could be reduced by
27% through effective child support enforcement.

The FSA does not resolve all issues surrounding child support
enforcement, however. Policy issues that remain are the adequacy
and equity of the formulas developed by states for establishing child
support awards, the resulting inequities across states, and the provi-

sion of a state guaranteed minimal benefit for each child regardless of parental earnings.

A less obvious issue is the impact of child support enforcement upon family relationships, particularly for poor families. Some argue that all fathers, regardless of their income, have an obligation to provide financial support for their children. By setting the amount as a percentage of earnings, poor fathers will be paying their fair share and will not be overburdened with child support payments. For poor families, however, the benefit of automatic wage withholding for child support is questionable at best. As Abramovitz (1988b) notes, for poor fathers, this provision "may be more like squeezing blood from a stone" (239) and it may establish incentives to work only in the underground economy. Further, this additional demand on an already very limited income may impair the relationship between the parents. A negative or adversarial relationship between parents has the potential for disrupting ties with the extended kin network, cutting off the mother and her children from important–if not vital–sources of informal instrumental and emotional support. The potential for destruction of these informal support networks is even more likely in instances where the mother must first establish paternity.

For many years, the states have had the option of operating AFDC programs for two-parent families and receiving federal financial support for related expenditures. With the passage of the Family Support Act, all states are required to operate an AFDC-UP program. The mandated inclusion of two-parent families for at least six months of AFDC support and for Medicaid coverage as long as the family is financially eligible applies to 23 states and represents an important legislative initiative to address one of the long-standing inequities of the AFDC program. However, the legislation allows states to require that at least one parent in an AFDC-UP family engage in a work activity, such as on-the-job training or a workfare program, for at least 16 hours a week in exchange for benefits. States are also permitted to require full-time participation in JOBS, which is discussed in the next section, by either parent in the AFDC-UP family. To the extent that JOBS activities are made available to fathers in two-parent families, resources may become less available to serve single mothers who, in general, have greater needs for services.

The provision of child care and Medicaid benefits for up to 12 months following ineligibility for AFDC recognizes the need for a transition period between receipt of full benefits and none at all. These transitional benefits are envisioned as a bridge for JOBS participants between welfare dependency and economic self-sufficiency. Important issues remain, however, regarding assuring access to these benefits as well as the charging of premiums in the last six months of Medicaid eligibility.

JOB OPPORTUNITIES AND BASIC SKILLS TRAINING PROGRAM (JOBS)

The JOBS program is the major vehicle by which FSA seeks to increase the economic self-sufficiency of AFDC recipients. By October 1990, all states were required to implement a JOBS program, the purpose of which is "to assure that needy families with children obtain the education, training, and employment that will help them avoid long-term welfare dependence" (102 STAT 2360). Placing primary responsibility for JOBS with the state's welfare agency, states are required to offer educational activities including high school or equivalent education, basic and remedial education, and English proficiency education; job skills training; job readiness activities; and job development and job placement. Additionally, states must provide at least two of the following: group and individual job search, on-the-job training, work supplementation, and community work experience.

Except in cases of exemption, or where the JOBS program is not available in a particular political subdivision, all AFDC recipients are required to participate if child care is available. In a significant departure from previous legislation, mothers with children age three years or older (or one year at state option) are required to participate if child care is available. Mothers under 20 years of age who have not completed high school or its equivalent are required to participate in educational activities, regardless of their children's age.

States must guarantee child care if it is necessary for an adult recipient to participate in the JOBS program. This care may be provided directly, contracted for with providers, or indirectly provided by cash payments or vouchers to recipients. Federal funding for child care is open-ended and matched at the Medicaid rate for the states, which ranges from 50% to 80%. States are also required to reimburse or to pay for transportation or other work-related expenses.

The federal law requires that employability plans be developed for each eligible participant based on a comprehensive assessment that includes not only the participant's skills, work experience, and employability but also the participant's educational, child care, and other supportive needs, the needs of her children, and the family's circumstances. States have the option of using contracts with clients to specify expectations and obligations. States may also use case management services in conjunction with JOBS.

To encourage states to focus on those most likely to become long-term welfare recipients and to avoid "creaming," the law specifies that 55% of the funds be spent on three target groups: (1) families in which the parent is under age 24 and has not completed high school or had little or no work experience in the preceding year; (2) families in which the youngest child is within two years of becoming ineligible because of age; and (3) families who have received assistance for 36 or more months in the past five years.

The JOBS legislation establishes overall participation rates in JOBS programs. Seven percent of the nonexempt caseload was required to participate by 1990; 20% by 1995. In addition to these participation rates, states will be expected to meet certain performance standards. These standards, to be developed by the Department of Health and Human Services by 1993, must be measures of program outcomes, not just participant activities. The performance standards will measure outcomes in terms of increased earnings, levels of economic self-sufficiency, and reductions in welfare use. (See Gowdy and Pearlmutter, Chapter 4 in this book, for a discussion of the meaning of economic self-sufficiency to poor women.)

More money is being allocated to a welfare employment program than was previously the case. The federal entitlement funding for JOBS was capped at $800 million in 1990, rising to $1.3 billion in 1995 for a total funding package of approximately $3.5 billion over

five years. The federal matching rate for the entitlement is 90%, up
to the amount allotted to each state for WIN in 1987. Additionally,
there is a minimum federal match of 60% for nonadministrative
costs and for the cost of full-time JOBS personnel. Other administrative costs are matched at 50%.

JOBS is an ambitious piece of legislation that may be considered
an agent for institutional change–a signal to welfare systems
throughout the nation that they should take on a mission and character that more heavily emphasizes services intended to reduce welfare dependency. In essence, the aim of the act is to convert what in
the most recent past were predominately cash assistance programs
into employment and training service systems to prepare AFDC
family heads, primarily mothers, for a job and to facilitate their
entry into the labor force.

And what are the prospects for this happening? Does JOBS have
the potential for bringing about meaningful changes in the lives of
AFDC mothers? Stoesz and Karger (1990) conclude that the likelihood of "significant change in the welfare system is virtually non-
existent" (147). Miller's (1989) analysis of previous work programs has led her to predict

> . . . marginal welfare savings, strong incentives for marriage,
> the perpetuation of women's dependence, and the continued
> denigration of "welfare mothers" because when the programs
> fail to meet expectations, administrators and politicians blame
> the participants–not the design of the programs (the real cul-
> prit). This "failure" will serve capitalism, patriarchy, and
> white supremacy by, once again, preserving a cheap pool of
> labor and by, once again, proving that women, especially black
> women, cannot make it on their own. (20)

These clearly are the dangers. And by itself, JOBS, at its best, can
have only a minimal impact on the poverty of AFDC mothers and
their children. Nichols-Casebolt and McClure (1989) accurately
point out that most welfare reform proposals, including JOBS, do
not take into account the availablilty of jobs or the structure of the
labor market. The projected area of growth for jobs in the next
decade will be low-wage, low-skill jobs (Nichols-Casebolt and
McClure 1989). Frequently these jobs do not offer health insurance

or adequate wages to support a family. About one-third of the full-time jobs now open to women do not pay enough to support a mother and two children above the poverty line. Additionally, both sexual and racial discrimination continue to characterize the job market, further limiting the opportunities for women, particularly women of color (Nichols-Casebolt and McClure 1989). Women are concentrated in a few occupations, with 47% in administrative support, including clerical positions and service jobs (Blau and Winkler 1989, 277). Women working full-time, year-round receive about 65% of men's earnings (Blau and Winkler 1989, 277). This pay gap, although improving, has persisted over time and is not fully explained by educational levels, work experience, and job tenure. It is estimated that sex discrimination "accounts for as much as half or more of the male-female pay gap" (Blau and Winkler 1989, 278).

Although constraints in the economy and the structure of the labor market must be recognized and addressed, JOBS does offer the *potential* for providing new opportunities for poor women to obtain the education and training necessary to compete for meaningful jobs in the labor market. Training, education, and child care are also a necessary part of the strategy to improve the well-being of women and their children. Achieving this potential depends upon the willingness and ability of states to commit their own resources to JOBS, as well as how the states choose to implement the JOBS programs.

The implementation of the JOBS program presents a major challenge to state and local governments. Welfare agencies will be required to perform the complicated task of providing cash assistance and delivering or coordinating a wide range of services: individual needs assessment, job search, placement services, education, training, and support services. Making the necessary alterations in their administrative structure, management activities, and attitudes will be a necessary prerequisite to increasing the employment of AFDC recipients. Will the JOBS requirements penetrate into welfare agencies and will agencies have the capacity to implement the ambitious purposes of this legislation? Will the education, training, and support services provided to recipients actually produce the anticipated outcomes of increased employment and reduced welfare use? Whether or not JOBS produces the anticipated outcomes will depend not on the AFDC mothers but on the design and administration of services by state and local welfare agencies. Is there a role for social work in this process of implementing JOBS?

ROLES FOR SOCIAL WORKERS

Some states have already begun to propose and implement progressive strategies for work with welfare mothers. Consider this selection of initiatives:

- California, Iowa, and Minnesota are using the opportunity provided by JOBS to provide college educations (Greenberg and Levin-Epstein 1989).
- New coordinating efforts between welfare, education, labor, and the Job Training Partnership Act (JTPA) are being undertaken. (Kansas appears to be unique in requiring a social welfare faculty member be part of its Interagency Coordinating Committee [Greenberg and Levin-Epstein 1989]).
- New designs for reducing service fragmentation are being developed, including New York City's new community-based initiative to provide social services where people live (Buder 1990).
- Administrators are beginning to expect that income maintenance workers provide some of the social services families need.
- Case management systems are being attached to some states' comprehensive employment and training programs (Greenberg and Levin-Epstein 1989).
- Iowa is targeting comprehensive social service interventions on multi-problem families (Bruner 1990).

All of these examples represent areas where social workers have expertise; some are initiatives that represent the profession's "bread and butter." Clearly, there are roles for social workers in the implementation of JOBS.

Direct Practice

The most obvious direct practice role for social work is in case management. At state option, states may use case managers to assist recipients in participating in the JOBS program. The specific models for case management as well as the roles of case managers will be developed at the state and local levels. Social work could have an instrumental role in developing models that build on participants' strengths, empower AFDC mothers, and not only broker services but also advocate on the client's behalf for necessary support services. These services may well extend beyond the education and training provisions of JOBS to include other social services that families may need.

Initial impressions indicate that in some instances case management is being viewed simply as monitoring client progress on paper only, a function sometimes performed by specially trained clerical staff. In other instances, personnel are drawn from other vocational education and training programs. In Iowa's program to serve multi-problem families, family development specialists are being used. To date, there is little social work presence.

The JOBS program also requires state welfare agencies to develop individualized employment plans and services for participants based on an initial assessment of their education, work experience, employment skills, family circumstances, and supportive services needs, including child care. At state option, the assessment may also include the needs of the children. Who are better prepared to conduct a thorough psychosocial assessment than social workers? In order to develop meaningful employability plans, these assessments must be comprehensive and involve the client as a mutual partner. Complex decisions will need to be made around such issues as child care arrangements and what types of family circumstances will constitute deferral from the JOBS program. This type of activity, if it is to be meaningful and to provide opportunities for empowerment, must be performed by a well-prepared professional.

The increased attention to child care offers additional opportunities for social workers. The legislation requires that child care be guaranteed if required for an individual to participate in JOBS programs. In arranging child care, the individual needs of the child are to be taken into account. Funding is also available to improve state licensing requirements and to allow for monitoring of child care to AFDC children.

Some of the employment-related programs also may be an appropriate arena for social work practitioners. Job development and job placement activities appear to be most successful when jobs are developed for specific individuals. Identifying and negotiating a match between employer and employee draws on a range of foundation social work knowledge and skills in community organizing as well as work with individuals. Social group work potentially lends itself to such activities as job readiness workshops and job clubs.

Vosler and Ozawa's (1990) preliminary findings from an evaluation of two pilot welfare-to-work programs in St. Louis suggest the importance of social work activity at the neighborhood and community level. Their findings suggest that a proactive and supportive community is a critical variable in enabling AFDC mothers to enter the work force. The neighborhood-based approach incorporates central tenets of social work practice and is characterized by

. . . targeting change at multiple system levels, focusing on enabling both personal and family system reorganization, empowering personal choice as the path to change, and a program based on grassroots leadership development and mutual self-help. (Vosler and Ozawa 1988, 20)

Vosler and Ozawa (1990) argue specifically for educating social work practitioners who are skilled at interventions on multiple system levels and who can operationalize the interconnections between practice knowledge, policy analysis, and human behavior in providing service to "already vulnerable women and children" (12).

Management

Perhaps the major administrative challenge facing welfare managers is to change the culture of the welfare organization from an emphasis on financial support and fiscal accuracy to an emphasis on service delivery. Or, as Kosterlitz (1989) describes the challenge: "States are struggling to get welfare agency officials to act more like social workers and less like accountants" (2943). Perhaps states should hire some social workers to assist in this transition to a more client-focused service delivery system.

Agencies will face at least three additional major management challenges in implementing JOBS that merit the attention of social work managers: intra- and interorganizational linkages, intensity and continuity of services, and management information systems. JOBS will require increased communication and coordination of services within the welfare agencies as ties between income maintenance, education and training services, and child care services must be linked for the participant to engage in JOBS. Welfare agencies and their personnel will be required to develop new mechanisms for organizational operations; they can no longer afford to keep all these units separate. And increasingly, there is talk of doing away with the separation of services from income maintenance. The JOBS legislation also requires coordination and cooperation with numerous other agencies, including child care providers, JTPA, and educational and training programs. The scope of this state and local coordination will challenge the most able administrator. What social work uniquely brings to this challenge is an awareness and appreciation that it is the client who is to be served, not the bureaucracy.

A key issue in previous welfare employment programs has been their capacity to process program participants in a timely manner. Often, participants' progress was delayed as they attempted to move from one program component to another. Some of the barriers to service continuity are participant barriers; for example, a change in family circumstances. But others are organizational barriers. Managers will need to develop methods to process clients from one component to another as well as to sequence program components in a logical fashion so they remain accessible to participants.

A third area is the development of management information systems. Many states will be required to develop new information systems in order to meet the federal reporting requirements. In designing these systems, consideration must be given to going beyond mere compliance with federal requirements. A well-designed system should be able to provide state policymakers with information about the program effects, patterns of usage, availability of services, and so forth. In addition, the system should be designed to be of use to the front-line workers in providing services to clients. A good system could incorporate data bases on educational programs,

training programs, and child care options, as well as other information important in designing individualized programs for each
mother and her children.

Staff Development and Training

The changes called for by JOBS will require extensive staff
development and training that extends well beyond knowledge
about the new rules and regulations. Many staff will be called upon
to assume new roles and functions that are more client-focused.
Given this change in expectations for front-line workers, social
workers may be uniquely qualified to provide staff training in areas
related to practice and human behavior.

For example, a particularly critical role will be played by the
income maintenance workers who not only perform the complex
task of eligibility determination but also provide access services
(Hagen 1987). As JOBS is implemented, it is anticipated that income maintenance workers will be increasingly called upon to provide access services and perhaps to conduct initial assessments. To
perform these functions effectively, income maintenance workers
will need extensive knowledge about human development and human functioning, an understanding of cultural and ethnic variables,
and information about the effect of poverty and associated socioeconomic conditions on individual and family functioning. They
will also need skills to engage the client in appropriate referral
activities, knowledge of both agency and community resources, and
case advocacy skills. All social workers should have a strong
foundation in these knowledge and skill areas and, as a profession,
social work should be able to offer the type of staff training required
for workers to assume these new functions.

Policy Analysis and Advocacy

Social work's policy analysis and advocacy roles will continue to
be critical as "welfare reform" is implemented. The policy analysis
must continue to point out the societal factors that restrict the ability
of individuals to be economically self-sufficient. Social work must
continue to highlight such factors as the geographic restrictions of

job availability, the extent to which full-time work fails to provide a "family wage," the pay differentials by gender and ethnicity, and the lack of societal supports for dependent care. And the vision presented must be the alleviation of poverty, not a reduction in welfare dependency.

Policy analysis must also focus on AFDC and the new JOBS programs. We will need to continue highlighting the inadequacy of welfare benefits, the inequities caused by maintaining state discretion in determining standards of need and levels of benefits, the potentially punitive components of the new legislation, and the possible unintended consequences of today's work/welfare programs.

Thoughtful and comprehensive policy analysis in keeping with the profession's values and commitment to the disadvantaged will frame the profession's advocacy agenda at both the national and state levels. This advocacy agenda will include increasing AFDC benefits, expanding the earned income and child care tax credits, providing govenment-subsidized dependent care, guaranteeing access to health care, developing parental leave policies, and establishing pay equity. It will also include advocating for intensive education and training services that will enable AFDC mothers to obtain jobs providing good salaries and benefits.

Research

Social work also has a role to play in the research on the JOBS programs. In the evaluation studies conducted on the welfare-to-work programs, little attention was given to their effect on program participants and their families. We have the technology to measure the net benefits from welfare-to-work programs. It is at least equally important to measure the programs' effect on people's lives and well-being. Research that includes the clients' assessments of the program's strengths and limitations is critical if these welfare-to-work programs are to be understood.

Social work researchers need to undertake the task of identifying those factors in JOBS programs that enrich people's lives as well as those that hinder and interfere with development and functioning. As the JOBS legislation undergoes revision, which it inevitably will, social work researchers should be in the forefront with findings on how welfare-to-work programs directly affect those who participate. Social workers can use these findings to promote programs that empower AFDC mothers and build on their strengths.

TOWARD THE NEXT CENTURY

The implementation of JOBS provides renewed opportunities for the profession of social work as well as for individual social work practitioners to become involved in public assistance policy and programs. This potential for involvement runs the gamut of social work practice areas from direct service to research. Further, as a profession, we have an obligation to become involved, to be a voice for the disadvantaged and poor in society. This obligation includes not only assuring that each client receives quality services responsive to both her and her family's needs, but also informing the public and policymakers about the limitations of welfare-to-work programs. The danger of JOBS is that AFDC mothers will be blamed should it fail. Work must begin now to prevent another episode of "blaming the victim."

Although the obligation is clear and the knowledge base matches the need, the probability of increased involvement in public welfare by social work is not immediately likely. The current reality of public bureaucracies, coupled with a conservative climate and the profession's focus on restricted practice technologies, does not lend itself to predictions of increased social work involvement.

What the profession does have, however, is a national association that continues to be concerned with poverty. The National Association of Social Workers (NASW) continues to advocate for progressive social policies and, through its national Center on Social Policy and Practice, has begun research on the implementation of JOBS and its effect on AFDC families. A few social work researchers and advocates are investing significant resources in evaluating and monitoring the implementation of JOBS in various states.

This type of activity, although limited, may be sufficient to provide a foundation for increased social work involvement in public welfare in the years ahead. My hope is that the 1990s may parallel the 1920s, a period frequently mischaracterized as devoid of social reform. Clarke Chambers, a noted social welfare historian, has termed the 1920s as the "seedtime of reform" in which

> . . . social workers kept alive and vital the crusade for social action, and thus formed a viable link between prewar progressiveness and the New Deal; they sparked many social action crusades that anticipated the reform programs of the following decade. (Quoted by Trattner 1984, 252)

The social workers to whom Chambers is referring were few in number. But they were women of vision, and their contributions were significant in designing the nation's current social welfare system. Perhaps the few social workers involved in public welfare today will contribute to progressive social policies designed in the next century for poor women and their children.

REFERENCES

Abramovitz, M. (1988a). *Regulating the lives of women: Social welfare policy from colonial times to the present.* Boston: South End.

Abramovitz, M. (1988b, September 26). Why welfare reform is a shame. *The Nation*: 236-240.

Bane, M. J., and D.T. Ellwood. (1983). *The dynamics of dependence: The routes to self-sufficiency.* Cambridge, MA: Harvard University. John F. Kennedy School of Government.

Blau, F. D., and A.E. Winkler. (1989). Women in the labor force: An overview. In *Women: A feminist perspective*, edited by J. Freeman, 265-286. Mountain View, CA: Mayfield.

Boneparth, E. (1988). Conclusion: Toward the year 2000. In *Women, power and policy*, edited by E. Boneparth and E. Stoper, 297-306. New York: Pergamon.

Bruner, C. (1990). Iowa's family grant program integrating family support and education with welfare-to-work (mimeo.).

Buder, L. (1990, April 26). Dinkins offers a plan to better social services. *New York Times*: B3.

Duncan, G. J., and J.N. Morgan, eds. (1979). *Five thousand American families: Patterns of progress*, vol. 4. Ann Arbor, MI: Institute for Social Research.

Ehrenberg, R. G., and J.G. Hewlett. (1976). The impact of the WIN 2 program on welfare costs and recipient rates. *Journal of Human Resources, 11*: 219-232.

Garfinkel, I., and S.S. McLanahan. (1986). *Single mothers and their children.* Washington, DC: Urban Institute.

General Accounting Office. (1987). *Work and welfare: Current AFDC work programs and implications for federal policy.* Washington, DC: G. A. O.

General Accounting Office. (1988). *Work and welfare: Analysis of AFDC employment programs in four states.* Washington, DC: G. A. O.

Greenberg, M. and J. Levin-Epstein. (1989). *The JOBS program: Good ideas and some concerns in the first round of state plans.* Washington, DC: Center for Law and Social Policy.

Gueron, J. (1986). *Work initiatives for welfare recipients.* New York: Manpower Demonstration Research Corporation.

Gueron, J. M. (1987). *Reforming welfare with work.* Ford Foundation Project on Social Welfare and the American Future, Occasional Paper 2. New York: Ford Foundation.

Hagen, J. L. (1987). Income maintenance workers: Technicians or service providers? *Social Service Review, 61*: 261-271.

Kopacsi, R., and A.O. Faulkner. (1988). The powers that might be: The unity of white and black feminists. *Affilia, 3*: 33-50.

Kosterlitz, J. (1989, December 2). Devil in the details. *National Journal:* 2942-2946.

Lurie, I., and B. Sanger. (1990). The family support act: Defining the social contract in New York (manuscript).

Miller, D. C. (1989). Poor women and work programs: Back to the future. *Affilia, 4*: 9-22.

Miller, D. C. (1990). *Women and social welfare: A feminist analysis.* New York: Praeger.

Nichols-Casebolt, A., and J. McClure. (1989). Social work support for welfare reform: The latest surrender in the war on poverty. *Social Work, 34*: 77-80.

Nightingale, D. S., and L. C. Burbridge. (1987). *The status of state work welfare programs in 1986: Implications for welfare reform.* Washington, DC: The Urban Institute.

Oellerich, D., and I. Garfinkel. (1983). Distributional impact of alternative child support systems. *Policy Studies Journal, 12*: 119-129.

Ozawa, M. N. (1982). *Income maintenance and work incentives.* New York: Praeger.

Ozawa, M. N. (1986). Nonwhites and the demographic imperative in social welfare spending. *Social Work, 31*: 440-446.

Ozawa, M. N., ed. (1989). *Women's life cycle and economic insecurity.* New York: Praeger.

Pearce, D. M. (1978). The feminization of poverty: Women, work and welfare. *Urban and Social Change Review, 11*: 28-36.

Rein, M. (1982). Work in welfare: Past failures and future strategies. *Social Service Review, 56*: 211-229.

Rodgers, H. R., Jr. (1986). *Poor women, poor families.* Armonk, NY: M. E. Sharpe.

Sidel, R. (1986). *Women and children last: The plight of poor women in affluent America.* New York: Penguin Books.

Stoesz, D., and H.J. Karger. (1990). Welfare reform: From illusion to reality. *Social Work, 35*: 141-147.

Trattner, W. I. (1984). *From poor law to welfare state.* New York: The Free Press.

Vosler, N., and M. Ozawa. (1988). An analysis of two approaches to welfare-to-work. *New England Journal of Human Services, 8*: 15-21.

Vosler, N. R., and M. N. Ozawa. (1990). Welfare reform: Educating for social work practice at multiple system levels. Paper presented at the annual meeting of the Council on Social Work Education. Reno, Nevada.

Weitzman, L. J. (1981). The economic consequences of divorce. *U.C.L.A. Law Review, 28*: 1181-1268.

Chapter 4

Economic Self-Sufficiency Is a Road I'm On: The Results of Focus Group Research with Low-Income Women

Elizabeth A. Gowdy
Susan R. Pearlmutter

INTRODUCTION

Women and their children are the primary recipients of welfare assistance in this country; more than 80% of families receiving Aid to Families with Dependent Children (AFDC) are headed by women. More than 60% of these women never completed a high school education; they have few, if any, marketable skills; and, although 90% of them have worked, their forays into the labor market include low-paying service sector jobs, temporary work, and other employment which does not permit them to provide for themselves or their families. Although AFDC was not planned as permanent assistance for husbandless families, it has become so for many who are impoverished. It is estimated that the AFDC grant has allowed less than 4% of welfare recipients to move out of poverty; in most states, the typical welfare grant provides families with less than 50% of the poverty threshold (Abramovitz 1988; Miller 1990; Pearce 1990; Sidel 1986).

The welfare system is demeaning, stigmatizing, and discriminatory (Pearce 1990). The routines and requirements of welfare departments are often rooted in purposeless bureaucracy. In Missouri, for example, the AFDC application is 12 pages long, seeking information which is required but not used. Until mid-1991, recipients were required to report on monthly income retrospectively, so that if a recipient had some employment in January, her AFDC check would be reduced in March or April when she no longer was working, and most needed assistance. Many welfare offices are, by design, crowded and uncomfortable; space is not provided for children, even though most women bring their very young children when they go to the welfare office. Often women must wait for long periods of time before seeing a worker. When the worker sees the woman, the visit is hurried, mechanisms for support and assistance are often unavailable, and the worker must move to the next client in a large and unmanageable caseload.

There is an even deeper inequity in the welfare system. Poor women, who often work in the "secondary" labor market–where there is little full-time work with health or other paid benefits, and where the pay is at or below minimum wage–are in a welfare system which is restrictive in its eligibility requirements and mandates impoverishment to receive benefits. Contrast this "secondary" income support program with a "primary" income support program such as Unemployment Compensation, which is available far more universally to those who have lost jobs, and does not require poverty for participation. In the primary support program, there are funds to "support the worker (and his or her family) during unemployment" and "to enable the worker to conduct a job search that will result in reemployment in a job that will maintain his or her skills, occupational status and income" (Pearce 1990, 269-270); in the secondary support program, women are encouraged to take a job, any job, regardless of the cost or benefit to the woman and her family. This welfare sector provides no incentives, makes it impossible for people to see a way out of poverty, and reinforces the disadvantaged position of women in the labor market (Pearce 1990).

Programs that have been designed to ameliorate welfare dependence often have used the same stigmatizing and discriminatory processes. Work programs such as the Work Incentive Program (WIN), the Comprehensive Employment and Training Act (CETA), and the Job Training Partnership Act (JTPA) have ignored the needs of women as they have sought to increase placement numbers.

Provision of child care, transportation assistance, work-related clothing, and ongoing support has been systematically excluded from these programs (Miller 1990). Training programs have prepared women for "traditional" employment, often in the service sector, where they are unable to earn sufficient wages to pay for health and child care, and thus, the welfare system becomes a "revolving door." More often, women have been encouraged or mandated to accept public sector jobs, as part of a Community Work Experience Program (CWEP). Again, substandard wages and benefits accrue and the women return to the welfare system. Employment in child care is often seen as a way out of the welfare system; again, wages do not meet the women's needs, but more importantly, women receiving welfare are not necessarily those who are prepared to provide quality care for young children. Supporting a woman's right to decide what she wants for herself and for her children is not a concern; the only concern is that the woman be out of the welfare system, if only for a short time.

The 1980s brought many changes to the welfare system as the Reagan economic agenda took hold. Entitlement programs in general, and the AFDC program in particular, were negatively affected: benefit levels were cut, work-incentive provisions were curtailed, eligibility for services was tightened. More recently, Congress passed the Family Support Act (FSA). As Jan Hagen describes, the purpose of the FSA is to convert what in the past were cash assistance programs into employment and training systems to prepare AFDC family heads, primarily women, to enter the labor market. (See Hagen, Chapter 3, for a complete discussion of the Family Support Act.)

Care and support have been provided for poor women and their families outside of the welfare system for many years. Most importantly, poor women have developed their own support systems in communities, public housing complexes, churches and other organizations. It is within these support systems that one can see and recognize the strengths of these women. They are survivors; they share wisdom about ways to manage within the welfare system; they know who will help, who they can count on; they provide for each other.

Programs that have worked successfully with women in the welfare system have recognized these strengths and used them to provide comprehensive services–services which "make it as easy as possible for the participant, and can also allow one staff group to work with the 'whole person' " (Okagaki 1989, 13). These programs are centered on meeting the needs of clients; they recognize the need to build self-esteem and help women believe in themselves. They understand that mutual respect and caring are essential, and that staff have to be warm, welcoming, compassionate, and clear about expectations and responsibilities. Women on welfare need to understand that they have choices in their lives, and they need to learn how to make those choices; experiences which teach life skills such as budgeting, problem-solving, and decision-making are essential. If clients are to participate in work experiences, they need career planning and coaching, an introduction to the world of work, and support services which will assist them in dealing with the barriers posed by the changes they must make. Finally, they need help and support in a job search process, and additional support once they locate a job (Okagaki 1989).

A FEMINIST RESPONSE:
THE WOMEN'S EMPLOYMENT NETWORK

The Women's Employment Network (WEN) fits Okagaki's criteria (1989). The organization was founded by a group of women who believe that the best way for women to get out of poverty is through work and the help of other women. It is a program based upon an empowerment model: "that each one of us has, as a fundamental right derived from a basic human need, the ability 'to speak one's own truth in one's own voice and have a part in making the decisions that affect one's life' [Pharr, 1988]" (as cited by Bricker-Jenkins 1991, 3). Designed to assist low income women in obtaining sustained employment so that they can achieve economic self-sufficiency, the program has served more than 1,200 women in almost six years of operation. More than 70% of those who have graduated from the program are working, and 65% of those placed have held jobs for six months or more. It is a program that is directly antithetical to the welfare system. It was created by women for women; the staff and board members are women who are committed to assuring whatever assistance it takes to move a woman beyond the need for welfare; it recognizes the discrimination and stigmatization faced by women in the welfare system and in the labor market. It works with clients so that they can make changes for themselves and it works within the welfare system alongside clients to change the system.

The Program

The program has several components:

1. Adult basic education (GED training) classes help high school drop-outs obtain the skills needed to pass the high school equivalency test. Classes are offered daily in the mornings and in the afternoons. An average of 30 women participate on a daily basis.
2. Employment readiness classes teach women basic job search and job keeping skills. Women attend for 90 hours and a new class begins each month. In addition to work-related behaviors, the class focuses on helping women increase their feelings of self-esteem, set short- and long-term goals, establish assertive communication skills, plan for budgeting earned income, meet child care and transportation needs, and make choices about what they want and need for their families. At the conclusion of each class, there is a commencement ceremony which recognizes the woman's completion of this component of the program and encourages her into the next phase.
3. Job search activities teach women to use self-directed job search techniques and to follow up on leads provided by the staff. Women who have had problems performing in mock interviews, or who have not maintained contact with the program after commencement, are encouraged to attend group job search workshops, so that they can develop more confidence in their abilities. Job placement usually occurs within three months after completing the job readiness class.
4. A year-long support system is in place to assist the women as they move from using welfare to economic self-sufficiency.

Included here are access to a counselor for personal and work-related assistance, an alumni group which meets quarterly, a monthly newsletter, a clothing bank, an emergency assistance fund, as well as child care and transportation assistance.

WEN's typical client is 25-28 years old, has two children, is a single parent and has worked sporadically in her adult years. Participation in the program is voluntary and usually occurs through referrals, now mostly from former participants, but also from the Missouri Division of Family Services (DFS–the welfare office). Women may call the office and be given an appointment with the intake staff person, or they may arrive without an appointment and be seen almost immediately. A staff member recruits participants through presentations at other agencies, Head Start centers, public housing units, and wherever she can get a group to listen. The program operates in a metropolitan area, with a population of 1.5 million. More than 80% of the participants are African-American women; 15% are Caucasian, and the remainder are Hispanic, Native American, or Asian.

As staff, we have created an atmosphere in which clients know they are valued: the waiting room is large and comfortable, children are welcome, pictures of graduates are everywhere, and graduates of the program are part of the staff (Rapp and Poertner 1992). We solicit client feedback, and value their responses, and we are consistently aware of their strengths, as well as the importance of all of our shared life experiences. Board leadership in this agency recognizes few limits; they, as well as we, believe that all things are possible for these women. Their tenacious advocacy and fund raising efforts have won great support for the program and its clients.

HEARING WOMEN'S VOICES:
EVALUATING THE PROGRAM

Early in 1988, members of the staff and Board of Directors began to explore mechanisms for evaluating the services WEN provides. In general, we wanted to know if the model we used was making a difference in the lives of the women we serve; we were concerned about whether we were any more successful in helping people move from poverty to self-sufficiency than was the welfare system. We knew informally from the women's stories that they considered themselves successful when they completed the classroom work in the program and initiated a job search. It was deeply frustrating to us that we were not able to fully define and measure service effectiveness (Patti 1987; Carter 1987). We knew that we could partially measure effectiveness by using placement and retention data; yet we recognized that this strategy could not provide information regarding the steps the women had taken to achieve economic self-sufficiency, nor could it indicate in any formal way what success meant to the women themselves. As staff members we believed that research *with* participants and graduates as partners had to be considered as the best alternative for the program. We believe that the voices of our clients are of primary value here (Rapp, Shera, and Kisthardt, in press). In our work with clients, we teach the importance of their voices and their perspectives. How could we fail to include them in decisions about the research and in the research itself? Members of the board, although skeptical at first, recognized that an evaluation/research project which was designed to explore and learn "about what holds value and meaning from the consumers' point of view" (Rapp, Shera, and Kisthardt, in press) could yield significant information regarding our program and its participants.

Our primary desired outcome for the first part of the research project was to define the abstract concept of *economic self-sufficiency* from a holistic, person-environment perspective that recognizes and includes the point of view of the women who use the program. Staff and board members had developed a definition of economic self-sufficiency based upon our values and experience with the program, but we had hesitated to adopt it given the absence of input from program consumers. This definition was very limited, and reflected our stereotypes for our clients' lives; it was only in soliciting participant input that we were able to see these limits.

A second and related outcome of the evaluation/research concerned gathering data to assist in program development and redesign. We recognized that the program needed a new perspective, an approach different from that of its original designers. Again, we believed that program participants and graduates could provide that.

By hearing the women's feelings, opinions, and ideas, we hoped to operationalize economic self sufficiency, so that (1) it could be effectively and efficiently measured over time, and (2) the program would have a way to inform all of its program constituents about overall program performance (Rapp and Poertner 1987; Rapp et al. 1988).

Methodology

Focus groups seemed an ideal method for our research. The use of focus groups emerged from marketing research, wherein groups of consumers are brought together to discuss their opinions of and experiences with particular products. This "consumer-centered" methodology readily translates to social service settings. The advantages of a focus group approach include: (1) personal interaction in a group setting fosters discovery of issues, ideas, and opinions that would not emerge from individual interviews; (2) participants often feel freer and safer to voice their experiences and opinions with peers than with an interviewer only; and (3) the group setting and process tends to normalize participants' experiences and opinions as the women offer each other validation, support, and feedback. The design and implementation of this research approach is based upon the work of Krueger (1988) and Morgan (1988).

Focus Group Design

We decided to conduct four focus groups, two comprised of WEN graduates who are employed and two of graduates who have had difficulty obtaining or maintaining employment. Potential participants were identified from lists generated by two staff persons most familiar with graduates' current status. To be included in the first two groups, a woman must: (1) have successfully completed the job readiness course; (2) be currently employed; and (3) have maintained at least minimum contact with program staff. Minimum contact was defined as one or more contacts with staff after her job placement. To be included in the second set of groups, a woman must: (1) have successfully completed the job readiness course; (2) have had difficulty obtaining and/or maintaining employment after graduation; and (3) have lost touch with the program during the postgraduation period. From these lists, a stratified random sample was drawn to include women who had graduated since the inception of WEN. In none of the groups did more than two women graduate in the same month and year in order to insure a greater range and diversity of experience and to minimize potential bias resulting from subgroup friendships.

A telephone interview form guided recruitment. The researcher attempted to contact over 60 women to participate. It quickly became apparent that many of these women lead transitory lives; many had moved with no forwarding address or telephone number. Others gave reasons for not being able to attend, such as family responsibilities, lack of transportation, or conflicting work schedules. While successful in recruiting enough currently employed women for the first two groups, it was possible to identify only enough unemployed or underemployed women to comprise one group.

Overrecruitment is standard practice for focus group research. Given the need for women to attend on a specific date and time, drop-off is expected due to unforeseen circumstances arising in participants' lives that bar them from coming. Thus, while 12 women were recruited for each group only one-half actually attended, so that six women comprised each group. Women who agreed to participate were sent follow-up letters to confirm the groups' purpose and meeting arrangements. Each group met once for two hours. Those who participated were provided with supper, ten dollars cash, and childcare reimbursement for those who needed it.

The groups were led by the first author and an assistant who was a WEN graduate. The sessions were audiotaped and these data were supplemented by written notes taken by the assistant facilitator. In addition, participants completed a short written survey to obtain demographic and income data. A guided interview tool was used to stimulate group discussion in the main areas of interest. (The questions used originated from collaboration among the researcher, the Board's research committee, and administrative staff). The research questions focused upon three broad concerns: (1) How do low income women define economic self-sufficiency for themselves? (2) How do they describe their lives in terms of pre- and post-WEN involvement? and (3) What opinions do they have about their program experience and what suggestions can they make for program improvement?

Description of Participants

The participants were representative of WEN's client population in terms of race, age, family situation, and economic status. Of the 18 women who participated, 14 were African-American and four were Caucasian. They ranged in age from early-twenties to late-fifties, with the average age being 35. In all groups the continuum of family living situations were represented. Some women lived alone, both with and without children, while others lived with a partner, both with and without children. Most women, however, were single and had either young or adult children.

Fourteen were currently employed and four were not. Of these four, one was attending school to earn a bachelor's degree, two were seeking immediate employment, and the remaining woman discussed her interests in starting her own business. The latter three women had no current income sources and had recently lost unemployment benefits. The former had $100 a month from personal savings.

Of the 14 who were employed, three were members of the focus group comprised of women having difficulty obtaining and maintaining employment. Of these three, one had been working as a waitress part-time for three years, earning $2.05 per hour plus tips and receiving no benefits. She had no other income. A second woman began work one week prior to the group as a self-employed hairdresser, renting a chair in a salon. She received no wages or benefits, but did list as income $472 a month in food stamps and her husband's monthly salary of $1,600. The third woman had worked for three months full-time as a files purger for a bank, earning $5.50 per hour plus health and life insurance and paid leave. She had no other income.

The wages for the remaining employed women in the first two groups ranged from $3.93 to $8.00 per hour, averaging $5.88. These women tended to work full-time and wages were slightly higher for those who had been continuously employed for longer time periods. Most of these employed women worked in a variety of community and social service settings. Only three women worked for a business or company. Five were secretaries and clerks; three women worked as non-professional helpers, and the remaining three were employed in the positions of data entry, cashier, and bookkeeper. Most of these women received fringe benefits from their current employer.

Findings

Analysis involved identifying the main themes of each discussion, and the range of agreement and disagreement among participants in each question area. The researcher took primary responsibility for preliminary data analysis. Initial findings from each group were presented to staff for review and additional interpretation. Findings from all groups were then summarized, resulting in identification of common themes. Final summation of findings reflects a collaborative effort among the researcher and staff, especially those who are WEN graduates. Focus group participants were also given drafts of the findings for their review and comment. A few did respond to follow-up calls from the researcher, and showed much more interest in what would be done with the findings than with the details of the results themselves.

The following sections present an overview of the findings. First, the concept of economic self-sufficiency is defined as a continuum and as comprising much more than a certain income level. Second, family issues related to economic self-sufficiency are presented. Ways in which participants benefited from program participation are then discussed, followed by a summary of implications and future activities based upon the research.

Economic Self-Sufficiency Is a Road I'm On

The women viewed the concept of economic self-sufficiency (ESS) as a continuum, as a road on which they travel. Far from being a dichotomous condition where one either is or is not economically self-sufficient, the women defined, often in great detail, how each is moving toward her own particular vision of this status. They discussed at length how economic self-sufficiency is a "personal thing," a process.

This finding is reinforced by the results of the survey question, "Do you consider yourself economically self-sufficient?" Nine women answered no, six answered yes, and three declined to answer. These responses cut across factors such as whether the woman was currently employed, the amount of income she currently received, or level of satisfaction with her current economic status. Further exploration of this issue led back to the central point that participants are "not there yet," but see themselves as moving closer to this goal.

In defining ESS in terms of their relative movement, the women placed surprisingly little emphasis upon the acquisition of specific amounts of money. Such concrete measures of economic self-sufficiency were usually dismissed as being a means to a greater desired end. According to the women, economic self-sufficiency is not captured merely by focusing on how many dollars one has. Rather it is what these dollars allow one to have and to do. The next section will illustrate this point.

What Being Economically Self-Sufficient Means

The women viewed economic self-sufficiency as comprised of three distinct but related components: (1) a concrete monetary and resource component; (2) a psychological aspect; and (3) a skill component. General consensus was found among all three groups regarding this definition. What differed was the emphasis they placed upon each component, which depended upon their current employment situation. For example, those who have been more successful in obtaining and maintaining employment tend to see themselves as having a career path and placed more emphasis upon changes in their sense of self-esteem than upon their current financial situation. Those who are in more immediate financial need focused more on concrete employment and resource concerns and viewed the psychological aspect more in terms of "surviving" than of accomplishment. Regardless of these subgroup differences, the basic definitional components remained the same.

Concrete Resources. Being economically self-sufficient means having "enough to cover the basic needs," and having the ability "to meet my obligations and to do what I want to do when I want to do it." The women were consistent in focusing upon the *experience* of being economically self-sufficient. This component of economic self-sufficiency includes: (1) being financially independent from both public assistance programs and significant others such as boyfriends, husbands, and parents; (2) being able to afford a car, a decent home, good food, clothes, and holiday trips; (3) being able to buy "extras" for their children and themselves, and to pursue their own interests and goals; and (4) being able to pay their debts and put money in savings, especially as a buttress against unexpected illness, old age, or job loss. Having freedom from worrying about living from paycheck to paycheck, staying out of debt, and staying on a budget were predominant in their discussions. The enthusiasm with which the women described their desire to be financially independent was palpable.

> I wouldn't say I'm economically self-sufficient yet. When it comes a point where I don't have to worry about the health care needs of my family, when I don't have to worry about the light bill, when the light man isn't knocking on the door saying "your bill is due." Not that you have a lot of money, but you're not worried about how your kid is going to get that next pair of shoes, or this doctor is not going to take them because I can't pay. Just the simple things, that may not be all that simple because we don't have them yet. Once I achieve that much it will be a whole lot easier and a whole lot better.

> A lot of people would look at me and would think I'd be very self-sufficient. I'm not married, I don't have children, I live alone. I take care of everything myself . . . [But] I live from paycheck to paycheck, and even with my part-time job [in addition to her full-time job] I don't even have a new car! But to not have a car payment you'd think I would have enough money to *save,* to buy the things I want, and I can't.

> Economic self-sufficiency for me is to be able to meet my obligations and to do what I want to do when I want to do it. I haven't gotten there, it looks a long way down the road, but I'm going to get there . . . We as women learn to rob Peter to pay Paul *early* in life, to keep our heads above water . . . You might have to eat beans and chicken wings this week, and neck bones and potatoes the next, but you don't go hungry . . . It may not be what you want, but you're always striving toward

the point of tomorrow being able to have steak and potatoes and salad.

Economic Self-Sufficiency Is a Frame of Mind. The women specifically identified a psychological part to economic self-sufficiency. The majority defined this aspect primarily as self-confidence and self-esteem. Some also used the term "survivor" to describe their capacity to "manage" the difficult times. Integral to this "frame of mind" are: (1) perceiving oneself as having choices; (2) appreciating the quality of one's present life situation while simultaneously striving for "more"; (3) viewing one's current employment situation or use of public assistance programs as stepping-stones to future career plans; and (4) attending to one's needs for happiness, satisfaction, and autonomy in the workplace along with wage and benefit levels. They also acknowledged the frustration and stress they experience when their personal and work activities are not psychologically satisfying. A few women mentioned reliance upon religious beliefs as giving them faith and hope during rough economic times.

> The place I live in is only $300 a month. It's a little bitty small thing. But I'm so satisfied with *me* and what *I'm* doing–I'm like *hey!* So that's why I feel I'm self-sufficient. Because I did this and I did that, and I'm doing this and doing that. So I don't think about what I'm *not* doing, or what I *don't* have, because what I don't have is not important. What I have now is what is important. I'm not going backwards.

> I've always managed since I was sixteen and I know I always will . . . In some ways I'm more self-sufficient than people I know that earn $35,000 a year yet are always worried about how they're going to pay their insurance and their car. So in some ways I'm already self-sufficient, psychologically, but as far as having a lot of money, I don't.

> I'm tired of taking these old "do nothing" jobs, just wasting my time, looking up at the ceiling, even though I have a paycheck. But the paycheck doesn't make me feel that good. It just does what it's supposed to do, pay the basic things. I don't intend to be a homeless person, so I've got to do something to

make things go, but it doesn't make me feel good on the inside, and that's what I'm looking for.

Acquisition and Use of Job-Related Skills. Economic self-sufficiency is also about having job-related skills and abilities. While only a few explicitly stated this was a component of economic self-sufficiency, they all talked about their skills and abilities. This component is comprised of: (1) formal education; (2) previous job experience; and (3) having a wide variety of interests and creative abilities. Several women discussed their abilities in terms of feeling competent to pursue entrepreneurial endeavors on their own.

There are two aspects of this component. First, there is the actual acquisition of specific knowledge, skills, and experience. Second, and no less important, is their ability to recognize, express, and act upon their job-related abilities and experience. In this respect, the psychological aspect of economic self-sufficiency appears to combine with the technical aspect, resulting in discussion by the women of what Bandura (1982) and others (Hackett and Betz 1981) refer to as self-efficacy. This finding will be elaborated upon later.

> Then there would be the ability, how I view myself ability-wise. Ability-wise I'd be a 5+!

> I feel like my learning, how to do the resume, and how to present myself, and how to answer difficult questions in the interview and things like that is very important.

> One thing I found out is that I use a lot of my skills, like being at home taking care of kids, and organizing, to that job. When I went through the mock interviews, in order to transfer those skills, I'd say, "I do this," and transfer it to what it would be in the work force.

Family Issues Related to Economic Self-Sufficiency

Discussions of economic self-sufficiency are interwoven with stories about family relationships and responsibilities. Their own financial situations are directly affected by the quality and intensity of their ties to children, parents, partners, and relatives. Being able to provide for their own children is a recurring theme for the mothers in the groups.

Most reported the very real sacrifices they make on a daily basis as they juggle multiple demands for their time, attention, energy, and financial resources. Getting by on two hours' sleep, being too exhausted to play with their kids after work, and trying to fit some "quality time" with children into an overloaded schedule are very real concerns for these women. Setting an example for their children that work is something of value was stressed several times.

Families help women on their road toward economic self-sufficiency by providing childcare, taking children to and from school, sharing living expenses, lending money, and providing emotional support. Participants struggled with the dilemma of often needing family support while concurrently seeking greater independence in their own lives.

Some anxiety and discomfort surrounded this area as the women attempted to reconcile the complex issue of interdependence with others. Ways in which women are doing so include: (1) paying family members and friends for child care they provide; (2) treating money given by family as "business transactions" to be repaid; and (3) being assertive with family about their long-term career goals and resisting their pulls to remain dependent on them emotionally and financially.

Several women touched on issues of traditional gender role expectations held by others and how this sometimes impeded their own efforts toward becoming economically self-sufficient. Being raised as "caretakers" was identified as a problem in that the message is to put others' needs before their own. Earning less than their husbands or partners also affected feelings of dependence and unequal power within relationships. A few women commented, with some anger, about the apparent double standard society holds for poor and middle-class women, i.e., poor mothers must work while middle-class women can choose to raise children full-time.

> There is no one really around me to help me. It's just me and my kids. They don't pay child support, and when you get on the courts about it, they'll say, "Well, we're on the case." So it's just me right now, and sometimes you feel all alone in this world. I have plenty of family in Kansas City, but it's like they want to bring me down because they want you to be at home taking care of your kids. And I believe I'm doing my job as a

mother but yet I want to show my kids that I don't have to sit at home and draw welfare.

I think I kind of have it made, because my mother said, "I'll be willing to take your kids all day, get them up, make sure they get to school." She watches them, takes care of them. I always tell her, "I don't know what I'd do if you weren't *here*." She helps with her income, we all pool our money together.

You feel like you're sacrificing your kids going to this job. You do feel that. I felt that when I was working days, and working at night you also feel the same way.

Changes in Their Lives Attributed to WEN

While general consensus was found among the three groups in defining economic self-sufficiency, there were disparities between the first two groups and the third regarding their experiences with the program. The following sections present an overview of what participants identified as the positive and negative attributes of their WEN experience, noting differences among the three group's opinions when they arose.

"They Made Me Feel Good About Myself." The majority of participants identified increased self-esteem as a significant and lasting benefit of the program. As noted earlier, what the women labeled as self-esteem appears to most closely fit the concept of self-efficacy, i.e., the combination of actual ability with a confidence or belief in one's ability (Bandura 1982). These are women who now know they have opinions and that their opinions matter. They were not afraid to speak out, disagree, push a point, explain further, seek support from other group members, and listen closely to what others had to say without feeling threatened. They spoke from their own hard-won experience and emphasized what they had learned from their economic and personal struggles.

Before I went [to WEN] I just had my second child and my self-esteem was very low, very low. I did not like myself, completely. It brought my self-esteem back up. Not to a high point, but to a point where I can deal with it.

Before I came to WEN, my self-esteem was low, because I didn't think I was a worthwhile person. The marriage to my girls' dad had failed and I thought it was my fault, so I went on ADC until my girls got into school full time. Then I decided to go to a local Business College and take up accounting. I graduated from there and was looking for accounting positions. I was told, "You don't have enough experience, you need a degree." And all I had was a diploma. Everywhere I went the door was slammed in my face and that brought my self-esteem down more.

I said, if they can make me feel so good about myself, then I can do anything. I even went to work, got fired, and I told him okay. If you fail, it's a lesson. So I'm able to go on.

I went through the program twice. The first time I had to quit because of the personal and physical problems that I had. I had absolutely no self-esteem or confidence. The second time, after I got things a little more under control, I still had low self-esteem and confidence. In fact, when we had to get up in front of the group and state our names, I had to face the chalkboard, I couldn't even talk to them. But by the end of the three weeks, not only could I face everybody, I could look at everybody in their eyes while I was talking.

The first two groups openly discussed and evidenced this positive self-concept in their behavior and interactions. The third group, in contrast, placed less emphasis on this outcome. The primary difference appeared to be that members of the first two groups have continued to obtain support and experiences to reinforce the positive changes in their attitudes and self-perceptions. This has not been generally true for members of the third group.

The women's "before and after" stories capture these differences quite clearly. Prior to their participation in WEN, the women in the first two groups generally described themselves as feeling like failures, as drifting aimlessly from one temporary situation to another, as lacking goals in the present or plans for the future, as feeling powerless over their own life circumstances, and as feeling detached and alone. Several women mentioned feeling stigmatized because they received AFDC or had criminal records. The picture they paint of life prior to the program is one of feeling burdened, alienated, and without hope for real change. In contrast, the majority of the women's "after" stories signify real and positive changes in their financial security, career plans, and psychological well-being.

Although similar themes were identified in the stories of the third group, the lack of lasting effects from program participation was evident. A few members of the third group continued to describe lives that resembled the "before" scenarios. They were scared their impoverished situations would not change and they would fail to succeed in the job market. They felt hopeless and alone with their struggles. Women in this group were frustrated by their lack of apparent benefit from WEN. What is true for all participants is that they were in a period of transition at the time they chose to come to WEN.

Connections to Self and Others. Women credit WEN for introducing them to a fellowship, sisterhood, and a bond with other women. Being able to communicate, to share personal problems, and see other women overcome the challenges they thought only they faced, were repeated themes. Developing mutual respect and trust, and overcoming prejudices were also mentioned as a part of this process. An underlying aspect of this perception of connection has to do with role-modeling; several women commented on things WEN staff and graduates said or did that helped them look at themselves in new, more positive ways.

Women in the third group also valued this aspect of the program, but to a lesser degree than the first two. Their discussion communicated less involvement with other WEN participants, both during and after the Job Readiness Class. However, the desire for human connection was voiced in this group as much as in the first two.

> Another interesting thing with the WEN program is they were able to bring success and failure stories *together*. If you look at the staff, some of them used to be part of the class and now they're doing an exceptional job. And to bring in past WEN graduates, and they're doing a fine job, and then you're able to relate to them. "God, if she can do it, then I can do it. If she was down and out, I can get back to that point too."

WEN gave me a fellowship with women. We still communicate. If I run into them downtown, we stop and chat, have a cup of coffee, send Christmas cards, and this type of thing. It was an enjoyable experience.

Access to Ongoing Support. This is the one area in which disagreement on an issue became evident among participants. While there was general agreement that they profit from having connections to other women after graduation, and from being able to call on staff for help with employment concerns on an ongoing basis, there were real differences in opinion around the issue of how to go about sustaining these connections. This was most apparent in the first and third groups, where quite a bit of discussion time centered on WEN's alumni meetings.

Being able to "go back" to the program for job leads, moral support, and emotional connection are valued. Maintaining friendships with other graduates and feeling they are part of a larger network are also valued "after WEN" experiences. What caused disagreement, especially in the first group, centered on who was responsible for staying in touch: the women or the staff.

Interestingly, members of the third group were just as likely to mention a desire for ongoing program connection, but tended to relate stories where such contacts had been negative, or failed to meet their expectations. A sense of "sisterhood" or mutual support among members themselves seemed lacking in the third group. In addition, several women, representing all three groups, identified the difficulty they faced in attempting to keep in touch with staff and attend alumni meetings while balancing work and family duties.

I feel I made a lot of good friends there. I feel in the event I need them again I can go back and brush up on the skills I don't have–grow that way.

I started working at Marion Laboratories. I worked there for 11 months and they laid me off. My self-esteem went back down again because I thought it was something with me. I went back to WEN to help me find a job. It seems just walking in the building helps you build something in yourself.

When they say network–you have to keep that line of communication open with the program. You have to make phone calls. Say for instance you lose a job, you tend to go back down, you tend to backslide. So, I'm not pushing the alumni meetings . . . but it really helps. Once I started going it was like dawn, it was really the uplifting feeling.

I run across someone every so often. I used to have contact but I think I let it slide. I had a lot of things going on over the last several years so I don't think I've been in touch with anyone.

Right after you get out of the class you go into this whirlwind, you're so excited you are really *too* busy to get back. So once things get settled you sort of forget.

I started with the Mentor Program, had to drop out for awhile, and my mentor never called me. I didn't feel a close relationship at all there.

Having Goals and Working Toward Them. A major difference in their lives after graduation was that of having goals, having a sense of direction, seeing their choices, and feeling more confident about knowing how to reach these goals. For some women learning what a goal *is* was in itself important. For others learning to take vague hopes for economic self-sufficiency and turn them into concrete steps and actions was of value. It was apparent as the women talked that they now know where they want to be in the future and feel they have the skills, resources, and persistence it takes to get there.

Where the third group differed was not related to the benefit itself, but rather that they had experienced a variety of external barriers to reaching their goals. Physical and mental illness, employment discrimination because of their age, child care responsibilities, and lack of specific marketable skills (such as computer literacy) were problems for this group. Overall, the third group refrained from discussing goals and career plans as such, and were much more likely to focus upon their immediate economic situations.

Now I can look at people and see if they have goals for themselves because that's what I do for myself. I set goals for myself and try to reach each goal as I go on with my life. I don't even talk to a man that doesn't have goals in his life!

You can have goals and ideals but do you take the fundamental steps to reach those goals–the WEN program made that possible for me.

I'd go apply for a position and they would ask me, "What's your goal?" and I never had a goal. They'd say, "You *have* to have a goal if you come apply for a job." I didn't know what a goal was, so I joined WEN.

If you want to take a trip to the Bahamas on your income you can do that. With *planning*. With a budget from day to day. Because I'm planning to go to London, England at the end of this year and I know I don't make that kind of money. But I'm *going*, that's what I want to do. It's because I'm getting ready right *now*. I'm making plans.

Dealing with Authority. This area seems directly related to the women's increased self-esteem, changes in their self-perceptions, and communication skills. They made reference to knowing what you need from the situation, knowing how to communicate your needs to people in authority, and being persistent in exploring available options. In the first group one woman's story about being overbilled by the gas company was used by other members as a reference point to discuss their ability to deal effectively with authority figures. In the second group, this issue played out in terms of feeling capable of interacting effectively with public assistance workers and now knowing how to present a past criminal record to potential employers. In the third group, discussion centered upon pursuit of a discrimination case against an employer.

See, I believe everybody uses something or someone within their lives. The Hyatt uses me to make more money. I can use them to gain more knowledge to get where I want to go. So that's why I have to go through what I have to go through.

You use the system to your advantage. You really end up beating it, but they don't know it.

The thing is, I have to be good with my words. That's the only way I get out of situations is that I talk to the gas company and tell them I can't pay that much now and then.

Acquisition of Specific Skills. All groups identified specific things they learned from the program that help them in the job market and contrast with their preprogram level of knowledge and skill. They talked about attending to their appearance and wearing dresses to job interviews. Several women identified as helpful learning how to complete applications, write resumes, and present past employment histories. Several women talked with fervor about the challenge of learning to speak in front of their classmates, giving graduation talks, and participating in public relations appearances on behalf of the program. Increasing their feelings of confidence and communication skills through this activity is a highly valued outcome of their WEN involvement.

However, all three groups, to varying degrees, also discussed the need for additional exposure to specific skills related to the job market. While recognizing that WEN is not designed to provide such targeted training, several women voiced their frustration at lacking technical skills related to clerical and computer work, and entrepreneurial activities.

It seemed like I'd go to places to put in applications and I couldn't fill out an application. I mean you can read one–I've always read, all the time, but just wasn't able to complete one. And a resume! I'd never even heard of one. I felt that the only people who had resumes are the ones who graduated from college or who'd been working long term.

They will show you *how* to job search, how to look for a job, help you ascertain *what* you want to do, and if you don't have the clothes for what you want to do they'll help you get them, plus give you car fare!

Well, it proved to me I need speech classes because I need to learn how to stand up in front of people. If you want to be a manager you have to have that control. I'm getting it slowly but surely, but talking in class pushed me a lot further than before.

The world we're living in today is being taken over by computers. Anybody that doesn't have some knowledge of computers, they better go to school. Because if not you're not going to have a job in the next ten years, five, maybe not even that long. In working, I said, "I better go to computer school, because if not, I'm going to be obsolete!" Extinct like a dinosaur!

Connections to Employment Opportunities. Another way their lives changed concerns having a clearer sense of what kinds of jobs they are looking for and having access to job openings through the program. As they shared their "before and after" stories, most of the women indicated they now know more about how to use their long-term goals to evaluate potential employment opportunities. Also, they see WEN as a connection to concrete job leads not otherwise available to them.

Women in the third group also recognized this as a benefit, but a few were dissatisfied with the quality or types of employment connections made. Expectations by some centered upon WEN's failure to produce: (1) a greater number of referrals; (2) jobs with higher wages and benefits; and (3) jobs tailored to their specific interests, regardless of a woman's qualifications.

[Before WEN] I was in places where I'd start at $4.00 an hour and go six months with no raises and no benefits. Employers don't even talk to you about those things, it didn't even cross my mind. And if my son got sick we went to Swope Park Comprehensive Center where they go by your income, and I was "below average income," and I'd think Oh my God!

Like when I worked for Marion Lab. People know that's a big prestigious company. Well when they laid me off it hurt me real bad, but I know it looks good on my resume. So I know that helps *me* in the long run.

WEN really started me on the road to where I am because at graduation they called me from the school district and I worked there temporarily for nine months. When I left there, by working for a temporary agency, she called again! And where I'm at now, they needed a bookkeeper, and I've been there almost a year, permanent. This position has allowed me to grow in the field I was in. I'd always been in the accounting field but I'd never been a full charge bookkeeper and now I am.

After graduation I worked for the IRS for two months, maintained contact with the WEN program, started working for the Salvation Army in my area of study, and have been with them for a year.

I do not feel I got very good placement assistance or referrals at all. I felt if I wasn't fitting into the standard run of the jobs they usually have, then that's just how it goes.

DISCUSSION AND IMPLICATIONS

For professionals committed to helping women gain greater economic self-sufficiency the lessons are clear. Economic self-sufficiency is much more than a job, a paycheck, or termination from AFDC. For low-income women to experience economic self-sufficiency they must have self-worth, confidence, and a sense of a future as much as concrete resources. Synonyms for "sufficient" include capable, competent, respectable, effective, and successful (*Webster's II* 1984). Unfortunately, job placement rates, AFDC payment limits, group literacy levels, eligibility rules, and vocational training duration continue to dominate professionals' discussions of economic self-sufficiency while systematic attention to helping women discover and act upon their abilities, competencies, and personal power is neglected.

Rethinking Our Assumptions

The findings from this study challenge professionals to scrutinize the assumptions upon which economic self-sufficient definitions are founded. Critiques of current ESS definitions have been offered by others (Greenburg 1990; Herr, Halpern, and Conrad 1991). Examination reveals three critical limitations. First, ESS is treated as a dichotomous state: a woman either is or is not economically self-sufficient. She either has sufficient earned income or she does not; she either is receiving public assistance or she is not. Thus, programs impose a view that becoming economically self-sufficient is a distinct event, hinging upon her ability to complete various job training, placement, or education programs.

In fact, some of the hardest work will occur long after "placement termination" as she negotiates the foreign worlds of work, school, skill and self development, and changing economic status. None of the women in this study identified with this "either/or" approach; regardless of employment status, income level, job history, education, race, age, or family composition, participants were clear in stating there is more to ESS than just having it or not. Satisfaction with their current economic situation and a view of themselves as making progress toward this goal were two factors that complicated these women's ability to respond with a simple yes or no to the question, "Do you consider yourself economically self-sufficient?"

Their responses lead to a second shortcoming with ESS definitions. Besides being dichotomous, they also tend to be absolute approaches to defining a complex developmental process. An "all or nothing" definition fails to offer a normalizing view of low-income women and sets their economic experiences apart from the nonpoor population. Typical ESS definitions imply a woman is economically self-sufficient only when she is providing *all* her resources (housing, food, child and health care, clothing, transportation, savings, recreation) through earned income. Accordingly, a woman could be working full-time, providing all these resources except one or two, and still be labeled economically dependent. There is no middle ground, no recognition of the normative process of accumulating these goods and resources over years, as all but the affluent do in our country.

These findings challenge professionals to move beyond traditional, categorical ways of thinking. In sharing our results with a social work educator, the response was, "but self-esteem and money are two different things entirely!" A pivotal lesson of this study is that dichotomous thinking by policymakers and service providers is part of the problem rather than the solution. Berlin (1990) criticizes social work research and practice for supporting bipolar thinking in situations where recognition of complex relationships among "opposites" would increase our understanding and effectiveness. A solution to blending the "opposites" of money and self-efficacy can be found in this study, and in similar research (Herr, Halpern, and Conrad 1991; Okagaki 1989), in which economic self-sufficiency is seen as a continuum and treated as a developmental process involving movement through various stages of personal and economic growth. "Different women will fall on different points in the continuum" (Okagaki 1989, 31) and will experience differing rates of movement and progress.

The final deficiency is that low-income women have been left out of the process of defining economic self-sufficiency. Clearly, professional assumptions have been made about what ESS means, what it is comprised of, and how to achieve it, without listening to the voices of those most affected. Numerous studies exist regarding the effects of poverty upon this population (Auslander and Litwin 1988; Axinn and Stern 1987; Donovan, Jaffe, and Pirie 1987; Wolock et al. 1986), their personal characteristics and behavior (Chrissinger 1980; Rein and Rainwater 1978; Shepard and Pence 1988) and program inadequacies (Dickenson 1986; Mason, Wodarski, and Parham 1985; Miller 1989; Ritter and Danzinger 1983; Moscovice, Craig, and Pitt 1987). Data regarding what low-income women say they want, how they define ESS, and their suggestions for ways programs can help them achieve this goal are absent (Miller 1989). Further research which captures and communicates answers to these questions is needed if we are to develop programs which are truly attuned and responsive to those we are called to serve.

The views of the women in this study concerning ESS are buttressed by other research. In a comprehensive study of 13 programs for low-income women that do work, Okagaki (1989) found that methodical attention to building women's self-esteem, life skills, economic motivation, social support, and sense of respect, integrated with job skills training, placement, and resource development, were key to successful outcomes. Similar findings are occurring at Project Match, an innovative welfare-to-work program operating since 1985 in Chicago (Herr, Halpern, and Conrad 1991). A central element of this program involves helping women (for up to three years) increase their self-esteem and confidence through recognizing and celebrating their incremental economic and personal gains.

Helping women believe in themselves, their abilities, and their future is the required practice approach, and one which necessitates a view of economic self-sufficiency as a personal journey that can take extended amounts of time and support (Burghardt and Gordon 1990; Herr, Halpern, and Conrad 1991; Okagaki 1989; Ritter and Danzinger 1983). As noted by Herr, Halpern, and Conrad (1991), a study of supported work programs found that individual achievement and programmatic success must be calculated not "by touchdown passes, but by grinding out two, three, four yards at a time" (Auletta 1982, 316). Effective practice requires a shift in perspective, where poor women are viewed as employed and unemployed citizens rather than "welfare mothers" (Zinn and Sarri 1984), where multiple routes out of poverty are recognized and supported (Burghardt and Gordon 1990; Herr, Halpern, and Conrad 1991), and where the upbuilding of the human spirit leads to growth and accomplishment (Reynolds 1975).

What we have seen at WEN, through operating the program and evaluating its effectiveness, is that, like economic self-sufficiency, changing the welfare system so that it truly hears participant voices is a road . . . a frame of mind. Policymakers need to hear from participants and their advocates if change is ever to occur in this at once unresponsive and totally over-burdened system. For those of us who are advocates:

> Developing and advocating agendas by, for and with poor women that are built around a recognition of interdependence, the value and importance of women's work to society, and the institutional character of gender discrimination is essential. It is especially crucial in a time of attack and retrenchment to have a vision of alternative sets of institutions, programs and policies that would bring about economic justice for women. Only with a vision can much less major actions be seen as meaningful, no matter how small; only with a vision and a set of principles to guide choices can we decide which small steps to take; only with a vision can welfare and all social policy be made into a system that is controlled by and for women. (Pearce 1990, 277)

Program and Practice Implications for WEN

Finally, based upon the women's recommendations from this study, significant changes have been made to the program and will be summarized here. First, WEN's Board of Directors officially adopted a revised ESS definition that recognizes the three aspects of ESS identified herein (Table 1). Second, an ESS survey tool was designed to use with women as they move through the program (Table 2).

Items were derived from the words women us 1 in the focus groups, and a five-point scale is used by women to rate themselves in relation to each item, thereby capturing the "movement toward" ESS. Baseline data is compared to quarterly follow-up data collected over a two-year period. The tool appears to be a meaningful measure, and is showing slight increases in women's reports of their ESS levels.

Program redesign and development are also underway. Activities in this area center upon the most problematic finding–that of the need to strengthen the postgraduation support component. Participants reported infrequent contacts from staff, a lack of attention to their needs once they had completed the job readiness class, and insufficient access to program resources after graduation. Staff discussed each of these issues and were able to develop a plan for responding to the women's concerns. First, staffing patterns were altered to allow the staff member who provides much of the postgraduation support to spend more time out of the office doing hands-on work with the women, while another staff member runs a weekly job-search group to augment individual job-search activities. Second, a volunteer (through the Jesuit Volunteer Corps) was assigned full-time to pursue extended support activities with women on a proactive basis, using phone and mail contacts to reach out in ways staff previously had not had time for.

Perhaps the two most radical changes to the program involve direct participation by the women themselves. A WEN Evaluation Committee, completely comprised of participants, meets monthly to review program development and evaluation activities, and to act upon the findings. Several committee members are women who participated in the focus groups. In conjunction with staff, the committee has planned and carried out two large social events for graduates, one of which highlighted women's personal and career suc-

TABLE 1

WOMEN'S EMPLOYMENT NETWORK
DEFINITION OF ECONOMIC SELF-SUFFICIENCY

A woman considers herself economically self-sufficient when she has:

1. Obtained sufficient earned income, benefits, and concrete resources to meet her (and her family's) basic needs. These needs are defined as: food, clothing, housing, transportation, health care, child care, leisure and social activities, debt payment, pursuit of personal goals and interests, and financial independence from public welfare agencies, family, and friends;

2. Achieved a definition of herself as a valuable, unique, and capable human being. This includes having the necessary self-confidence, support, and abilities to operate successfully in her work and home environments;

3. Acquired an array of knowledge, skills, and experiences. These include: academic and vocational education; career development and job-related knowledge and skills; on-the-job training and experience; problem-solving and goal-setting skills; resource acquisition strategies; and interpersonal influence and negotiation skills, among others.

Economic self-sufficiency exists on a continuum upon which women travel toward greater economic and personal autonomy over time. It is a fluid and dynamic process involving movement toward increasing levels of sufficiency relative to each woman's individual circumstances. According to this definition, low-income women become increasingly self-sufficient economically as each "small" financial and personal success occurs, is reinforced, and is sustained over time. Systematic environmental support throughout this process is necessary to facilitate achievement of this desired outcome.

---

cesses. The committee was also instrumental in designing a novel peer-support network for graduates called the WEN Sisterhood. Members were clear in stating "we don't want more services–help us help ourselves." The Sisterhood's goal is to decrease the social isolation so many women experience, increase their exposure to peer role models, and create a venue for women to share their experience, strength, and hope with each other after structured program involvement has abated. Women who graduated from WEN over one year ago are matched with more recent graduates to spend several hours together each month engaged in various social, recre-

TABLE 2. WEN Economic Self-Sufficiency Survey

Name: _____ Date: _____ Class #: _____

Think about your PERSONAL economic situation over the last 3 months. For each of the following items, circle the number that most clearly indicates where you rate yourself, using this scale:

1 = NO, NOT AT ALL   **4** = MOST OF THE TIME
2 = OCCASIONALLY   **5** = YES, ALL OF THE TIME
3 = SOMETIMES

My current financial situation allows me to:

ITEM	SELF-RATING				
1. Meet my obligations	1	2	3	4	5
2. Do what I want to do, when I want to do it	1	2	3	4	5
3. Be free from government programs like AFDC, foodstamps, general assistance, etc.	1	2	3	4	5
4. Pay my own way without borrowing from family or friends	1	2	3	4	5
5. Afford to have a reliable car	1	2	3	4	5
6. Afford to have decent housing	1	2	3	4	5
7. Buy the kind and amount of food I like	1	2	3	4	5
8. Afford to take trips	1	2	3	4	5
9. Buy "extras" for my family and myself	1	2	3	4	5
10. Pursue my own interests and goals	1	2	3	4	5
11. Get health care for myself and my family when needed	1	2	3	4	5
12. Put money in a savings account	1	2	3	4	5
13. Stay on a budget	1	2	3	4	5
14. Make payments on my debts	1	2	3	4	5
15. Afford decent child care (leave blank if you don't have children)	1	2	3	4	5

ational, and goal-related activities. Private funds were acquired to fund the project, including a full-time staff member to oversee the project and to attend to any special needs of Sisterhood participants. Finally, a unit of four social work students will be acquired to extend the amount of personalized support available to graduates and demonstrate the value of extended support through improved program outcomes.

REFERENCES

Abramovitz, M. (1988). *Regulating the lives of women.* Boston: South End Press.

Auletta, K. (1982). *The underclass.* New York: Vintage Books.

Auslander, G. K., and H. Litwin. (1988). Social networks and the poor: Toward effective policy and practice. *Social Work, 33:* 234-238.

Axinn, J., and M. J. Stern. (1987). Women and the postindustrial welfare state. *Social Work, 32:* 282-286.

Bandura, A. (1982). Self-efficacy mechanism in human agency. *American Psychologist, 37:* 122-147.

Berlin, S. B. (1990). Dichotomous and complex thinking. *Social Service Review, 64:* 46-59.

Bricker-Jenkins, M. (1991). Introduction. In *Feminist social work practice in clinical settings,* edited by M. Bricker-Jenkins, N. R. Hooyman, and N. Gottlieb, 1-13. Newbury Park, CA: Sage Publications.

Burghardt, J., and A. Gordon. (1990). *More jobs and higher pay: How an integrated program compares with traditional programs.* New York: Rockefeller Foundation.

Carter, R. K. (1987). Measuring client outcomes: The experience of the states. *Administration in Social Work, 11*(3/4): 73-88.

Chrissinger, M. S. (1980). Factors affecting welfare mothers. *Social Work, 25:* 52-56.

Dickenson, N. (1986). Which welfare strategies work? *Social Work, 31:* 266-272.

Donovan, R., N. Jaffe, and V. Pirie. (1987). Unemployment among low income women: An exploratory study. *Social Work, 32:* 301-305.

Greenburg, M. (1990). What's happening in JOBS: A review of initial state data. Washington, DC: Center for Law and Social Policy.

Hackett, G., and N. E. Betz. (1981). A self-efficacy approach to the career development of women. *Journal of Vocational Behavior, 18:* 326-339.

Herr, T., R. Halpern, and A. Conrad. (1991). *Changing what counts: Re-thinking the journey out of welfare.* Evanston, IL: Northwestern University Center for Urban Affairs and Policy Research.

Krueger, R. A. (1988). *Focus groups: A practical guide for applied research.* Newbury Park, CA: Sage Publications.

Mason, J., J. S. Wodarski, and T. M. J. Parham. (1985). Work and welfare: A reevalution of AFDC. *Social Work, 30*: 197-203.

Miller, D. C. (1989). Poor women and work programs: Back to the future. *Affilia, 4*: 9-22.

————— (1990). *Women and social welfare: A feminist analysis.* New York: Praeger.

Morgan, D. L. (1988). *Focus groups as qualitative research.* Newbury Park, CA: Sage Publications.

Moscovice, I., W. Craig, and L. Pitt. (1987). Meeting the basic needs of the working poor. *Social Service Review, 61*: 420-431.

Okagaki, A. (1989). *Women and self-sufficiency: Programs that work, policy that might.* Washington, DC: The Corporation for Enterprise Development.

Patti, R. (1987). Managing for service effectiveness in social welfare organizations. *Administration in Social Work, 11*: 1-6.

Pearce, D. (1990). Welfare is not *for* women: Why the war on poverty cannot conquer the feminization of poverty. In *Women, the state and welfare*, edited by L. Gordon, 265-279. Madison, WI: University of Wisconson Press.

Rapp, C. A., and J. Poertner. (1987). Moving clients center stage through the use of client outcomes. *Administration in Social Work, 11*: 23-38.

————— (1992). *Social administration: A client centered approach.* New York: Longman.

Rapp, C. A., W. Shera, and W. Kisthardt. (in press). Research strategies for consumer empowerment. *Social Work.*

Rapp, C. A., E. A. Gowdy, P. Sullivan, and R. Wintersteen. (1988). Client outcome reporting: The status method. *Community Mental Health Journal, 24*: 118-133.

Rein, M., and L. Rainwater. (1978). Patters of welfare use. *Social Service Review, 52*: 511-534.

Reynolds, B. C. (1975). *Social work and social living.* Washington, DC: National Association of Social Workers.

Ritter, M., and S. K. Danzinger. (1983). *After supported work: Post-program interviews with a sample of AFDC recipients.* New York: Manpower Research Demonstration Corporation.

Shepard, M., and E. Pence. (1988). The effect of battering on the employment status of women. *Affilia, 3*: 55-61.

Sidel, R. (1986). Welfare: How to keep a good woman down. In *Women and children last*, edited by R. Sidel, 77-99. New York: Penguin Books.

Webster's II New Riverside University Dictionary. (1984). Boston: Houghton Mifflin Co.

Wolock, I., L. Geismar, B. Lagay, and P. Raiffe. (1986). Forced exit from welfare: The impact of federal budget cutbacks on public assistance families. *Journal of Social Service Research, 9*: 71-96.

Zinn, D. K., and R. C. Sarri. (1984). Turning the clock back on public welfare. *Journal of Women in Culture and Society, 10*: 355-370.

Chapter 5

Women Who Work Outside the Home: Multicultural and Multigenerational Influences on the Family Adjustment Process

Edith M. Freeman

INTRODUCTION

Between 1950 and 1980, the number of women employed outside the home increased from 34 to 52% (U.S. Department of Labor 1983). Projections indicate that by 1995, approximately two-thirds of all new workers in the labor force will be women (Johnston 1987, Congressional Budget Office 1988). This trend primarily reflects the rising numbers of employed women in two categories: single heads of households and married women with children under the age of six. The most rapid increase was from 12 to 45% among women in the latter category, an increase of 375% since 1950 (England and Farkas 1986). Rates for married women with children between the ages of six and 17 are not as dramatic (rising from 28 to 62% during this period), but they represent a similar upward trend.

Generally, because a woman's entry into the labor force has consequences for all members of the family, this trend has been viewed as a problem (Freeman, Logan, and McRoy 1987; Weintraub, Jaeger, and Hoffman 1988). The definition of the problem, however, has changed over the years. As policymakers and researchers grappled with the increased labor force participation of women in the 1970s, a major concern was the proper supervision of children. The term "latchkey" children was coined to illustrate their high-risk status and the danger of their falling through the "cracks" between family, school, and community systems. Special afterschool enrichment programs, child care cooperatives, and public awareness campaigns were the result.

The focus then shifted to how the trend was affecting the world of work. For instance, some women wished to enter previously male-dominated or nontraditional areas of work. As a consequence of having more women in the labor force who were challenging existing practices, issues of sexual harassment and gender discrimination became more visible (Rosen 1982; Balamaci 1991). Laws and personnel policies had to be broadened to clarify what behaviors constitute sexual harassment. Moreover, gender-related employee benefits, such as family leave and child care services, required a reallocation of financial resources.

More recently, the issues of employed women have been framed in terms of problems that occur within the family when women attempt to manage multiple role responsibilities (Repetti, Matthews, and Waldron 1989). Unfortunately, this focus has served to obscure some important issues outside of the family. It has made it easy, for example, to ignore the more global underlying reasons many women have entered the labor force. With the rising inflation rate, it has become an economic necessity for women to work outside the home, whether they are in two-parent families *or* single heads of household (Freeman, Logan, and McRoy 1987; Shortridge 1987). As long as the focus continues to be on how women manage to "juggle" existing *and* added role responsibilities, only women take the blame when this process does not work.

Moreover, such a focus presents a narrow perspective of employed women isolated from the cultural context in which they live. It ignores, for instance, aspects of gender, family, and ethnic culture that influence the reasons and consequences of their entry into the labor force as well as the community and societal changes that are needed as a result. Given the biases inherent in how the issues of employed women have been framed in the past, it is important to view the situation in a more strengths-oriented and ecological manner.

The purpose of this chapter, therefore, is to examine the total ecology of the family adjustment process when women are employed outside the home. Multicultural and multigenerational factors that influence this process and some important policy and practice implications have been addressed.

THE FAMILY ADJUSTMENT PROCESS

Hartman and Laird (1983) have defined the family as "two or more people who have made a commitment to share living space, have developed close emotional ties, and share a variety of roles and functions" (30). This definition encompasses families that do not have legal ties along with those recognized by a court of law. While this definition presents a clear conceptualization of the family at this time, it represents a shift from the more traditional definitions of the family, as assumptions about the family have also changed.

Assumptions About the Family Adjustment Process

Change is a common, ongoing aspect of family life whether in reference to how families are defined or how they function. It can be assumed that the family adjustment process is an important, dynamic component of a unit's functioning that changes over time. This process is defined as a unit's ability to respond positively and adaptively to changing internal needs (e.g., the birth of children or a member's need for increased support) *and* external conditions (e.g., industrialization, urbanization, and technological advances that affect employment) (Freeman, Logan, and McRoy 1987).

Another assumption is that the extent to which internal and external demands are congruent or can be accommodated often determines the quality of a family's adjustment. At any point in time, the family's process of adjusting to changes provides a "snapshot" of "moment-to-moment interactions" among family members. It also reflects similar momentary interactions between the members and other systems in their environment such as the extended family, neighborhood, social or community organizations, schools, social agencies, and the workplace.

As in all systemic processes, a third assumption is that these interactions are circular rather than linear. Emphasis is placed, therefore, on the goodness of fit between the person and environment rather than on what caused a given problem. Germain's (1979) ecological perspective further clarifies the adjustment process with its dual concerns about "the adaptive potential of people and the nutritive qualities of family and community environments" (8).

Illustrations of the Adjustment Process

As changes occur, the family adjustment process and the situation which is initiating the changes continuously influence one another in both positive and negative ways. The following brief case studies illustrate this process of circular causality, although, on the surface, various changes related to employment seem to be triggering the adjustment process in a linear manner. (All of these are composite case studies with fictitious names.)

> The Kelsos are an African-American couple in their late 20s. This is Mr. Kelso's first marriage; he is from a poor family and is very ambitious. His job with a large corporation requires extensive travel. Thus, he finds it difficult to help with household responsibilities except occasionally. Ms. Kelso has two children under age six from her first marriage who live with the couple. She recently went from part-time work and college classes to full-time work with the federal government. She is bored with this job. After her divorce from her first husband, Ms. Kelso had begun to feel she was more in charge of her life both financially and emotionally. Since their marriage, Mr. Kelso handles the money because he feels women in general are poor managers, although he is supportive of his wife in other areas. Ms. Kelso would like to have more input into decisions about the family now that she is contributing more toward their income.

> The Bennetts are a well-to-do white couple in their 40s. She is from an extremely poor family in southern Appalachia in which women had little power in their marriages. She has been happily married most of the time; she sees Mr. Bennett as very

giving in material things but also very controlling. He is from a middle-income family and is very self-assured. He owns his company and knows a lot about many things. Ms. Bennett entered graduate school, and after several months, Mr. Bennett asked her for a divorce. He felt she was placing her interests first since she no longer did as much caretaking for her family. Also, he has ridiculed her desire to obtain a masters' degree and has not been supportive of her efforts to involve the four children (12 to 17 years old) in household chores. He convinced her that he should have custody of the children because of his higher income. Three of the four children decided to live with the father after the divorce. With her greatly reduced family income, Ms. Bennett has to struggle to finish graduate school in order to obtain adequate employment.

Mr. and Ms. Rivera are a Hispanic couple in their 30s. He is a high school drop-out who recently lost his auto assembly job in a general layoff. He has never wanted his wife to work, and continues to feel this way in spite of the fact he has been able to obtain only part-time work. She had agreed she would not work outside the home. Then when he was unable to find a full-time permanent job, she found a secretarial job based on her vocational training during high school. Mr. Rivera agrees to baby-sit with their two younger children (three and four years old), but he will not do household chores and continues to be resentful of her employment. Ms. Rivera and the two teenage children share the housework and other chores.

The Elgarths are a Jewish couple in their early 40s. He is a nursing home administrator who has recently been offered employment out of town that requires more responsibility and provides more income. Ms. Elgarth went to work after their children were older and has just received a promotion. She suggests he turn down the job offer or that she should not move with him because of her career. Her parents have encouraged her to be supportive of her husband, indicating that she can get a job anywhere. Their son supports the father in his desire to move. He also believes that a move east will help him get into the college of his choice in two years. The older daughter thinks they should all have some input into the decision since all will be affected. Ms. Elgarth handles most of the household responsibilities, with the children doing a small amount and Mr. Elgarth helping out periodically.

In reviewing these case studies, an "intricate dance" is apparent, involving ongoing issues and changes related to employment. The situations present each family with an opportunity for positive change and growth that may not be realized due to the ways in which power is being handled within each system. This dance of power affects how these families allocate roles and how they adjust to and cope with stress.

HOUSEWORK AS A METAPHOR FOR OTHER ISSUES

Issues of power, role allocation, and coping with stress in the case studies are most apparent in how housework was being handled within those families. Housework is a recurring theme throughout each of the case studies. In this sense, housework can be viewed as a metaphor for the other issues which are identified. To understand this metaphorical relationship, it is necessary to explore the value of women as well as the value of what is considered to be "their work" within this society.

Gender Socialization and Values

Housework, or domestic labor, is generally viewed as difficult and unglamorous, but as a necessary part of family life. Women have always been devalued in this society relative to men; it may have been a simple step to relegate them to the most undesirable work. As a consequence, women and housework have been closely associated through the process of gender socialization to which both males and females are subjected (England and Farkas 1986). Devaluation of the person (females) has resulted in a similar devaluation of the work even though it is essential to an acceptable quality of life. With this circular devaluation process has come a withholding of power and status from women and an assumption that these qualities are a given for men, especially for white men.

It follows that most couples will assume that the wife is responsible for housework, except where circumstances make this impractical temporarily, such as when a child is born into the family. England and Farkas (1986) note that this type of assumption is an implicit marital contract, although Stafford, Backman, and Dibona (1977) note that even among unmarried cohabiting couples the woman is responsible for the majority of the housework.

Relationship Between Housework and Employment

Implicit contracts between couples about housework tend to be adhered to without regard to changes in a family's circumstances. This tendency includes those circumstances in which the woman becomes employed or enters an educational or training program. A general consequence, according to Geerken and Gove (1983), has been a decrease in total housework when women are employed rather than increased rates of housework by males. Research has revealed some specific factors that affect the husband's or partner's participation in housework and power-sharing when the woman is employed:

1. The presence, number, and ages of children in the family affect how much housework men will do. Said another way, if there are a sufficient number of children living in the home who are old enough to do housework, the man is less likely to participate.
2. When men do take on some of the housework, it is primarily in the child care area (e.g., playing with the children while the woman prepares a meal).
3. Some men who participate in housework, in areas other than those included in #2 above, do only a slight amount in response to the woman's employment outside the home and usually only when she is not available (e.g., she works a different shift from the husband's).
4. Men model underlying gender values and roles in terms of their reactions to and participation in housework.
5. When women enter the labor force, their power base in the family does not automatically increase. Often, they are unable

to use their contribution to the family income to increase the man's participation in housework or their own input into decisions about the family (Vanek 1974; Robinson 1980; Ferber 1982; Farkas 1976; Rexroat and Shehan 1987).

Theoretical Underpinnings and Housework

England and Farkas (1986) indicate that "this failure of males to increase their housework participation is one of the major puzzles of research in this area" (94). The most common explanations of allocation of family labor fail to fully explain men's relatively low participation in housework.

For example, some authors believe that the gender role ideologies which men model vary across social class subgroups, with working class individuals holding more traditional sex role values and expectations than those of other income levels (Elkin and Handel 1978; Stockard and Johnson 1980). The more traditional the ideology, the less a man would be expected to shift roles and participate in housework when the woman is employed. Findings of other researchers, however, suggest that any observed class differences are manifested more in attitudes than in actual behavior (Beer 1983; Coverman 1983).

Others suggest that the relative potential wage of women and men is an important predictor of their division of labor within and outside the home (Becker 1981). Each person is expected to contribute an equitable share of the family labor. There may be an implicit computation of the value of each person's work in the home versus his or her wage from paid employment (Mansur and Brown 1979). Thus, if the woman's wage is close to that of the man, he will be more likely to engage in housework than if his wage is much greater than hers. However, evidence suggests that while women with wages comparable to their partners may be able to increase their power in other ways, they have not been able to use this power to increase men's participation in housework except very slightly (England and Farkas 1986).

There is also an exchange theory related to power and housework. Although similar to the theory of relative wages on the surface, exchange theory is based on the principle of control. It posits that the partner who brings more resources to the relationship wields the most power. According to England and Farkas (1986), wages are one measure of resources that can be withdrawn if a relationship ends. It is assumed that the person with less power will do more of the housework since he or she has more to lose if the relationship dissolves. According to exchange theory, a shift in woman's ability to withdraw resources from the relationship when she becomes employed should cause a shift in power. Again, the evidence suggests that in such situations many males continue to refuse involvement in housework.

In summary, these theories do not fully explain the low level of male involvement in housework when a woman's roles include outside employment. As indicated earlier, the metaphorical relationship between housework and other family relational issues which result from gender socialization may better account for this phenomenon. Rigidity about housework as the female's responsibility is clearly a metaphor for women's devalued status and lack of power. Such rigidity indicates the problem is deeply woven into the fabric of society and family life, and that it can negatively influence the adjustment process. A systemic view goes beyond the restricted focus imposed by some of the theories discussed previously. It helps to focus on a broader range of positive and negative influences on a family's adjustment, including multigenerational and multicultural factors.

MULTICULTURAL AND MULTIGENERATIONAL FACTORS

Multicultural and multigenerational factors are those factors that are involved in a family's and racial/ethnic group's culture across the generations. They include a consistent set of values, roles, behaviors, and societal conditions that permeate the system over time in an interrelated and predictable manner.

Gender Values

Gender values refer to the belief systems of families across generations that determine the relative worth of men and women within the family as well as within the society (Freeman and Landesman 1992; Devore and Schlesinger 1987). The focus is on issues of equity (dissimilar contributions may have the same value) and on complementarity (the value of contributions is based on how well they fit together to meet a unit's needs). The following questions help to focus on some intergenerational factors that influence gender values:

1. How are women and men in a family or racial/ethnic group perceived in terms of their relative power and powerlessness?
2. What are the sources of their power?
3. Is violence against women and children accepted or condoned (physical or emotional) based on power differentials within a family?
4. Can males support females emotionally (and the reverse) across generational boundaries without negative sanctions?
5. Are females allowed or encouraged to develop their own sources of power without negative sanctions?
6. What values, language, rituals, and customs related to race and ethnicity have been maintained by family and what is the role of women in terms of these phenomena?

In some families and racial/ethnic groups, women are assumed to not possess or value power; consequently, there may be generational secrets about how women have obtained and used power covertly. Sons may not be able to provide emotional support to their mothers directly because that would acknowledge female sources of power to influence relationships; this could threaten the power of the males within a family.

The Elgarth family, discussed earlier, was in the process of deciding how to respond to the father's opportunity for employment in another city. The family provides an example of conflicts over gender values. The son supported the father's desire to move without regard to the mother's career needs, indicating that each spouse's contributions and needs might not have been valued equitably. In addition, the wife's parents urged her "to support her husband" which did not allow her to validate her view of the situation. In a positive sense, the wife and daughter were united in an attempt to change the unit's gender values and power differentials. A source of support for such positive changes was the husband's periodic participation in housework. However, an important barrier was the couple's traditional roles in decision making and the cross-generational influence of her parents in reinforcing those roles.

A similar positive analysis can be developed in regard to racial/ethnic values and how they can influence family adjustment. For instance, in the African-American culture, because of institutionalized racial barriers, various positive coping strategies have been developed and valued by members. One such strategy is to support and reinforce those members of the group who have the best opportunity to achieve in a given area. In many situations, this is an effective strategy, especially for black women for whom racial barriers have often been less rigid than for black men. In the Kelso family, Mr. Kelso is doing well in his career, but the situation does not seem to be working as well for Ms. Kelso. She has shifted from part-time work and college to support Mr. Kelso's career and is now in a full-time position with which she is bored. Moreover, there is a traditional value of role sharing in terms of housework and the handling of money that is frequently part of this supportive coping strategy. But role sharing is not occurring within the Kelso family, causing some strain for Ms. Kelso. While stressful, this type of situation may be qualitatively different for black women versus women in general. A strength may be that black women have a longer history of being employed outside the home than women of other racial groups. Therefore, group supports in the form of rituals for sharing housework among women, combining child care resources, and developing mentoring relationships may be more available to Ms. Kelso and other black women in similar circumstances than to white women, for example (Freeman, Logan, and McRoy 1987).

Gender Roles

Roles for men and women are often predetermined and acted upon across family generations. They may be based primarily on gender rather than on ability and needs. Freeman and Landesman (1992) note that such multigenerational and multicultural influences on family adjustment can be discerned through exploration of the following questions:

1. What do the family or racial/ethnic group define as acceptable and valued roles for men and women?
2. How are "deviations" from those roles responded to?
3. To what extent are roles for men and women interchangeable and under what circumstances?

In the case of the Bennetts, it was clear that the roles of employee outside the home and high-income wage earner were the most valued male roles in the husband's family of origin. In comparison, women's roles as workers within the home were not valued by the wife's southern Appalachian, impoverished family, nor were women expected to work outside the home. Moreover, these valued and devalued ethnic and generational roles for men and women permeated the current family and did not allow the wife to assume a different role through graduate school attendance and becoming a professional. Her gender-determined role and relative powerlessness as a wife limited her ability to bargain with her husband and children in order to encourage them to take on some aspects of the caretaker role (housework, nurturer, or supervisor/supporter of children's recreational activities).

Guilt about giving up the caretaker role and taking on a new wage earner role may have encouraged Ms. Bennett to agree with the husband's unilateral custody decision. However, there was also a positive aspect to the family divorce. Visitation with their mother provided a new set of circumstances for the noncustodial children to cope with. The mother's life-style (less leisure time or time for focusing primarily on the children's needs) altered their relationships and required the children to be understanding of her needs more than in the past. Moreover, the children had to take responsibility for some of their own caretaking due to moving from one parent's household to the other. They now had to care for laundry and keep track of personal possessions. The focus was on the changes needed in their total life-style as a result of the divorce rather than only on the changes caused by the mother's recent education and employment. As a consequence, the family adjustment process was enriched.

In terms of interchangeable roles, the Rivera family exhibited gender roles that were rigidly adhered to in an inflexible manner. The wife's role precluded work outside the home even after the husband lost his employment. In addition, when she became the primary wage earner against his wishes, he agreed to assume the child care role but would not participate in the housework. The presence of older children who helped with the housework was, no doubt, a factor in his continued refusal to participate and in the overall family adjustment process. Within this family, only one gender role assigned to the wife (child care) was interchangeable when she became employed outside the home. This type of rigidity in role assignments within a given family or racial group is often a result of gender socialization.

Gender Socialization

Gender socialization has been discussed more fully in a previous section, particularly with regard to how it influences the division of labor for housework within families. The following questions help to focus on the role of gender socialization more generally (Freeman and Landesman 1992; Devore and Schlesinger 1987):

1. What behaviors are men and women differentially reinforced for?
2. How does the family or racial/ethnic group empower males and females (if at all)?
3. What goals or boundaries are predefined for males and females?

In many families, men and women are socialized through the reinforcement of particular behaviors. Women may be socialized to be other-directed; in those circumstances they are often heavily reinforced for caretaking roles across the generations within a family or racial/ethnic group. In other families, men or women may only become empowered through the denial or withholding of power from one another, as when male members dominate because women are considered to be inferior. The opposite is true for families in which individuals are empowered or feel good about their experiences in controlling their lives based on abilities rather than on gender. For example, the men in one family have enjoyed and excelled in cooking over three generations. They have been socialized to pursue this and other non-gender-determined activities and, in the process, have empowered themselves based on the family culture's flexibility about gender roles and interests. In this sense, their gender boundaries have not been rigidly prescribed for them by the family or by their racial/ethnic group.

However, a different picture emerges in the case of the Kelso family. Within the husband's family of origin, men have been socialized to handle money, based on an assumption that women cannot manage adequately. This practice allows men in that family to have a prescribed type of power that is not available to women. It reinforces the racial group's emphasis on "macho" behaviors as another source of empowerment for black men. Ms. Kelso, on the other hand, has developed a sense of empowerment from her previous experience as a single mother in managing her income successfully. In the current family, her gender boundaries have been predetermined in this area based on the cross-generational influences of the husband's family of origin. Along with these influences, this family also illustrates the influence of some interrelated societal conditions that are affecting their adjustment process.

Current Societal Conditions

Although the familial and racial group factors that have been discussed are important, another more critical variable involves social policies that affect cultural dynamics and adjustment within families. An example of a question that helps to focus on this particular influence is how do economic and political conditions in society differentially impact particular families and their adjustment–racial and ethnic minorities, women of color, single mothers, lesbian women, and other vulnerable groups?

Discriminatory policies that have led to high unemployment and underemployment among blacks, Hispanics, and women, for example, create additional stressors that impact on the adjustment of individual families within those and other cultures (Nilsen 1984;

Schervish 1983). The expectations for women within such families may lead to cultural conflicts that make coping and adjustment within the family more difficult. The Rivera family illustrates this type of cultural conflict and is generalizable to the other groups of vulnerable women *and* men identified above. Ms. Rivera was confronted with the conflicting expectations of her family and ethnic group that limited problem-solving around housework and her outside employment. The cultural and societal stereotypes emphasize that Hispanic women are passive and that they play the major role in homemaking. Employment discrimination (an unwritten policy) has reduced the potential job market for Mr. Rivera, thus making it necessary for her to work outside the home in addition to her homemaking duties. These conflicting expectations are barriers to Ms. Rivera's employment outside the home. The purpose of her employment is to decrease stress related to finances. However, these barriers can increase stress between the couple because both her working *and* her efforts to involve him in housework are likely to be viewed by him as a threat to his role as head of the household. Thus, institutional racism, poverty, and a lack of adequate resources such as child care and health insurance benefits for women were part of important societal conditions that inhibited the family's coping (Beller 1984; Corcoran, Duncan, and Ponza 1984). Such conditions also tend to keep the problem and its resolution focused at the level of the individual woman and her family only, and not at a societal level as well.

HOW CAN THESE CONDITIONS BE CHANGED?

Given the conditions described in the previous sections, concerted efforts need to be directed toward change at both micro- and macro-levels. At the macro-level, more comprehensive and gender-sensitive social policies are needed, while methods for enhancing the strengths of individual women and their families are important at the micro-level.

Micro-Level Interventions

Interventions targeted for individual women, their families, and local communities should involve community education that can impact the multicultural and multigenerational influences that have been discussed. For instance, churches, schools, community centers, and the media can be used for community education programs. The sessions should be open to the general public. They could involve values-clarification exercises and information about how gender socialization can predetermine male and female behavior and inhibit effective family adjustment. Education about a particular racial group's history of oppression, values, and rituals can highlight its strengths and create understanding about shared and effective ways of coping (Devore and Schlesinger 1987). It may also provide examples of role sharing, division of labor related to housework, and power bargaining that are useful for employed women of all races and ethnic groups (Freeman, Logan, and McRoy 1987).

Micro-level interventions also may be directed toward women who request services from social agencies for help with the family adjustment process. For maximum effectiveness, those interventions should be mutually determined and focused on helping to provide opportunities for women to empower themselves. Because of the nature of the issues with which these women may request help, there should be some exploration of who else in the current family, family of origin, and other areas of social support should be included in the sessions (Freeman, Logan, and McRoy 1987). Examples of potential mutually determined interventions involve teaching clients how to do the following:

1. Bargain as a coping/change strategy to impact the power balance in the family. (The goal is to make the couple's or single parent's and children's contract for housework, decision making, and other issues as explicit as possible.)
2. Enhance their awareness of sources of strengths and strain within the family that result from multicultural and multigenerational influences. (This allows the woman to set clear expectations about her own needs as a valuable person, to give up the guilt sometimes associated with working outside the home, and to be less available for roles such as housework that she would like to interchange with other family members.)
3. Develop a multigenerational resource network within the relevant racial or ethnic culture or cross-culturally as a result of

increased awareness. (Such networks increase self-help and support resources across the generations, provide role modeling opportunities, and help to develop competencies for handling the identified sources of strain.)

4. Enhance the woman's self-in-the-world orientation or the selection of a perspective that views women as unique and worthwhile human beings whose common emotionally bonding experiences are unifying. This bonding can relate to the set of actors in the woman's immediate environment *and* to the larger population of women. It can involve organized sources of bonding such as the women's movement, meditation, spiritualism, or other sources. The goal is the development of an intrinsic self-esteem which is not based on gender role performance.

Macro-Level Interventions

In addition to these prevention and intervention strategies, change is needed at the social policy and large-system level (Scarr, Phillips, and McCartney 1989). Two major macro-level strategies involve changes in traditional education and workplace policies. A policy of preventive education could be useful for refocusing textbooks, curriculum, school practices, the physical environment, and the values of school personnel (kindergarten through the twelfth grade) to reflect an appreciation for multicultural and gender differences (Allen-Meares, Washington, and Welsh 1986). This perspective could be integrated throughout the education curriculum of school districts, in addition to being the focus of self-contained units of curriculum. It could include many of the areas discussed in this chapter, including the strengths and unique qualities of women. Other areas of focus involve the roles of men and women, gender socialization, gender values, and positive aspects of a multicultural perspective.

Important workplace policies might include preventive education about sexual harassment and sexual discrimination. Education would be more effective in small work groups, where team-building could occur, rather than in the large heterogeneous groups that typically comprise staff training units in work settings. The application of the concept of comparable worth could be useful for addressing pay inequities between male and female employees (Treiman and Hartmann 1981). Such a policy would bypass arguments about quotas for female hirees in particular male-dominated positions. Finally, a national policy for family leave is essential at this time. By adopting a gender-sensitive, but not gender-specific, policy, the implication is that both parents have responsibility for family adjustment issues. Such a policy supports the type of bargaining at the individual family level which has been discussed in the previous section of this chapter.

CONCLUSION

The increasing numbers of women entering the paid labor force today provide unique opportunities for growth at the level of individual families, staff in employment settings, community members, and society. Women and their families can be helped to empower themselves and to enhance the adjustment process through identifying strengths and sources of strain from multi-generational and multicultural factors. The complexity of the adjustment process can be appreciated through recognition that these two types of factors often interact in a given family's situation. Moreover, it is often difficult to prevent such factors from affecting the workplace itself, through reinforcement of sexual discrimination and other negative practices. Increasing numbers of working women indicate that the resolution of many of these issues must occur at a societal level where they are maintained through institutional racism and a negative gender socialization process. Only then can the growth and development potential of women and their families be fully realized.

REFERENCES

Allen-Meares, P., R. O. Washington, and B. L. Welsh. (1986). *Social work services in schools.* Englewood Cliffs, NJ: Prentice-Hall.

Balamaci, M. (1991, October 28). The price of saying no. *People Magazine, 36*: (16): 44-50.

Becker, G. S. (1981). *A treatise on the family.* Cambridge, MA: Harvard University Press.

Beer, W. R. (1983). *Househusbands: Men and housework in American families.* New York: Praeger.

Beller, A. H. (1984). Trends in occupational segregation by sex and race, 1960-1981. In *Sex segregation in the workplace: Trends, explanations, remedies,* edited by B.F. Reskin, 11-26. Washington, DC: National Academy Press.

Congressional Budget Office. (1988, March). *New report on family income.* Washington, DC: Author.

Corcoran, M., G. J. Duncan, and M. Ponza. (1984). Work experience, job segregation, and wages. In *Sex segregation in the workplace: Trends, explanations, remedies,* edited by B.F. Reskin, 171-191. Washington, DC: National Academy Press.

Coverman, S. (1983). Gender, domestic labor time, and wage inequality. *American Sociological Review, 48*: 623-637.

Devore, W. and E. G. Schlesinger (1987). *Ethnic-sensitive social work practice.* 2nd ed. Columbus, OH: Merrill.

Elkin, F. and G. Handel. (1978). *The child and society: The process of socialization.* 3rd ed. New York: Random House.

England, P. and G. Farkas. (1986). *Households, employment, and gender: A social, economic and demographic view.* New York: Aldine.

Farkas, G. (1976). Education, wage rates, and the division of labor between husband and wife. *Journal of Marriage and The Family, 41*: 473-483.

Ferber, M. (1982). Labor market participation of young married women: Causes and effects. *Journal of Marriage and The Family, 44*: 457-468.

Freeman, E. M. and T. Landesman. (1992). Differential diagnosis and the least restrictive treatment. In *The addiction process: Effective social work approaches,* edited by E.M. Freeman, 27-42. New York: Longman.

Freeman, E. M., S. Logan, and R. McRoy. (1987). Clinical practice with employed women. *Social Casework, 68*: 413-420.

Geerken, M. and W. R. Gove. (1983). *At home and at work: The family's allocation of labor.* Beverly Hills, CA: Sage.

Germain, C. (1979). *Social work practice: People and environments.* New York: Columbia University Press.

Hartman, A. and J. Laird. (1983). *Family-centered social work practice.* New York: The Free Press.

Johnston, W. B. (1987). *Workforce 2000: Work and workers for the 21st century.* Indianapolis, IN: Hudson Institute.

Mansur, M. and M. Brown. (1979). Bargaining analyses of household decisions. In *Women in the labor market,* edited by C. Lloyd, E. Andrews, and C. Gibroy, 3-26. New York: Columbia University Press.

Nilsen, S. (1984). Recessionary impacts on the unemployment of men and women. *Monthly Labor Review, 107*: 21-25.

Repetti, R. L., K. A. Matthews, and I. Waldron. (1989). Effects of paid employment on women's mental and physical health. *American Psychologist, 44*: 1394-1401.

Rexroat, C. and C. Shehan. (1987). The family life cycle and spouses' time in housework. *Journal of Marriage and the Family, 49*: 737-750.

Robinson, J. P. (1980). Housework technology and household work. In *Women and household labor*, edited by S.F. Berk, 53-68. Beverly Hills, CA: Sage.

Rosen, B. (1982). Career progress of women: Getting in and staying in. In *Women in the work force*, edited by H.J. Bernardin, 70-99. New York: Praeger.

Scarr, S., D. Phillips, and K. McCartney. (1989). Working mothers and their families. *American Psychologist, 44*: 1402-1409.

Schervish, P. (1983). *The structural determinants of unemployment*. New York: Academic.

Shortridge, B. G. (1987). *Atlas of American women*. New York: Macmillan Publishing Co.

Stafford, R., E. Backman, and P. Dibona. (1977). The division of labor among cohabitating and married couples. *Journal of Marriage and The Family, 39*: 43-54.

Stockard, J. and M. M. Johnson. (1980). *Sex roles: Sex inequality and sex role development*. Englewood Cliffs NJ: Prentice-Hall.

Treiman, D. J. and H. I. Hartmann. (1981). *Women, work, and wages: Equal pay for jobs of equal value*. Washington, DC: National Academy Press.

United States Department of Labor. (1983). *Time of change: 1983 handbook on women workers*. Bulletin 298. Washington, DC: U.S. Government Printing Office.

Vanek, J. (1974). Time spent in housework. *Scientific American, 231*: 116-120.

Weintraub, M., E. Jaeger, and L. Hoffman. (1988). Predictive infant outcome in families of employed and non-employed mothers. *Early Childhood Research Quarterly, 3*: 361-378.

Chapter 6

Child Welfare:
A Woman's Issue

Elizabeth D. Hutchison

INTRODUCTION

Twenty years ago, when I became a mother for the first time, I began to understand child welfare as a woman's issue. The process by which I developed this understanding conceptually over the years can best be described as halting. For the past 30 years, this country has engaged in its second child-saving movement, and in this climate of child-saving–in spite of an active feminist movement–few attempts have been made to construct child welfare as a woman's issue. To many, feminists as well as nonfeminists, analyzing child welfare as a woman's issue implies a lack of concern for the vulnerability of children. But to some of us, such analysis was unspeakable because, if pursued, it might raise the painful question: Must the welfare of children come at the expense of the welfare of women?

Indeed, almost from the outset, the child welfare system has accepted without question the consequences for children, particularly poor children, of the unequal power structure of a patriarchal society. Child welfare scholars, policymakers, and practitioners, historical as well as current, have too often studied, planned for, and served children and their families without giving special attention to the needs of female caregivers–as if children's needs could be met whether or not their caregivers had access to the resources for providing sufficient care. The child welfare literature is notable for its failure to address the possibility that the well-being of children might, under current societal structures, come at great costs to their female caregivers–assuming instead that mothers' needs and children's needs are met by the same programs.

This assumption has been challenged on occasion. Grace Abbott, chief of the United States Children's Bureau from 1921 to 1934, noted the possible conflict between children's needs and women's needs in a memorandum regarding a proposed child welfare program:

> Women and children are frequently spoken of as though the interests of both could be served by the same measures. The reverse is true. Women and children have both suffered by the assumption that they and their problems should be classed together. (Cited in Costin 1985a, 197)

In a more recent analysis, *Child Welfare* devoted an entire 1985 issue to exploration of a feminist perspective on child welfare (Costin 1985b). Dorothy Miller's 1987 article entitled "Children's Policy and Women's Policy: Congruence or Conflict?" echoed Abbott's warning about conflict in the needs of women and children.

In recent years, feminist scholars have contributed fresh analyses of the general social welfare system (Abramovitz 1988; Sidel 1986). Specific child welfare issues have also been explored from a feminist perspective, but the child welfare system has not been scrutinized with the same intense gender analysis as is applied to the general social welfare system. This chapter draws heavily on earlier feminist analyses of the general social welfare system and specific child welfare issues to frame a more comprehensive gender analysis of child welfare.

To accomplish this task, an ecological perspective, suggesting connections among several societal systems, is taken. Although this approach allows for a more holistic understanding of child welfare, it does not provide in-depth discussion of specific issues. Partialization of issues has obscured the complexity of child welfare and led to piecemeal solutions that necessarily fail. For this reason, the present discussion uses a broader brush to stimulate more integrative thinking about child welfare policy. The following sections present historical as well as current gender biases in policy related to child welfare and discuss the oppression of selected categories of women in the child welfare system. Policy implications and practice guidelines that flow from this analysis are outlined.

At least three important reasons can be given for using a gender lens to analyze the child welfare system. First, as long as patriarchal society delegates the care of children exclusively to women in the private sphere, individual women are held accountable for the welfare of individual children. Second, as long as women serve almost exclusively as the caregivers of children, the question of allocation of resources to the caregiving function of society is a woman's issue. Third, current child welfare policy and practice is built on the oppression of several categories of women.

HISTORICAL PERSPECTIVE

The current public discourse often distorts child maltreatment as a new problem. Linda Gordon's (1988) recent historical analysis suggests the opposite–"the ebb-and-flow pattern of concern about family violence over the last century suggests that its incidence has not changed as much as its visibility" (2). Like Gordon, I argue that child welfare has been "historically and politically constructed" (3) and a tracing of this construction informs the current situation. Although the following discussion of historical themes is not exhaustive, it highlights the major issues of gender bias in the development of child welfare policy.

There is a strong belief in the United States that individual families serve as the primary social service system for all children (Kadushin and Martin 1988). From colonial times, local, state, and federal governments struggled with the question of whether, and if so, how, to aid families who are not capable of meeting the needs of children without organized assistance. After the Revolutionary War, there was a general feeling that families should not be aided in their own homes–that to do so would destroy initiative and the necessary fear of poverty (Sidel 1986). Colonial law allowed the separation of children from parents for reasons of "destitution, ungovernable conduct, and improper guardianship" (Abramovitz 1988, 91) to protect the common good. Two major methods of overseeing these dependent children developed: "placing out" and institutional care.

Local poor law officials were authorized to "rescue" vulnerable children and indenture or apprentice them into "responsible" homes. After the Revolutionary War, it became more popular to place young, as well as old, economically dependent persons in almshouses. Children could be placed in almshouses with or without their "unfit" mothers.

As conditions in the almshouses deteriorated, however, public outcry demanded separate means for caring for dependent children. Again, the alternatives were placing out or institutional care. Some children were sent to homes in the country, even from the East to the Midwest, while others were sent to orphanages. Beginning in the 1870s, Societies for the Prevention of Cruelty to Children (SPCCs) began to develop, and state legislatures expanded the authority of the court to remove children from families in the 1890s (Abramovitz 1988; Sidel 1986). Children of indigent and neglectful parents, as well as orphans, were the targets for removal, and early records indicate that any woman who did not live with a male breadwinner was particularly susceptible to being declared "unfit" and having children removed from her care (Gordon 1988).

As the SPCCs matured and began to professionalize, dissatisfaction grew with existing alternatives of care for vulnerable children. In 1906 the Massachusetts Society for Prevention of Cruelty to Children (MSPCC) began to integrate the developing social casework method with anticruelty work to serve families with children in their own homes (Anderson 1989). This new approach received a big boost when the 1909 White House Conference on the Care of Children recommended that children should not be removed from home for reasons of poverty alone (Abramovitz 1988).

This new approach to promoting the welfare of children, serving them within the context of their own homes, raised the awkward question: How can indigent children be maintained in their own families without providing economic resources to their caregivers? Support was growing for a program of aid to mothers and children but was met with the old fears about undermining family responsibility by providing aid to the "unworthy." Dissatisfaction with existing methods of child saving converged with other social forces, however, to lead to the passage of Mothers' Pension laws during the early twentieth century (Abramovitz 1988; Sidel 1986).

Separate Spheres Ideology

One of the social forces that contributed to the development of mothers' pensions was the "separate spheres" ideology that accompanied the industrialization of work. During the colonial period, the home was the economic base and economic productivity intermingled with reproductive tasks. Although women were secondary to men in the family power structure, both men and women were typically involved in economic productivity and fathers carried some childrearing responsibilities such as discipline, education, religious, and vocational instruction (Abramovitz 1988; Sidel 1986).

As economic productivity was industrialized and moved out of the home, a more highly differentiated gender division of labor was established. Women were assigned to the "private sphere" of home and men to the "public sphere" of work. A social philosophy grew up around these changes in the organization of economic productivity. The home, no longer the primary site of economic production for most families, was constructed as a "domestic haven" where economic providers could retreat. The new social philosophy also prescribed that women were needed to staff this domestic haven because they were blessed biologically with the traits of the "domestic wife"–"tenderness, gentleness, affection, sweetness, and comforting" (Hareven 1982, 454). The ideology lent support to the idea that children needed the care of their mothers in their own homes.

In the labor market, the separate spheres ideology led to the idea that men should be paid a "living wage" to support children and a domestic wife. If women were in the labor market, they were located in the secondary market doing different jobs than those performed by men and making secondary wages, less than a living wage. Protective labor laws supported the ideology that women and children belong in the private sphere of home and men in the public sphere of work. This separate spheres division of labor assigned the care of children totally to women, made women and children economically dependent on men, and justified the treatment of women as secondary workers when they did enter the public sphere. The separate spheres ideology led to the development of social welfare policies that supported the gender-based division of labor–policies such as mothers' pensions, AFDC, survivors' benefits, and protective labor laws. The economic support policies permitted the state to fill in for the man economically when he faltered or was absent, allowing the woman to remain in the private sphere. The image of the domestic wife became the model for distinguishing deserving mothers from undeserving mothers in the social welfare system (Abramovitz 1988).

Day Care

It should be no surprise that child day care has been slow to develop in a society committed to the domestic wife. Day nurseries, sponsored by churches and voluntary social agencies, were developed from the 1880s to World War I to care for the children of poor working mothers–as an alternative to institutional placement. During this same period, nursery schools were developed to provide an early childhood educational experience for middle-class children. Rapid growth in the day-care movement occurred for the first time during the depression when the federal government funded nursery schools, but the real expansion in day care occurred during World War II when women became essential to the labor force (Steinfels 1973).

The World War II experience with day care demonstrates our national capacity to develop innovative family support programs when women are needed in the labor force. During the war, state governments and private industries supplied day-care funds. The most notable example is the day-care program at the Kaiser Shipbuilding Corporation in Portland, Oregon, where two centers were open 24 hours per day year round. Besides caring for the children, the centers mended clothes, shopped for the mothers, provided low-cost carry-out dinners, and even took in children with minor illnesses (Close 1943). Social workers and child welfare agencies remained strong opponents of working mothers and child day care because they believed that children could be best cared for by their mothers in their own homes; 2,800 day care centers closed at the end of the war when they were considered to be no longer necessary (Steinfels 1973).

The Child Protection Movement

As will be discussed later, child welfare is currently constructed narrowly as child protection. Gordon (1988) has made a significant contribution to the child welfare literature by using a gender lens to analyze the child protection movement. After reviewing case records of the MSPCC from 1880 to 1960, Gordon identifies five stages (through the 1970s) of the political construction of child maltreatment in the United States. The first stage (1875-1910) is the nineteenth-century (or first) child-saving stage. During this stage, family violence was defined as cruelty to children and emphasis was placed on the "depraved immigrant man"–often under the influence of alcohol–as perpetrator. According to Gordon this was the only stage in which child welfare reforms represented gains for women as well as children. Examples of such gains are public-health programs, public education, and child-custody reforms.

During the second stage, the Progressive Era and its aftermath (1910-1930), child welfare was defined in terms of child neglect. Concern focused on the weakening of the family, particularly the increase in single-parent families. With the professionalization of social work, the earlier concern about brutal men seemed "moralistic and unscientific" (21) and spousal violence was portrayed as interactive. Case records generally indicated a cover up of wife-beating.

During the Depression, the third stage described by Gordon, emphasis was on supporting nuclear families. Social service organizations deemphasized family violence and focused on economic neglect of children. The deemphasis on family violence continued through the fourth stage (World War II and the 1950s), but now it took another turn. Social work, heavily influenced by psychiatry, viewed interpersonal problems through the lens of individual personality structure. Agency records indicate that during this stage wives were often blamed for being abused by their husbands. Child neglect continued to be emphasized, but was now seen to derive from parental neurosis. Emotional neglect was introduced as a new category of child maltreatment.

During the final stage identified by Gordon (1960s and 1970s), a second child-saving movement refocused attention on physical abuse and neglect and brought public attention for the first time to sexual abuse of children. During this era, an active feminist movement garnered recognition that family violence often involves violence to women.

CURRENT THEMES

The second child-saving movement, which began in the late 1960s, is in the paternalistic tradition of earlier child welfare efforts. This movement, stimulated by the media presentation of the "battered child syndrome," defines child welfare narrowly as child protection (Kamerman and Kahn 1990). Protective policy was based on the assumption that child welfare policy could be divorced from general social welfare policy, or more specifically, from anti-poverty policy (Nelson 1984). The evidence is clear that this was a faulty assumption–one that has been costly for poor families in general but particularly costly for women and children. Historically, child maltreatment has been associated with low family income. This continues to be true (U.S. Department of Health and Human Services 1988).

Child Maltreatment and Poverty

The current child protection movement focuses on policing family life rather than enhancing the resources for family caregiving. The recent construction of child maltreatment inspired a child welfare system that relies on mandatory reporting laws as the case-finding method, emphasizes involuntary rather than voluntary services, and seeks solutions to cope with individual caregiver deficiencies (Hutchison 1990). The continuing allegiance to the separate spheres ideology ensures that it is usually women's deficiences that are noted in the child welfare system and, even when men are the perpetrators of maltreatment, it is women who are held accountable for controlling the maltreating behavior. In recent years, with the skyrocketing rates of reporting, increasing portions of child welfare budgets have gone toward the process of investigative disposition, with little left for services (U.S. Department of Health and Human Services 1988; Kamerman and Kahn 1990).

These policy directions become even more troubling when one considers the social context in which they were implemented. This social context included changes in family structure leading to more female-headed single-parent households, changes in the labor market with women participating more but still as secondary workers, and assaults on social welfare programs that serve women and children.

Between 1970 and 1988, as the second child-saving movement was being implemented, the number of female-headed single parent families increased by 98%, and in 1988, 21.4% of all children under 18 lived with their mothers without fathers present. The rate for black children was 51%. Census Bureau projections suggest a continued increase in single-parent households headed by women (Balchen 1989). It is well-documented that a large portion of children living in mother-headed single-parent households receive no financial assistance from their fathers. In 1985, almost two-thirds of mothers caring for minor children whose father lived elsewhere received no child support payments (Rix 1989).

These changes in family structure are juxtaposed against the increasing presence of women in the work force. Currently, only 28.6% of children under 18 live in two-parent families with only the father employed. Between 1976 and 1987 the percentage of married women in the labor force increased from 33% to 46% and single mothers increased from 62% to 69% (Saluter 1989). Despite their increased presence in the labor force, women are still considered secondary workers receiving a secondary wage, whereas men in some sectors of the labor market are still paid a "living wage" that they may or may not share with their children. Although media attention focuses on the progress of professional women, the majority of women workers can be found in 20 of the 420 occupations listed by the Bureau of Labor Statistics. In 1987, the number of women with their own income was slightly larger than the number of men with their own income, but the total income for women was 47% of the total income for men (Balchen 1989).

As mandatory reporting laws were being implemented, the numbers of poor children were increasing, and governmental spending for poor families with children was declining. Between 1978 and 1987, federal expenditures for programs for children declined by

4% (Danziger 1990). During the Reagan years, while the numbers of maltreatment reports were on a sharp incline, federal funds for Medicaid, maternal and child-health programs, family planning programs, food stamps, child nutrition, housing, and day care were cut significantly. Many households lost AFDC eligibility (Abramovitz 1988; Sarri 1985). Recent analyses of service trends indicate that the incline in maltreatment reports over the last decade matches the decline in service provision in both the income maintenance and the child welfare systems (Datallo 1992; Kamerman and Kahn 1990).

A convergence of these changes in the family system, the labor market, and the social welfare system has intensified the climate of vulnerability for women and their dependent children. In 1987, the poverty rate was 41.6% for all female-headed single-parent households, 38.7% for white female-headed single-parent households, 59.5% for black female-headed single-parent households, and 60.7% for Hispanic female-headed single-parent households. These poverty rates become even more jolting when they are analyzed for their impact on children. In 1987, one of every five children under the age of 18 in the United States was living in poverty. The rates are higher for minority children and children under the age of six (Saluter 1989).

Ambivalent Federal Initiatives

During the past few years, policymakers at all levels of government have become alarmed at the extent of child poverty and have directed legislative efforts to address this national problem. In 1988, Congress enacted the Family Support Act with the intent to promote economic self-reliance of low-income families, particularly those headed by single mothers through three primary programs: education and training provided under the Job Opportunities and Basic Skills Training (JOBS) program; short-term support services, including health benefits and child care for families in transition from welfare use to economic self-reliance; and child-support enforcement to ensure that noncustodial parents provide financial assistance to their families (P.L. 100-485). (See Hagen, Chapter 3, for a full discussion of the Family Support Act). The Omnibus Budget

Reconciliation Act of 1990 offers further promise of relief for poor families with children. The main ingredients of this act are increased earned income tax credit (EITC), gradual expansion of Medicaid to cover all children in poverty, and block grants that allow states to improve the quality and accessibility of child care (Chilman 1991; General Accounting Office 1991).

Although these recent initiatives offer some promise for the improved welfare of poor women and their children, most of them are crippled by historical ambivalence about how to aid children without aiding parents. Five factors are particularly germane to this discussion:

- Poor women tend to need more education if they are to secure jobs that will bring them out of poverty (General Accounting Office 1991). However, early evidence suggests that implementation of JOBS in most states will emphasize job search and public service activities and deemphasize education and training (Lurie and Sanger 1991). The JOBS program mandates that poor women with young children belong in the public sphere, but its conservative implementation will ensure that they are locked into the secondary job market making less than a living wage.
- Although improved child-support enforcement does make men more responsible for the children they father and will significantly improve the life-style of some poor women and children, it will provide little or no assistance to the many families in which the father is unemployed or marginally employed. Much child poverty and family disruption is related to the economic plight of men, particularly minority men, in a changing labor market (Axinn and Stern 1987; Chilman 1991). The Family Support Act mandate of AFDC-UP (unemployed parent) to all states may help prevent some family disruption related to fathers' employment problems.
- Increases in EITC will improve the prospect for poor families, but because benefits do not vary for families with more than two children and because benefits are still inadequate, this legislation is limited in its capacity to bring families out of poverty (Chilman 1991; General Accounting Office 1991).

- Extension of Medicaid coverage to all children living in poverty sounds promising until one notes that this legislation excludes coverage for adult caregivers. It is important to note that a recent longitudinal study suggests that 35% of poor single mothers have no health coverage in the low-wage jobs they secure (General Accounting Office 1991).
- Increased federal money for child care is a positive step, but it is still unknown whether we have the will to provide child care services that approximate the quality of World War II programs.

In the recent past, women have worked more than in previous eras at jobs that pay less than what men receive. They have served more often as the sole support to children while being held increasingly accountable for adequate nurturance of children by a system that has cut social welfare benefits and refused to develop alternative methods of child care. Recent federal legislation has made positive, though ambivalent, efforts to reduce these problems. Early evidence suggests that current problems with the economy coupled with state autonomy over many aspects of implementation will result in inadequate benefits to children and their caregivers (Chilman 1991; General Accounting Office 1991; Lurie and Sanger 1991; Rovner 1991).

WOMEN IN THE CHILD WELFARE SYSTEM

Gillian Dalley (1988) describes the role of women under the separate spheres ideology as revolving around "enforced dependency and compulsory altruism" (17). That description, unfortunately, is an apt one for many of the women who play central roles in the current child welfare system. To understand the construction of child welfare as a woman's issue, one must look more closely at some of the women involved.

Mothers

When children's needs are not being met, mothers are scrutinized and held accountable. To the many women who already blame themselves for not being able to provide for their children, this comes as a double insult (Sidel 1986). Although child maltreatment reports often include a mixture of allegations of neglect, physical abuse, and sexual abuse, it is informative to examine the mothers involved in these categories of allegations separately.

Allegations of Neglect

Throughout child welfare history, neglect has been the most frequent type of child maltreatment known to child welfare agencies. Neglect has consistently been more strongly correlated with poverty than any other category of child maltreatment, and mothers have been considered the perpetrators of neglect in a large majority of cases (Gordon 1988; Kadushin and Martin 1988). This, of course, fits the separate spheres division of labor. Single mothers have been particularly vulnerable to the label of child neglect, although the noncustodial father is typically far more neglectful than the custodial mother. Gordon (1988) found that approximately 83% of single mothers known to child protection agencies in Boston between 1880 and 1960 were known for child neglect.

Neglect is the vaguest of the categories of child maltreatment, and sometimes allegations arise around differences in definition–especially with allegations of failure to supervise. To paraphrase Dorothy Miller (Chapter 2), every day mothers have to make choices about what to neglect. Although sometimes children are neglected, mothers, particularly poor mothers, probably neglect their own basic needs more often. Hill and Stafford (1984) found that when mothers increase their hours in paid work, they typically decrease their own leisure time or time at houshold tasks to avoid decreasing time spent with children.

Allegations of Physical Abuse

Although the second child-saving movement was predicated on the imagery of the "battered child syndrome," now, as in the past, most cases of physical abuse documented by child protection agencies involve excessive corporal punishment (Gordon 1988). Again, issues of definition arise. In contrast with neglect, approximately equal numbers of women and men are alleged to be the perpetrators of physical abuse. Gordon (1988) found that mothers were perpetrators in 46% of physical abuse cases and fathers in 54%. These data are consistent with more contemporary findings (Howing, et al. 1989). Clearly, women are capable of violence within the context of the family, but caution must be exercised in interpreting the finding of similar rates of physical abuse by mothers and fathers, recognizing the far greater amount of time mothers spend with children. It is important to note that even when women are not the perpetrators, they are held accountable for monitoring the man's violence toward children. Protective service workers usually meet only with the mother, and their assessment focuses on the mother's ability to protect the child from the perpetrator (Gordon 1988). Again, this is in keeping with the gender-based division of labor.

Allegations of Sexual Abuse

Although it is only in the last 15 years that child sexual abuse has been recognized as a phenomenon with more than rare occurrence, Gordon (1988) found in the early days of the first child protective movement at least 10% of case records referred to incest. Men were the perpetrators in 98% of the incest cases in this historical analysis. Since the "discovery" of child sexual abuse, the literature has been replete with allegations that mothers collude with fathers in the sexual abuse of their daughters (Wattenberg 1985). Although Gordon (1988) found that some mothers felt they had no options for protecting their daughters, many others took vigorous measures to protect their daughters. Gordon also noted a strong correlation between incest and wife-beating. This correlation is substantiated by recent research (Elbow and Mayfield 1991; Sirles and Franke 1989; Truesdell, McNeil, and Deschner 1986). Across time, many mothers have been advised by a variety of "helpers" that their husband's abuse of a daughter is a reflection of the mother's sexual inadequacies. There has been a reluctance on the part of the child protection system and society in general to hold men accountable for their own sexual behaviors.

Foster Mothers

When a birth mother is judged to be not "good enough," children may be removed from her and placed with a foster mother–

someone approved as "good enough" by the child welfare system. While children are placed in foster *families*, it is primarily the women whose parenting qualities are assessed. Many foster families have made heroic contributions to children, but they have done so with insufficient resources for the difficult task they perform. Foster parents must cope with excessive family transitions with little support, even though family theorists identify such family transitions as major stressors contributing to family dysfunction (Carter and McGoldrick 1988). Carol Meyer (1985) paints this poignant picture of the life of a foster mother:

> To be a woman, to be a mother, to be lower middle class or poor, to be in a minority group, to work for (with? under?) a child welfare agency, to be paid a pittance, to be asked to parent a child whom no one else is able to parent, to try to love that child and to lose him or her when loving has been achieved, to be supervised by a 22-year-old social worker, to have to deal with school teachers, police, courts, medical appointments, angry biological parents, and the impact of all of this upon one's own family–that is the lot and life of a typical foster mother in America. (252)

As Meyer (1985) and Kamerman and Kahn (1990) suggest, it is time to explore the possibility of reconstructing foster care, especially specialized foster care, from a pretend natural family to an adequately compensated social service.

Child Welfare Workers

At the direct service level, public child welfare agencies are staffed predominantly by young white women who have no children of their own (Hegar and Hunzeker 1988; Kadushin and Martin 1988). They have little or no professional education (Lieberman, Hornby, and Russell 1988), receive comparatively low pay, and are under constant public attack for being both overintrusive and underprotective. As Hegar and Hunzeker (1988) suggest, they, like other public sector workers, are "at risk for inadvertently taking the identity of benefactors" (500). They are mandated to intervene in the lives of families, and for a variety of reasons, their most intrusive services are directed toward women who are poor, often minority, single parents–women who are already seriously disempowered. Social workers, who themselves feel disempowered in a system with too few resources, can easily fall into the habit of using their limited power to act "for" (or against) their clients rather than "with" them.

Day Care Providers

Societal ambivalence about child day care derives from a strong commitment to the separate spheres ideology as well as to the philosophy of "individualistic familism" (Dalley 1988) which makes each family responsible for the needs of its members. This ambivalence about alternative forms of child care has resulted in mothers transferring their delegated responsibilites for the care of children to day-care providers–another exploited group of women. Day-care work is one of the lowest paid jobs in the labor market. Moreover, day care workers suffer from job insecurity as a result of the political conflict over funding for day care (Frankel 1991).

Adolescent Females

Gender bias is evident in programs for pregnant and parenting adolescents. Birth rate data are reported for female adolescents, and research about adolescent sexuality, contraception, pregnancy, and abortion has focused primarily on females. Social service programs that deal with adolescent sexuality, pregnancy, and childrearing seldom involve young men (Chilman 1985). The clear message to adolescents of both genders is that women are responsible for the sexual behavior of men as well as for themselves–and they carry sole responsibility for the care of children. These are subtle but powerful messages to deliver at a time when gender roles are being formalized.

Minority Women

Middle-class, white, heterosexual women often fail to recognize that their efforts to rid themselves of the domestic wife role do not adequately represent the struggles of minority women. The separate spheres ideology is not useful for understanding either the historical or current situation of poor women, especially poor women of color. These women have always been responsible for both spheres and learned early what many middle-class white women have only recently discovered–that the separate spheres ideology makes them secondary laborers in the labor force while robbing them of their sense of successful role performance in their assigned domestic domain. Women of color suffer the double jeopardy of race and gender discrimination, and when they cope well, as they often do, their strength is used against them. Policymakers and direct service practitioners often consider services unnecessary because the clients are "strong black women" or because black neighborhoods and black extended families do such a good job of assimilating unmarried mothers and their offspring (Gould 1985). Recent research indicates that the child protective system responds more slowly and less comprehensively to crises in minority families. Once they do respond, however, their assessments and interventions are harsher than those directed toward white families (Hogan and Siu 1988).

POLICY IMPLICATIONS
FOR THE TWENTY-FIRST CENTURY

Because the welfare of children is influenced by a convergence of trends in several systems, including the family system, the labor market, the general social welfare system, and the child welfare system, changes are needed in all systems to improve the general well-being of children. As we move into the twenty-first century, these societal changes require adaptive changes in three major areas: elimination of gender-based division of labor; redistribution of income to reduce, if not eliminate, child poverty; and reallocation of societal resources to give more support to the caregiving functions of society. A diverse set of policy initiatives is required to meet these goals.

Elimination of Gender-Based Division of Labor

Even though elimination of gender-based division of labor in the private sphere of the family lies outside the realm of public policy, changes in the public sphere can enhance and support efforts of families to move in this direction. Policy initiatives in the labor market can ensure that wages are based on comparable worth. Eliminating the dichotomy of a "living wage" for men and a "secondary wage" for women would encourage the equal participation of men and women in both the public sphere of work and the private sphere of home. To ensure the equal participation of men in family life, paternity leave should be made available in the labor market. To ensure the equal participation of women in the labor, attempts to attract women to traditional male occupations should be intensified.

In the general social welfare system, accessible, affordable, high-quality day care and afterschool programs are critically needed to assist in eliminating the gender-based division of labor. Our national failure to develop such programs in the quantity and quality needed to ensure the well-being of children is a vestige of the twentieth-century separate spheres ideology. For the twenty-first century, we need child care policy that is more responsive to the contemporary reality of family and work life.

The child welfare system should examine policies and programs for instances where gender bias blinds decision makers to the responsibilities of men for the well-being of their children. Such examination would identify policy and practice that holds women accountable for men's behavior to children, consequently failing to hold men accountable. Efforts in the child welfare system should also be directed toward eliminating gender bias in programs for pregnant and parenting teens. Programs should provide active outreach to teen fathers to encourage shared responsibility for the well-being of children.

Reduction of Child Poverty

Reducing child poverty requires changes in the labor market as well as the general social welfare system. In the labor market, wages based on comparable worth would assist the many children who live in female-headed single-parent families, a group found disproportionately among the working poor (Klein and Rones 1989). With the twentieth-century dichotomy of a "living wage" for men and a "secondary wage" for women eliminated, children living in single-parent families headed by women will be less economically disadvantaged in the twenty-first century.

As discussed above, although legislation for several important social welfare policies designed to reduce child poverty has been recently passed, it will have little success without some modifications. Social service workers should attempt to influence state implementation of JOBS to ensure sufficient emphasis on adult education and training. Continued and increased funding for EITC should be encouraged, and future legislation should stipulate that benefits vary according to family size. Health insurance needs to be available to all citizens in the twenty-first century.

Reallocation of Resources to Caregiving Function

Changes in the labor market, the general social welfare system, and the child welfare system can help to reallocate national resources to the caregiving function in the twenty-first century. With the elimination of the separate spheres ideology, improved parental leave and more flexible workplace policies are needed in the labor market to allow for management of family life. Labor market policy must become more responsive to the realities of work and family life.

In the social welfare system, the most crucial policy imperatives are affordable, high-quality child day care and improved maternal/child health programs. The social welfare system and the labor market should share the responsibility of providing quality day care in sufficient quantity to meet the needs of all families with children. The social welfare system must ensure that quality child care is available to families in the public sector. As we develop new systems of health-care financing, the social welfare system must ensure that adult caregivers of children will be adequately covered.

The child welfare system must come to grips with the crisis that has ensued from the narrow construction of child welfare as child protection. It must begin to promote and provide more voluntary family-enhancing services and fewer involuntary family-policing services. This will probably require a narrowing of the scope of the reporting laws (Hutchison, 1993). It will also require tighter coupling of the child welfare system and the general social welfare system.

PRACTICE GUIDELINES

Gordon's (1988) historical analysis corroborates the author's recent observations that, in spite of the oppressive context in which child welfare services have been offered, individual mothers have been able to seek and obtain some of what they need from child welfare programs. And individual social workers have been able to respond to the pain of mothers, as well as children, in the child welfare system. Several important practice guidelines are suggested by historical and current analysis.

- Focus on women as people rather than just on women as mothers–know as much about their hopes and their dreams as you know about their parenting skills.
- Focus on the strengths rather than the inadequacies of mothers–on their efforts to solve problems.
- Work in the least hierarchical fashion possible with clients–involve women in decision making even when providing involuntary services.
- Recognize and validate the emotions expressed by women.
- Work with women and agencies to recognize when a private woe should be constructed as a public problem.
- Be sensitive to and challenge "blame the victim" assessments of women clients presented by other professionals.
- Help women develop an "internal locus of control and an external locus of responsibility" (Hegar and Hunzeker 1988, 499).
- Share information with clients honestly–even when the news is bad.
- Develop networks of support for families (in churches, workplaces, neighborhoods, schools, etc.) to enhance their caregiving functions–use those networks intensively and creatively in times of family crisis.
- Ensure that all contacts with families support women in their development as persons–and support, to every extent possible, the sharing of the caregiving load. Help women create a space (at least a small space) for themselves.
- Approach foster mothers with an honest exploration of the complex demands of their roles.

- Evaluate programs for pregnant and parenting adolescents for their gender bias.
- Do not hold women accountable for acts of maltreatment that they did not perpetrate.
- Empower yourself by organizing your scarce resource of time to allow the development of some innovative service that you care about.

CONCLUSION

The second child-saving movement has produced some gains for women and children, but, on balance, has been more costly than beneficial. On the benefits side, the juxtaposition of an active feminist movement with the second child-saving movement finally focused attention on the phenomena of incest and spouse abuse. These important gains have been offset, however, by the reconstruction of child welfare as child protection. Under this construction, families have witnessed shrinking voluntary services and expanding coercive services. Their chances for being investigated for child maltreatment have increased and their chances for receiving goods and services have decreased (Hutchison 1993; Kamerman and Kahn 1990). Such policies have been costly to men, as well as women and children, but a disproportionate share of the burden has been borne by impoverished female-headed single-parent households because these households are overrepresented in the child protection system.

Gender bias is not the only factor contributing to the current child welfare crisis, but the child welfare system cannot be put on course without recognizing that the unequal power structure of the patriarchal society has negative consequences for many children. Luepnitz' (1988) ironic characterization of the contemporary American family as both patriarchal and father-absent serves as useful theory for child welfare policy as well as clinical practice. Not all acts of maltreatment of children would be eliminated if the patriarchy were eroded and poverty were eradicated. However, the general welfare of children would be greatly enhanced if economically disadvantaged and/or dependent women were not assigned sole responsibility for their care. Cross-cultural studies provide convincing evidence that societies in which caregiving is shared have the lowest rates of child maltreatment (Korbin 1981). Until we move in that direction, the welfare of children will continue to come at considerable cost to the welfare of women–and the welfare of women will come at the expense of the welfare of children.

REFERENCES

Abramovitz, M. (1988). *Regulating the lives of women: Social welfare policy from colonial times to the present.* Boston: South End Press.

Anderson, P. (1989). The origin, emergence, and professional recognition of child protection. *Social Service Review, 63*: 222-224.

Axinn, J. and M. Stern. (1987). Women and the postindustrial welfare state. *Social Work, 32*: 282-286.

Balchen, A. (1989). *Fairchild fact file: Consumer market developments.* New York: Fairchild Publications.

Carter, B. and M. McGoldrick. (1988). *The changing family life cycle.* 2nd ed. Boston: Allyn & Bacon.

Chilman, C. (1985). Feminist issues in teenage parenting. *Child Welfare, 64*: 225-234.

Chilman, C. (1991). Working poor families: Trends, causes, effects, and suggested policies. *Family Relations, 40*: 191-198.

Close, K. (1943). Day care up to now. *The Survey, 79*: 194-197.

Costin, L. (1985a). Introduction. *Child Welfare, 64*: 197-201.

Costin, L., ed. (1985b). Toward a feminist approach to child welfare (special issue). *Child Welfare, 64*(3).

Dalley, G. (1988). *Ideologies of caring: Rethinking community and collectivism.* London: Macmillan Education Ltd.

Danziger, S. (1990). Antipoverty policies and child poverty. *Social Work Research and Abstracts, 26*: 17-24.

Datallo, P. (1992). The gentrification of social welfare. *Social Work, 37*: 446-453.

Elbow, M. and J. Mayfield. (1991). Mothers of incest victims: Villians, victims, or protectors? *Families in Society: The Journal of Contemporary Human Services, 72*: 78-85.

Frankel, A. (1991). The dynamics of day care. *Families in Society: The Journal of Contemporary Human Services, 72*: 3-10.

General Accounting Office. (1991). *Mother-only families: Low earning will keep many children in poverty* (GAO/HRD Publication 91-62). Washington, DC: U.S. Government Printing Office.

Gordon, L. (1988). *Heroes of their own lives: The politics and history of family violence.* New York: Viking.

Gould, K. (1985). A minority-feminist perspective on child welfare issues. *Child Welfare, 64*: 291-305.

Hareven, T. (1982). American families in transition: Historical perspectives on change. In *Normal family processes*, edited by F. Walsh, 446-465. New York: Guildford Press.

Hegar, R. and J. Hunzeker. (1988). Moving toward empowerment-based practice in public child welfare. *Social Work, 33*: 499-502.

Hill, C. and F. Stafford. (1984). Parental care of children: Time diary estimates of quantity, predictability, and variety. In *Time, goods, and well-being*, edited by F. Juster & F. Stafford 415-438. Ann Arbor: University of Michigan Survey Research Center.

Hogan, P. and S. Siu. (1988). Minority children and the child welfare system: An historical perspective. *Social Work, 33*: 493-498.

Howing, P., J. Wodarski, J. Gaudin, and P. Kurtz. (1989). Effective interventions to ameliorate the incidence of child maltreatment: The empirical base. *Social Work, 34*: 330-338.

Hutchison, E. (1990). Child maltreatment: Can it be defined? *Social Service Review, 64*: 61-78.

Hutchison, E. (1993), Mandatory reporting laws: Child protective case-finding gone awry? *Social Work*. 38:56-63.

Kadushin, A. and J. Martin. (1988). *Child welfare services*. 4th ed. New York: Macmillan.

Kamerman, S. and A. Kahn. (1990). If CPS is driving child welfare–where do we go from here? *Public Welfare, 48*: 9-13.

Klein, B. and P. Rones. (1989). A profile of the working poor. *Monthly Labor Review, 112*: 3-11.

Korbin, J., ed. (1981). *Child abuse and neglect: Cross-cultural perspective*. Berkeley and Los Angeles: University of California Press.

Lieberman, A., H. Hornby, and M. Russell. (1988). Analyzing the education backgrounds and work experiences of child welfare personnel. *Social Work, 33*: 485-492.

Luepnitz, D. (1988). *The family interpreted: Feminist theory in clinical practice*. New York: Basic Books.

Lurie, I. and M. Sanger. (1991). The family support act: Defining the social contract in New York. *Social Service Review, 65*: 43-67.

Meyer, C. (1985). A feminist perspective on foster family care: A redefinition of the categories. *Child Welfare, 64*: 249-258.

Miller, D. (1987). Children's policy and women's policy: Congruence or conflict? *Social Work, 32*: 289-292.

Nelson, B. (1984). *Making an issue of child abuse: Political agenda setting for social problems*. Chicago: University of Chicago Press.

Rix, S., ed. (1989). *The American woman 1988-89: A status report*. New York: W.W. Norton & Co.

Rovner, J. (1991). Raising the curtain on welfare reform. *Governing, 4*: 19-22.

Saluter, A. (1989). *Changes in American family life*. Washington, DC: Bureau of Census.

Sarri, R. (1985). Federal policy and the feminization of poverty. *Child Welfare, 64*: 235-247.

Sidel, R. (1986). *Women and children last*. New York: Viking.

Sirles, E. and P. Franke. (1989). Factors influencing mothers' reactions to intra-family sexual abuse. *Child Abuse and Neglect, 13*: 131-139.

Steinfels, M. (1973). *Who's minding the children? The history and politics of day care in America*. New York: Simon and Schuster.

Truesdell, D., J. McNeil. and J. Deschner. (1986). Incidence of wife abuse in incestuous families. *Social Work, 31*: 138-140.

U.S. Department of Health and Human Services. (1988). *Study of national incidence and prevalence of child abuse and neglect*. (DHHS Publication, Contract #105-85-1702.) Washington, DC: U.S. Government Printing Office.

Wattenberg, E. (1985). In a different light: A feminist perspective on the role of mothers in father-daughter incest. *Child Welfare, 64*: 203-211.

Chapter 7

Older Women: Policy Issues for the Twenty-First Century

Brenda Crawley

INTRODUCTION

The shifting role of women in society is significantly reflected in the policy issues of older women. This chapter focuses on policy issues related to socioeconomic status, e.g., older women's work lives and histories, limitations of private pension provisions, inequities in the social security system, and poverty's disproportionate effect on older women in general and older minority women in particular. A second set of issues emanate from family life policy concerns, e.g., the increasing role of older women as primary caregivers, the cost of divorce to the older woman, and elder abuse. The chapter opens with a sociodemographic profile of older women, is followed by a discussion of the policy concerns mentioned above, and concludes with multidimensional policy recommendations and questions.

SOCIODEMOGRAPHIC PROFILE

Of the 30.4 million persons 65 years of age or older in 1988, 59.2% (18 million) were female (American Association of Retired Persons and Administration on Aging, undated A). To speak of the issues of the aged population is to recognize that the issues of women must be addressed. Thus, whether speaking of marital status, financial aspects, social/living arrangements or any aspect of life for older Americans, older women figure prominently in the policy discussion.

Marital Status

Older men are almost twice as likely to be married as older women–78% and 41% respectively. Almost one-half of older women are widowed, compared to only 14% of older men (American Association of Retired Persons and Administration on Aging, undated B).

Differences in the marital status of older males and females are generally explained in one of the following ways: (1) older women are more likely to have married older men *and* because older males have a shorter life expectancy than females, the males die before the females; (2) older men have broader age ranges from which to select mates–should they become widowed or divorced and desire remarriage they may choose from virtually any age group of women; or (3) it may be that once a woman has completed her reproductive and coupling responsibilities and finds herself widowed she does not as actively seek to be reconnected with the household and spousal imperatives of her younger years (National Institute on Aging and National Institute of Mental Health 1980).

The above figures reflect more than an interesting picture of male and female differences in marital status. There is a well-documented link between marital status and financial well-being for older females (Minkler and Stone 1985).

Economic Status

Older women's median income is 57% of older men's median income, $6,734 and $11,854, respectively. Older women's average Social Security benefit is 76% of that for older men–$462 compared to $604. Similarly, the median income of older widowed women is 76% of that of older widowed men, $6,993 and $9,258, respectively. Regardless of the characteristics of older women, they, like younger and midlife women, persistently lag behind men in terms of income (American Association of Retired Persons and Administration on Aging, undated A, B; Women's Initiative 1988,1989).

When racial and ethnic characteristics are factored in, the income picture becomes more dismal. The median income for all elderly African-Americans is 59.6% of their elderly white counterparts. In 1985, the median income of African-American elderly women was 67.6% that of elderly white females–$4,441 and $6,571, respectively (U.S. House of Representatives Select Committee on Aging 1987).

Income sources vary widely between older men and women and are clearly implicated in their financial well-being. For example, older men receive private pensions at twice the rate of older women. Older women are much more dependent on federally administered Supplemental Security Income than older men (Women's Initiative 1988). As shown below in the section on poverty, amounts and sources of income play a significant role in the poverty experience of older women.

Living Arrangements

Older women are much more likely than older men to live alone or with nonrelatives. For the last decade the pattern has been that 43% live alone or with nonrelatives; 40% live with spouses; and 17% live with other relatives. In contrast, for older men, 75% live with spouses; 18% live alone or with nonrelatives; and 7% live with other relatives (American Association of Retired Persons and Administration on Aging, undated A). As pointed out in the data on poverty, those who live alone or in nonrelative households are at greater risk of poverty and economic vulnerability than those in other living arrangements. The poverty rate for elderly women who live alone is 26.8%. This is over twice the overall elderly poverty rate of approximately 12.6% (Villers Foundation 1987, 15).

POLICY ISSUES RELATED TO ECONOMIC STATUS

The socioeconomic profile of older women suggests that there are critical issues related to their economic security, e.g., work history, private pension provisions, inequities in the social security system, and poverty's disproportionate effect on older women.

Work History Factors

Household responsibilities often prevented today's cohorts of older women from entering the labor force. The economic or market value of their domestic labor and work was not calculated or viewed as relevant to wage issues. For some, it may not have been an issue of not working, but rather of interrupted or sporadic incursions into the paid labor market that determined their economic lives. For example, they may have selected peripheral types of jobs such as seasonal or part-time work, or low-paying but convenient-for-family-responsibilities types of work, which were likely to lack pension plans, and had little opportunity for advancement. In short, for some the focus was on money-earning opportunities and not jobs with good career advancement, job stability, good pay, and benefits. Certainly one well-known result of these labor market experiences is that the wage levels were low and allowed for little, if any, development of a solid retirement foundation (White House Conference on Aging 1981; Kahne 1981; Minkler and Stone 1985; Older Women's League, undated).

Limitations of Private Pension Provisions

Building a solid retirement foundation was indeed out of reach for many older women during their work years. In addition to low wages, which likely provided little if any money for retirement investments, private pension plans were predicated on the assumption that the male/husband was the household's primary earner and conditions of the pension reflected this view. As pointed out by Leonard (1988), "pension plans reward the long-term, steady worker with low mobility and high earnings. This happens to conform best to the white male work pattern" (3).

Most older women could not and did not share the long-term, full-time or full-year work experiences of men (Coalition on Women and the Budget 1984). However, it has not only been the lack of long-term work histories that has disadvantaged women in the private pension system, but the nature of the private plans themselves. For instance, companies do not have to provide employees with pension plans. Numerous companies have, however, offered pension plans as part of an employee's benefit package. Up until the early 1970s, there was very limited federal attention to the operations or distribution of such private pension plans. Fortunately, over the past couple of decades, private pension provisions have been affected by several major laws: Employee Retirement Income Security Act (ERISA), Retirement Equity Act of 1984 (REACT) and the Tax Reform Act of 1986 (TRA). Each of these acts has addressed, albeit inadequately, issues of paramount concern to older women. While the provisions of these acts will not assist today's older women, it is important that we discuss them because of their policy implications for older women in the twenty-first century (Leonard 1988; Warlick 1985).

Because of the discontinuous nature of women's work histories, three areas of concern regarding private pension provisions will be highlighted: vesting rights, part-time/part-year workers, and break-in service. These have been chosen because they most directly address the conditions that characterize female work patterns, such as interrupted work histories and the juggling of family responsibilities and work.

Vesting is the criterion used to determine an employee's eligibility to receive a pension from an employer. Prior to TRA, ten years of employment was required by most firms before an employee would be vested, that is, qualified to draw benefits upon retirement. TRA reduced the eligibility period to five years of employment, on average, before an individual is vested.

There are work patterns which are not as yet covered by the five-year vesting criterion. Some women work long-term, but only part-time. Leonard (1988) cites, for example, the bookkeeper who works two days every week for decades while maintaining household responsibilities. Such a work pattern has not as yet been taken into account by legislative reform. Finally, even though the five-year vesting criterion is a vast improvement over a ten-year period, it is necessary for some employees to assume significant breaks in their work life. This is especially true for women–they are more likely than men to experience breaks in service for care of children, spouses, parents, and other family members (Older Women's League 1989). REACT permits no loss of vesting credits if the *break-in-service* does not exceed five consecutive years or the period of earlier employment (Leonard 1988).

While these and several other reform features are beginning to recognize women's unique employment patterns due to family and childrearing responsibilities, it is necessary that more reforms be aimed at the private pension issues of women in general and older women in particular. The fundamental issue is whether and how all employees' work histories should be connected to their retirement economic security (Birren and Bengston 1988; Hughes 1991).

Social Security System Inequities

In addition to obstacles in private pension plans, built-in inequities in the social security pension system bode ill for older women and, in fact, curiously contribute to their subsistence life-style. According to Horn (1988), "a major reason elder women are more frequently poor than elder men is the way social security and pension benefits are paid out" (8). Her illustrations include the following: (1) if an older woman receives social security based on her earnings, the benefits are generally low due to her low wages; (2) if married, she and her husband must give up one of their social security checks though both would have paid into the retirement system (usually, because the woman will have had the lower paying job, her pension is the one dropped); and (3) if a woman's husband dies, she then receives only one-half of the calculated amount.

Women are further disadvantaged by social security if they are divorced before ten full years of marriage, e.g., they cannot collect on the spouse's earnings. This is true regardless of the family life contribution the wife made to facilitate the husband's career development and earnings potential. If the marriage is less than ten years old, she may pursue civil legal remedies as part of the divorce settlement, but the social security system does not recognize her contributions. Additionally, neither women's nor men's paid employment in farm labor, domestic work, and some low-wage part-time jobs are covered by social security.

Women who are married to spouses who are eligible for certain state or local public pension benefits may find themselves poorer because of social security's dependent (spousal) offset rule. This allows social security benefits to be reduced by up to two-thirds of the value of the public pension. The following example from Leonard (1988) illustrates the offset rule.

> If she receives a $1,000 per month civil service pension for example, and is entitled to $500 per month Social Security as a widow, her widow's benefit will be cut to nothing, because 2/3 ($666) of the public pension, completely offsets the Social Security benefit. (11-12)

While not specifically aimed at women, this offset rule disproportionately affects them because they are more frequently the dependent beneficiary.

Poverty: Its Disproportionate Effect on Older Women

When the income picture of older women is viewed from the perspective of poverty, the following profile emerges: while they comprise approximately 60% of the aged population, older women comprise 72% of the elderly poor, i.e., they fall below the official poverty line for the elderly. This means that 15% of older women live in poverty compared to 9% of older men–2.5 million and 1 million, respectively. Not all women are equally likely to live in poverty. Thirty-six percent of African-American elderly women are poor, 25% of elderly Hispanic women are poor, while 13% of elderly white women are poor (Worker Equity Department 1991). Elderly rural women of all racial/ethnic groups are a most impoverished group (American Association of Retired Persons and Administration on Aging, undated A, B; Women's Initiative, 1988).

Among the aged, 39.5% of whites are poor or economically vulnerable. In contrast, 71.1% of African-Americans are so classified (U.S. House of Representatives 1987). The number rises to 87.9% for single elderly African-American women, e.g., those ". . . living in single-person households or with nonrelatives" (U.S. House of Representatives 1987, 8). It is not only elderly African-American women who are affected by living status. As the Older Women's League (OWL) (undated) reports, "among the elderly, living alone is strongly correlated with poverty. While 30% of all persons aged 65 and over live alone, 61% of the elderly poor do. Given that the majority of the elderly poor are women, it is no surprise that 71% of older women with incomes below the poverty level live alone" (10).

The high poverty rate of older women in general and in particular subgroups of older women may be traced to factors already mentioned. Older women employed outside of the home worked mostly in pink-ghetto industries such as secretarial/clerical, teller, clerks and numerous service-type businesses, and the secondary labor market, with jobs characterized by low wages, little or no fringe benefits such as life or health insurance, low status, and limited or no career advancement opportunities (Bandler 1989; Coalition on Women and the Budget 1984; Older Women's League, undated). Their work histories have prevented them from accumulating any or adequate personal retirement income. Furthermore, many employed women have found themselves (1) without private pension plans, (2) as tenuous beneficiaries to their spouse's private pension plans (which in some cases were terminated or significantly reduced upon his death), (3) having discontinuous work histories which resulted in low pension amounts for the approximately 20% of women who qualify for private pensions, and (4) subject to inequities in the social security system.

POLICY ISSUES RELATED TO FAMILY LIFE

There is no clear demarcation between policy issues related to economic status and those related to family life, e.g., caregiver issues, cost of divorce for older women, and elder abuse. Rather, each area flows into the other. For example, one could easily classify or cross-reference issues pertaining to divorce under the economic status category. Similarly, caregiving and income status are interconnected as caregivers to the elderly are disproportionately poor (Older Women's League 1989).

Caregiving

Several factors make caregiving a critical twenty-first century policy issue. These include increased chances for living longer accompanied by increased risk of illness, a lack of a national family (spousal, child, parent) caregiver policy, a severe shortage of noninstitutional personal care services such as day care, home health care and respite care, and women's growing participation in the workforce.

This latter point cannot be understated, as women are the primary family (spousal, child, parent) caregiver. A composite profile of the average caregiver is a married woman in her mid-forties. Slightly over one-third of caregivers of the elderly are over 65, while 10% are over 75 (Older Women's League 1989). Of present female caregivers who are caring for children and elders, over one-half are also in paid employment. Men and women caregivers differ in the responsibilities they assume. Men will generally assist by doing home repairs, providing transportation, or engaging in financial management. Women will, in addition to these tasks, provide extensive and often long-term personal care.

Women cannot, as in the past, be assumed to constitute a free and readily accessible caregiver workforce. As they enter the labor force in greater numbers, they must contend with multiple pulls on their capacities for parenting, household management, spousal relations, care of elders, civic responsibilities, and other demands of daily and community living. Evidence is mounting that caregivers, especially long-term caregivers or caregivers to the terminally ill, are experiencing health problems and/or emotional difficulties. This potentially places the caregivers themselves in jeopardy. Moreover, conflicts between the demands and responsibilities of work and family caregiving are growing. Because employers provide little, if any, support to employees who are caregivers, there is speculation that job productivity and work behaviors can deteriorate (Creedon 1988; Older Women's League 1989).

It is in the interest of several parties, not the least of whom is the caregiver, that the federal government's and employers' roles in providing for and supporting the family unit undergo significant restructuring as we approach the twenty-first century. Creedon (1988) suggests that a general lack of awareness of employees' eldercare needs at the executive-level, the failure of employees to "demand" assistance, tight budgets, and a reluctance to undertake new benefits prevent businesses from responding to caregiving issues. Yet, as has been pointed out, companies benefit when employees are not preoccupied and burdened by the demands of caregiving. Absenteeism is reduced, productivity is maintained or upgraded, and employees have a more positive outlook.

The Cost of Divorce for Older Women

Leonard (1987) offers one of the most succinct but poignant descriptions of the plight of the older divorcing woman.

> Of paramount importance to the older divorcing wife is the family home. Unlike her spouse, she may have no credit history, no income except alimony, and almost no prospect of recovering her lost earning capacity. Yet all too commonly the court orders the home sold, in order to divide its value and to pay attorney's fees. For the older woman, especially a career homemaker, this is a major cruelty; upon divorce, she loses her husband, her occupation, and then–all too often–her home. This nearly comprises her universe. In those states which do permit the sale of the home to be delayed, it is usually only in situations where minor children are involved. (6)

Older women may be career homemakers (i.e., no paid employment, as homemaking is their career), homemakers whose paid employment has accommodated family and spousal needs and demands, and homemakers with career-focused paid employment. The latter group were popularly referred to as supermoms in the 1980s. Homemakers in this latter category are likely to have jobs that provide good life and health insurance coverage as well as retirement pensions. Homemakers in this category also are likely to plan for their older years in retirement. While it is not intended that this group be excluded from the following discussion, it must be recognized that these homemakers/career-track workers will not encounter some of the more difficult situations faced by divorced career homemakers and homemakers who work under non-career track conditions.

Except in rare, but highly publicized, Hollywood or Palm Beach-type divorces, most divorced women experience dramatic financial losses, major living arrangement shifts, traumatized social lives, and damage to self-identity, self-worth, and self-esteem (National Institute on Aging and National Institute of Mental Health 1980). Women are much more severely financially disadvantaged than men after divorce (Levitan 1988; 1990). Some subgroups of divorced women suffer more than others. Divorced women with minor children experience a perilous drop in income and often fall into poverty status. Divorced older career homemakers also encounter major income losses as well as severe losses in status.

Two issues, spousal support and marital property, are central to understanding the effects of divorce on women, in general, and older women, in particular. Historically, spousal support was viewed as a means to care for a dependent spouse. Leonard (1987) and Weitzman (1985) point out that the advent of no-fault divorce coupled with a superficial response to the women's liberation movement weakened historical views in awarding spousal support. Today, spousal support is viewed as a privilege and/or temporary condition that continues only until the woman finds employment. An older woman cannot automatically expect to be compensated for her contributions which made it possible for her husband to pursue a high-paying career. Rather, she may find herself liberated from the marriage, which has been her sole means of financial support, and required to find employment whether or not she has skills, education, or work experience. As a result, over the past decade-and-a-half, many midlife and older women have learned to identify themselves as displaced homemakers.

Even when spousal support is awarded, a women may lose it when her former spouse remarries or retires (Leonard 1987; Weitzman 1985). This again reflects the view of spousal support as a privilege. When viewed as a privilege, the awarding (or lack of awarding) of spousal support depends on the whims of the court or the savvy of the former husband's legal counsel. As will be recommended below, financial support for career homemakers must be derived from more stable sources than those involved in the marriage or divorce. Additionally, the view that women receive spousal support as a privilege rather than a right is questioned.

The division of tangible marital property is much less subject to manipulation by either spouse than is the awarding of spousal support. Since the laws of each state determine the equal or equitable distribution of tangible property (Leonard 1987), less discretion is left to courts, judges, and spouses.

Two intangible properties, which can have significance for older women's financial well-being, remain hotly contested in divorces, however (Weitzman 1985). Neither pension benefits nor education/ licenses have been definitely identified as divisible property (Leonard 1987, 6). However, more divorce cases and rulings are grappling with the issue. Older women, especially those who have been career homemakers or homemakers with non-career-focused paid employment, have a great stake in how pension benefits are ultimately legally defined. For many, if pension benefits are defined as marital property they will be treated as divisible property. It is also possible, under the concept of enhanced earning power, to think of a spouse as being entitled, as a right, to some of the financial value of education and/or licenses if she/he contributed to such being obtained and used in ways which enhanced their value (Leonard 1987; Weitzman 1985). For the older woman, the legal conclusions drawn in this area have important consequences for her financial well-being.

Elder Abuse Among Older Women

The final family life issue to be addressed in this chapter is elder abuse. Because older women are the most likely victims, it is critical that any consideration of older women's issues in the twenty-first century reflects the growing pattern of "granny bashing" (Silverman 1987, 226).

In the developing literature on various forms of abuse in families, there is a moderate but growing segment on elder abuse. Four types of elder abuse have been identified: physical abuse, negligent abuse, exploitative abuse, and psychological abuse (Silverman 1987, 226). Each type diminishes the quality of life of the elder victim. Because of their generally low visibility, vulnerable elderly women do not often receive attention or treatment until the situation is either at the crisis or emergency stages (Brubaker 1990; Margolis 1990; Steinmetz 1988). More often than not, abuse of elders goes unreported.

Research on the perpetrator is mixed. Some studies indicate that females are the more likely abuser, while others report that males are more likely the source of abuse (Silverman 1987; Steinmetz 1988).

While it is established that women are the more frequent victims of elder abuse, it is likely that class and ethnic/racial status also influence victimization. More research is necessary to expose the linkages among distinct patterns of abuse, under what conditions various types of elder abuse occur, and the responses to abuse by family members and communities.

Several factors make the issue of elder abuse a grave concern to social workers. Of course, the abused individuals are of paramount concern. It is unacceptable, after a lifetime of family, social, and community contributions, to end one's remaining years terrorized by abuse. Equally regrettable is the reality that those we most expected to count on when aged, vulnerable, and needy may be least capable of adequately providing such care and, even worse, capable of plunging one into even greater misery—in short, the family context may be an unsuitable environment for care and nurturance in an older woman's declining years.

DISCUSSION AND CONCLUSION

Older women of today and those of the twenty-first century will face their aging years in a society decidedly different than that of their counterparts in the twentieth century. No longer can the average older woman expect to be embedded in kinship networks which promise economic protection from marriage through death. Such arrangements (1) usually provided strong cultural constraints against the dissolution of marriage, (2) were an imperative for spousal and family care in older age, (3) provided no institutional arrangements for pensions, (4) viewed paid work outside of the home as less than, and secondary to, homemaker responsibilities, and (5) treated elder abuse as nonexistent or as a personal trouble, not a public issue. These cultural norms no longer operate with the strength or vitality they possessed in the first half of the twentieth century.

The breathtaking changes which have occurred in the latter half of the twentieth century are reflected in twenty-first century policy

concerns. Women have moved into the labor force in massive numbers–in 1960 approximately one-third of those in the labor force
were females, by 1995 about one-half will be females. Other
changes include high divorce rates–one in two new marriages will
fail; revolutionary redefining of the family, accompanied by the
redefining of expectations of who cares for whom and under what
circumstances; high mobility as a way of life; the modern super-
mom phenomenon of expecting women to work, develop careers,
and engage in homemaking; the advent of federal attention to and
regulation of private pension plans; the institutionalization of the
social security system; and the growing recognition that violence in
society is disproportionately directed at women.

There is a common thread cutting across each of the policy areas
discussed–the need for economic and income equity for older
women. A major issue is whether an older woman's economic
viability should be functionally related to her paid labor force experiences. This is a critical issue in a modern industrial and technological society that continues to socialize women for spousal and domestic roles (Chafetz 1988; Hyde and Rosenberg 1976). These
non-labor-force activities usually occur during the peak work/career
years of women. In lieu of progressing by training, experience, and
promotion through a career while contributing to the buildup of a
retirement pension, women are raising families. If society benefits
when women raise families, is it equitable compensation to peg
their financial and retirement future to one-half of their spouse's
earnings?

Other options may be more equitable and reflect women's real
social contribution. It may be more equitable to peg women's remu-
neration in old age to 100% of the spouse's public pension benefit.
Public pensions may be based on the value of the household/home-
maker/family life labor. They may combine some mix of a woman's
own earnings record and the value of family life labor. These issues
must be addressed for future older women.

For today's older women, a simple solution is to discontinue the
current policy of reducing a dependent spouse to poverty on the
death of the pensioner. Rather than basing public policy on the myth
that one can live cheaper than two, models need to be designed
which reflect the realities faced by many older women. They live

alone. Housing, utility, and automobile costs are not reduced with the death of a spouse. In short, some durable costs remain constant, whether for one or two persons. Public pension policy which links wives to their husbands' pensions must recognize this fact and maintain an adequate survivor's pension level. The United States could join several European nations and recognize homemakers as a legitimate category of beneficiaries in their own right within the social security system. Even a moderate level of pension support for being a career homemaker would be a first step on the appropriate policy path for older women.

Attention must also be given to private pension provisions. While the qualifying period for vesting in private pensions has been reduced from ten to five years, the U.S. House of Representatives Select Committee on Aging Report (1987) recommends a further reduction to three years. There is, as they point out, ample evidence that such a policy would be useful in addressing some of the income needs of elder women. They also suggest that, since women, far more than men, are dependent on Supplemental Security Income (SSI), it should not be the policy to reduce that SSI income by one-third when an individual receives in-kind support from a multi-person household. Why impoverish individuals through SSI reductions because they live with others? This is an especially relevant point when one thinks of the impoverished conditions of those who live alone or with unrelated individuals.

There are some other more controversial approaches to reducing the poverty of older women. Poverty among older women might be treated on a categorical basis. This means older women would be targeted as a group requiring special identification and attention in legislation and policies which deal with poverty. The obvious reasons to avoid this type of policy focus is that categorical poverty programs are usually highly stigmatizing, generally not particularly effective in eliminating poverty, and often create taxpayer resentment. On the other hand, a category does single out the special features and needs of a group, thereby gaining attention for their particular interests and remedies. Another suggestion is to treat older women as casualties of an era of radical social change. This would recognize that older women were socialized into behaviors that are no longer functional for them: (1) to place family responsibilities above preparation for retirement, (2) to assume work that was peripheral to domestic activities and as such did not contribute to pension investments or accrual, and (3) to expect a place within the family for care and safety in older age. As casualties, they may be subject to special reparations either as a one-time lump sum or as a lifetime monthly annuity over and above SSI and/or social security payments.

As pointed out earlier, the primary issue for older women who are divorced is whether spousal support should be legally redefined as a right rather than a privilege. There is also the question of whether some means can be devised to ensure equitable treatment among women regarding the award of spousal support. Must final decisions be left to the discretion of an individual judge? If so, what can be said when divorcing women of similar profiles find themselves with very different judicial outcomes because of the judges who heard their cases? One woman may receive minimal or token spousal support and another may be adequately or even abundantly compensated through spousal support. Both would have raised families, performed domestic responsibilities, and assisted their spouses' educational/license and career/earnings development. Serious reform is needed to provide guidance to the legal system to deal equitably with this issue which so gravely affects older women and their standard of living.

Throughout the chapter focus has been given to the policy issues facing older women in the twenty-first century. Concern with these issues grew out of the sweeping social changes which revolutionized the lives of today's older women and will significantly alter the lives of young and midlife females as they age. It is imperative that social workers' dialogue on the policy issues continue–to this end the following questions are offered. These questions are not meant to be exhaustive, but rather a reflection of both the six policy areas discussed and their interactive effects on each other. Grappling with these questions can assist us in pushing for greater economic equity for older women and for safer, more humane environments for them to live out their later years. Finally, the questions below are intended to fuel the debate over what constitutes an adequate balance of individual and societal responsibility for well-being, and the proper balance between personal troubles and public issues.

- Will female employees' paid work histories be the basis for determining eligibility for vesting rights or will male employment patterns (i.e., long-term, uninterrupted work periods) continue to be used as the standard? Or will some standard which recognizes inherent differences in worklife experiences be adopted?
- If women's income levels continue to reflect institutionalized disparities with those of men, will the offset mechanisms in the social security system be modified to exclude women of certain low income levels so they are not doubly disadvantaged by losing all or part of their public pension payments?
- If society continues to expect (require?) women to maintain their current disproportionate share of responsibilities for homemaking and childrearing–a twenty-four-hour, seven-days-a-week involvement–will the imputed value of their labor be factored into the social security system under their own record of earnings?
- Will the definition of marital property include spouse retirement benefits as well as the future earnings potential of education and licenses obtained under conditions where one spouse maintained a household to allow the other spouse to obtain these resources which increased his/her earnings potential?
- Under what conditions must society recognize caregiving as a public issue and not a personal trouble? What should be the key elements of a national caregivers policy, family leave rights, and provisions for respite care?
- Should elder abuse be criminalized or should it be treated as a matter of family conflict and trouble? What actions are needed to decrease the incidence of elder abuse?

REFERENCES

American Association of Retired Persons and Administration on Aging, U.S. Department of Health and Human Services. (undated B). *A profile of older Americans 1989*. Washington, DC.

American Association of Retired Persons and Administration on Aging, U.S. Department of Health and Human Services. (undated A). *A profile of older Americans 1990*. Washington, DC.

Bandler, J. (1989). Family protection and women's issues in social security. *Social Work, 34*: 307-311.

Birren, J. and V. Bengston. eds. (1988). *Emergent theories of aging*. New York: Springer Publishing Company.

Brubaker, T., ed. (1990). *Family relationships in later life*. Newbury Park: Sage Publications.

Chafetz, J. (1988). *Feminist sociology: An overview of contemporary theories*. Itasca, IL: F.E. Peacock.

Coalition on Women and the Budget. (1984, March). *Inequality of sacrifice: The impact of the Reagan budget on women*. Washington, DC: Author.

Creedon, M. (1988). The corporate response to the working caregiver. *Aging, 358*: 16-19, 45.

Horn, P. (1988). Elders on the edge. *Dollars and Sense, 33*: 8-9.

Hughes, W. (1991). Private pension coverage declining. *Aging Today, 12*: 9.

Hyde, J. and B. Rosenberg. (1976). *Half the human experience*. Lexington, MA: D.C. Heath.

Kahne, H. (1981). Women and social security: Social policy adjusts to social change. *International Journal of Aging and Human Development, 13*: 195-208.

Leonard, F. (1987). *Divorce and older women*. Washington, DC: Older Women's League.

Leonard, F. (1988). *Older women and pensions: Catch 22*. Washington, DC: Older Women's League.

Levitan, S. (1988). *Working but poor: America's contradiction*. Baltimore: Johns Hopkins University Press.

Levitan, S. (1990). *Programs in aid of the poor*. 6th ed. Baltimore: Johns Hopkins University Press.

Margolis, R. (1990). *Risking old age in America*. Boulder: Westview Press.

Minkler, M. and R. Stone. (1985). *The feminization of poverty and older women, 25*: 351-357.

National Institute on Aging and National Institute of Mental Health. (1980). *The older woman: Continuities and discontinuities*. Washington, DC. NIH Publication No. 80-1897. Washington, DC.

Older Women's League. (1989). *Failing America's caregivers: A status report on women who care*. Washington, DC: Older Women's League.

Older Women's League. (undated). *The road to poverty: A report on the economic status of midlife and older women in America*. Washington, DC: Older Women's League.

Silverman, P., ed. (1987). *The elderly as modern pioneers*. Bloomington, IN: Indiana University Press.

Steinmetz, S. (1988). *Duty bound: Elder abuse and family care*. Newbury Park: Sage Publications.

U.S. House of Representatives Select Committee on Aging. (1987). *The status of the Black elderly in the United States*. (Comm. Pub. No. 100-162). Washington, DC: U.S. Government Printing Office.

Villers Foundation. (1987). *On the other side of easy street*. Washington, DC: Villers Foundation.

Warlick, J. (1985). Why is poverty after 65 a woman's problem? *Journal of Gerontology, 40*: 751-757.

Weitzman, L. (1985). *The divorce revolution*. New York: The Free Press.

White House Conference on Aging (1981). *Concerns of older women: Growing number, special needs*. Final Report of Committee II, Volume 3 - Recommendations, Post Conference Summary of Delegates.

Women's Initiative, American Association of Retired Persons. (1988). *Facts about older women: Income and poverty*. Washington, DC: American Association of Retired Persons.

Women's Initiative, American Association of Retired Persons. (1989). *Facts about older women: Twelve powerful statistics on older women*. Washington, DC: American Association of Retired Persons.

Worker Equity Department. (1991). Nine facts about older women. *Working Age*. Available from Worker Equity Department, American Association of Retired Persons, 1909 K Street, N.W., Washington, DC 20049.

Chapter 8

Changing Women's Narratives: Taking Back the Discourse

Joan Laird

Night after night my mother would talk-story until we fell asleep. I couldn't tell where the stories left off and the dreams began. At last I saw that I too had been in the presence of great power, my mother talking-story. Her mother taught her to grow up a wife and a slave, but the talk-story has the power to remind. She also taught me the song of the warrior woman. I would have to grow up a warrior woman.

–Maxine Hong Kingston, *Woman Warrior*

INTRODUCTION

Gender, we have learned, is socially constructed. The meanings of being male and of being female are fashioned, in varying cultures, through language, social discourse, the stories we tell about ourselves and the stories that are told about us. These sociocultural stories tell us what we are like and what we are to be like, how we are to think, with whom we should choose to be, and even how we do and should speak. In reciprocal and circular fashion, these narratives both reinforce what already is and create it anew, as we speak our lives within the constraints of prevailing public discourses.

Portions of this chapter have been excerpted from J. Laird (in press). Women's silences–women's secrets. In *Secrets in family therapy*, edited by E. Imber-Black. New York: Norton.

The stories in the larger sociocultural surround provide the contextual repertoire we draw upon to construct our autobiographies, the life narratives that we build and revise as we construct, deconstruct, and reconstruct ourselves. The shape of these self-narratives is influenced in particular by the prevailing folklores in our families and other important groups, that is, by the unique ways our families and other primary reference groups have translated larger social constructions into prescriptions for living.

Clearly the relationship between the personal and the social story is an interactive one. Larger social discourses are constructed from what Geertz (1983) calls "local knowledges" and these larger social discourses, in turn, provide contexts in which local knowledges may flourish or, conversely, become extinct or go underground. Local knowledges–sets of ideas, explanations, and interpretations about the world–gradually take hold and may gain increasing numbers of adherents. These local knowledges/stories, as they become part of the surrounding discourse, guide our everyday words, thoughts, and actions. They shape the lives of women in very powerful ways, guiding and constraining their speech and even their thoughts.

For example, the popular idea that women encourage sexual exploitation on the part of men is one of the many "stories" that has kept generations of women silent about their experiences of harassment, molestation, and rape. The Hill-Thomas episode demonstrates just how influential this set of ideas is and how difficult it is to dislodge it. Similarly, we now have a prevailing social discourse, reinforced by a largely white-male dominated fashion industry, that dictates women's own body images (Faludi 1991). In the social construction of beauty, women are to be extraordinarily thin and, paradoxically, voluptuous. Anorexia and other eating disorders, as well as the current popularity of silicone breast implants, at least in part, may be interpreted in the context of these larger social stories that prescribe and proscribe women's bodies.

There is, of course, a remarkably intimate relationship between knowledge and gender, and between power and gender (Goodrich 1991). One of the most powerful lessons of feminist research over the last two decades has been that ways of knowing and speaking are gendered and are socially reproduced through mothering (Chodorow 1978), education (Belenky et al. 1986), story and folklore (Laird 1989), ritual (Imber-Black 1989; Laird 1988), the popular media and in the arts, indeed in all of the contexts in which our lives are defined. It is white, middle- and upper-class males who largely control the making of local knowledges and of social discourse and social meanings. The making of women's narratives and women's silences, then, cannot be explored without constant attention to issues of gender and power, and to how these forces operate in the constituting of women's lives.

The language of the mental health professions, which I would also call "stories" or "local knowledges," has also had enormous influence in shaping the public's ideas about people and about individual and family functioning. For example, widespread "depression" among women is rarely termed "oppression," which is more difficult to "treat." Instead of directly naming the molestation and violence that men commit against women, we tend to name the effects on women, directing attention to women's symptomatology and away from the original offenses and offenders. Thus, many women sexually abused as children are now termed "borderline personality disorder" or "multiple personality disorder" or "anorexic." In the process, attention is diverted from the offenders. What might be more appropriately storied as wife beating is named "marital discord," "spouse abuse," or "family violence." Such euphemisms, argues Lamb (1991), implicate mental health professionals in a powerful obfuscation of language which masks gender oppression and detours social solutions to massive social problems. Furthermore, storying these experiences as problems in individual and family functioning is one way the mental health field assures its own perpetuation and expands its influence over thought, language, and the social construction of gender.

In this chapter, I examine how the story metaphor can provide a tool for both understanding and transforming women's lives. I am particulary interested in how women can and cannot use their voices, how women's language is constituted and perceived, how women are silenced, how they can and do resist oppression through finding their voices and using their silences in strengthening ways, and how they can and do transform their stories and thus themselves.

Two examples of the relationship between public discourse and individual story and the impact of that relationship on women are used–the incest story and the lesbian story. In each case, I look at some of the ways that women have been silenced, as well as some of the ways that they have begun to restory their lives and to influence the larger public story.

Many postmodern thinkers argue that the self is constituted through the narratives we construct to explain our lived experiences, through the self-bearing witness to the self, through a mutually affirming sharing of stories with others with like experiences, and through the narratives others construct about us (Bauman 1986; Bruner 1986; Gergen and Gergen 1983; Polkinghorne 1988). Story, then, or restorying, is an important pathway to change. Just as gaining the power to influence social discourse and social meanings can bring about change on the societal level, so the restorying process on the individual or family level offers powerful potential for change, not just for the individuals involved but in initiating and strengthening alternative local knowledges. For example, as the women's movement has helped to shape our consciousness concerning the patriarchal nature of the traditional family, so many individual women, strengthened by feminism, have restoried and restructured their family lives in very important ways.

Similarly, the clinical context can offer an opportunity for the reshaping of women's personal and familial narratives and thus for the beginnings of new local knowledges. Throughout this chapter, questions for social work clinicians are generated. I end with some suggestions about how restorying can be applied to a formulation for clinical practice that builds on women's strengths and helps women to take more charge of their own meaning-making. This restorying phenomenon, I argue, is one of the major ways that clinical practice and the collaborative helping relationship contain transformative power.

Story, Knowledge, and Power

In the era of the "scientific" paradigm, sometimes called logical positivism, we were told that our task, as scientists, scholars, and professionals, was to discover, measure, test, prove, validate, generalize, and be accountable for something "out there," to tease out the "truth," the real story. In the postmodern era of constructionism, constructivism, and deconstructionism, another view of "reality," or rather a different way to think about reality, has gained favor across many disciplines of scholarship. In this story it is the narrative itself, not the raw data "out there," that assumes primary importance. Edward Bruner (1986), an anthropologist, frames this view as follows:

> It is not that we initially have a body of data, the facts, and we then must construct a story or theory to account for them. Instead . . . the narrative structures we construct are not secondary narratives about data but primary narratives that establish what is to count as new data. New narratives yield new vocabulary, syntax, and meaning in our ethnographic accounts; they define what constitute the data of those accounts. (143)

Bauman (1986), a linguist, makes a similar point when he argues that fact or fiction, historical truth or mythical truth, are not useful dichotomies. He suggests that perhaps events are not the raw materials from which we construct our stories but rather the reverse, that events may be abstractions from narrative.

> It is the structures of signification in narrative that give coherence to events in our understanding, that enable us to construct in the interdependent process of narration and interpretation a coherent set of interrelationships that we call an event. (5)

Polkinghorne (1988), a cognitive psychologist, argues that "historical narratives are a test of the capacity of a culture's fictions to endow real events with the kinds of meaning patterns that its stories have fashioned from imagined events. Thus, historical narratives transform a culture's collection of past happenings (its first order referents) by shaping them into a second-order pattern of meaning" (62). Story or narrative (terms I use interchangeably here), then, are not simply reflections about real events but they are themselves *constitutive* of those events; events only gain meaning when they are storied. Thus stories are extremely powerful categories for individual and social meaning-making and action. There is, then, an intimate relationship between story, knowledge, and power (White and Epston 1990).

Indeed Foucault (1980), as discussed in White and Epston (1990), argues that power and knowledge are inseparable. Through those "knowledges" that claim to hold "truth" or "objective reality" we are

> . . . judged, condemned, classified, . . . destined to a certain mode of living or dying, as a function of the true discourses which are the bearers of the specific effects of power. (1980, 94)

Tomm (1990), in the foreword to White and Epston (1990), describes the knowledge/power relationship as follows:

> . . . our personal identities are constituted by what we "know" about ourselves and how we describe ourselves as persons. But what we know about ourselves is defined, for the most part, by the cultural practices (of describing, labeling, classifying, evaluating, segregating, excluding, etc.) in which we are embedded. As human beings in language, we are, in fact, all subjugated by invisible social "controls" of presuppositional linguistic practices and implicit sociocultural patterns of coordination. In other words, if family members, friends, neighbors, coworkers, and professionals think of a person as "having" a certain characteristic or problem, they exercise "power" over him or her by "performing" this knowledge with respect to that person. Thus, in the social domain, knowledge and power are inextricably interrelated. (viii)

This interrelationship is, of course, highly complex. One of the problems with constructivist epistemology or philosophy, as MacKinnon and Miller (1987) so aptly point out, is that it is often assumed that we all participate equally in the construction of social knowledge. Knowledge-making, or what I call storying or mythmaking, is not a value-free or influence-free endeavor. It is a political process. Clearly, all stories are not equal. Foucault argues, however, that we are *all* caught up in a web of power/knowledge.

Indeed, it is not possible *not* to exercise power/knowledge, as "we are simultaneously undergoing the effects of power and exercising this power in relation to others" (quoted in White and Epston 1990, 22). Various groups gain dominance by controlling social discourses, by qualifying particular knowledges and sanctifying them. There are, of course, significant differences, both overt and covert, in the power that particular groups have to ensure that certain narratives will prevail. This is the case in our families, in our communities, in our society, and in the world. Language does not simply mirror society; it is used to construct and maintain various distinctions and inequalities, in the case at hand, between men and women.

WOMEN, LANGUAGE, AND STORY

Women's lives have been largely defined and described by men. Furthermore, women's language has been defined, interpreted, and demeaned by men and by women themselves. For women are also influenced by the larger social discourse that defines them. The contemporary feminist movement and important work in women's studies has taught us well how women's lives have been measured with yardsticks designed by and for men and have been found wanting (see, e.g., Chodorow 1978; Gilligan 1982). Women learn to regard themselves according to the prevailing story for their lives, to gauge their performances against available socially constructed stories. A few examples make the point.

Belenky and her colleagues (1986), in their interviews with some 100 women of differing ages, educations, and social classes, found that many women feel "voiceless" and unheard in educational contexts that do not value women's ways of learning and knowing, contexts in which "truth" is sought through objective, rational search rather than through intuition, self-understanding, and connection. Throughout *his*tory, a meaning-making process (Spence 1983) dominated by men, women have often been denied their stories which, as Heilbrun (1988) points out, deprives them of the narratives by which they might take control of their own lives. For Heilbrun, to gain the right to tell one's own story is contingent upon the ability to act in the public domain. Women's storying, in contrast to men's, has been limited largely to the family, a domestic or largely private storytelling context. In revisiting the autobiographies of a number of famous women, Heilbrun concludes that "male power has made certain stories unthinkable" for women (44). Women who do not make their lives contingent upon their husbands or children, who seek adventures or quests independently of men, have few stories to follow, for "lives do not serve as models; only stories do that" (37). Conway (1983) notes the narrative flatness in which women of the Progressive Era in the United States, such as Jane Addams or Ida Tarbell, wrote their lives. In their public stories, their autobiographies, they portray themselves as feminine, that is as intuitive, passive, and nurturing. Their causes and their successes occur almost fortuitously, accidentally, not as the result of a conscious vision or purposeful quest. Other notable women, if they are grandiose enough to follow a vision and to describe it without qualification, risk public ridicule (Laird 1986). Their literature or their science or their psychology may be storied as faulty and sentimental (or, if it is terribly good, perhaps someone else wrote or invented it). Such women are often described as having failed as mothers, as promiscuous and, to place the final nails in the coffin, as unfeminine, manly, or perhaps even lesbian. Such women, it is implied, are not real women.

Certain storying *genres* have also excluded women. Written language, until the invention of the novel, was largely the province of men. In eastern European Jewish culture, for example, women spoke Yiddish, the spoken language of the commoner, but were forbidden Hebrew, the language of writing and of the scholar (Zborowski and Herzog 1952). (One colleague told me the story of her grandmother, who confessed on her deathbed that as a child she had secretly learned Hebrew by peeking in through the window of the boy's *schul*. Never in her life had she dared to tell anyone of her hidden power).

Women have also been excluded from other forms of public storying. For example, until recently the female comedian was a rare occurrence, limited to situation comedy and domestic humor. The public storyteller, the community humorists, have been men, and what their humor is frequently about is women. Jewish mothers, mothers-in-law in general, and wives are particular targets.

(I've never heard a Jewish father joke and fathers-in-law are rarely targeted.) In this age of measuring success through Nielsen ratings and sound bites, it is men who largely control the stories, the images, and the icons we are bombarded with daily on television and in print. These popular "stories" often portray women benignly as creatures who clean and need to be cleaned, and less benignly as sexual objects and targets for violence. The popular media is, according to the title of a powerful film commentary, "still killing us softly."

Certainly there are exceptions. Television series such as the now defunct *Cagney and Lacey* feature women who are tough, courageous, and competent–women who are more androgynous, who learn how to speak in the deeper voices of men, to swear, to take risks, to assert themselves, to act with bravery in dangerous situations. While Lacey tries to balance her role as woman cop with that of mother-wife, frequently a heartwrenching problem, Cagney has great difficulty allowing herself to be soft or loving or vulnerable. Like Hong Kingston, and Thelma and Louise in the recent controversial movie, she recognizes the contradiction between the choice of wife/slave or woman warrior.

> As the old couple said to the young woman who followed the bird up the mountain:
> "You can return to pull sweet potatoes, or you can stay with us and learn how to fight barbarians and bandits." (Kingston 1975, 27)

The woman warrior learns to not let menstrual days interrupt her training; she learns that motherhood and warriorhood seem not to mix, that she must put off having children for a few more years.

> No husband of mine will say, "I could have been a drummer, but I had to think of the wife and kids. You know how it is." Nobody supports me at the expense of his own adventure. (Kingston 1975, 57)

Women-Talk

Women, in their historical assignment to the domestic sphere, have clearly had a far less powerful role than men in the development of the public, collective stories that in turn shape domestic stories. Folklores, local knowledges, take shape and gain sanction in communities (Kirshenblatt-Gimblett 1970, 1987). Not only have women had less access to the powerful shaping sources for social definitions of gender as well as to certain discourse genres, but those ways of speaking identified as "women's talk" have frequently been demeaned and less valued. Women as talkers have been variously labeled gossips, chatterboxes, or naggers (Coates 1986). Their speech, in various studies of and commentaries on language, has been seen as vacuous and restricted, full of useless adverbs and hyperbole; women have been said to be expert in the use of euphemism (Lakoff 1975). Yet, said Rousseau, their writing lacks eloquence and passion. "They may show great wit but never any soul" (quoted in Coates 1986, 28). Women have been said to have much more restricted vocabularies, yet to talk too much. As one old English proverb would have it, "many women, many words; many geese, many turds." Another old English proverb suggests the ideal: "Silence is the best ornament of a woman."

Men, on the other hand, are in charge of eloquence. One has only to attend a university faculty meeting, a meeting of the legislature, or a corporate board gathering today to observe that oratory eloquence, in the best tradition of the Roman Senate, is still the province of men. Our national debating societies, such as the U.S. Congress or the Supreme Court, serve as public forums featuring the voices of men, as prevailing public discourse is made and remade. It is male voices that determine women's lives and even women's bodies, as men consider whether women will have the right to control the use of their own bodies.

Coates (1986), in a study of historic folklinguistic beliefs about sex differences in language, articulates the "androcentric rule":

> Men will be seen to behave linguistically in a way that fits the writer's view of what is desirable or admirable; women on the other hand will be blamed for any linguistic state or development which is regarded by the writer as negative or reprehensible. (15)

In the last 15 to 20 years, many scholars of language have turned their attention to the study of the relationships between gender and language, to the study of male and female voices. Like one of the central arguments in feminist theory itself (Are men and women *really* so very different from each other?), it is not clear whether women's language (voice) is fundamentally very different from that of men or is only stereotyped and reinforced as different. But for our purposes here, three points should be stressed. First, what is important is the fact that women's language and women's storying are perceived and marked as different or "other" to the unmarked language and storying of men (Andersen 1988; Coates 1986; Graddol and Swann 1989). Second, women have less access to the shaping of local knowledges and the larger social discourses that define them as women, to themselves and to others. And third, women are represented, and thus created and recreated, very differently than men in and by language.

There is a Chinese word for the female I–which is "slave." Break the women with their own tongues. (Kingston 1975, 56)

LANGUAGE AND THE MENTAL HEALTH PROFESSIONS

A series of professional "movements" have defined women's lives in the last century. For example, the medicalization of birthing restoried birthing from a process in which women were expert into one which transferred both definition and process into the hands/instruments of men. Women were now told to lie down, to take drugs, to play a passive role, and to remove themselves from the company of other women (Rich 1976). The home economics movement turned wives/mothers into household scientists, dedicated to full-scale and full-time war against household dirt, to scientific housekeeping, to the artful making for men of a haven from the difficult and sometimes cruel world of industry (Mintz and Kellogg 1988). The mental hygiene movement extended and reinforced the notion of mothering as a self-conscious, scientific process in which mothers became entirely responsible not only for the physical but also for the emotional lives of their children.

Mother-wife blaming has been an important part of almost every major school of developmental and clinical theory, including family theory and therapy (Luepnitz 1988). In fact, some argue that the blaming of women and the assignment of "responsibility" for individual and family development to women is an essential part of preserving and extending the influence of the mental health professions. To be "womanly," argued Chesler (1972) in her pathbreaking book, is to risk hospitalization for mental illness.

The storying of women's physical and mental health also illustrates the intimate connections between story, knowledge, and power. The power assumed by and granted to "professionals" to pathologize women's experiences of oppression extends even to women's abilities to define and understand their own bodies. Many women, even in contemporary times, have grown up without ever knowing the words for their own genital parts; they cannot speak important parts of themselves (Lerner 1988).

As professionals, it is difficult for us to extricate ourselves from the cultural/linguistic surround that shapes what we see and hear. We, too, influence and are influenced by our professional languages, which make possible what we see and hear or do not see and hear. For example, depending on our favorite human behavior theories, the behavior of an angry, hostile, and rebellious 14-year-old girl toward her single-parent mother may be seen as part of normal development, as the consequence of turmoil and loss following an acrimonious divorce, as the girl's faulty object relations, as a result of the mother's lack of sensitivity or firmness, or as faulty family structure or communication. Rarely do clinicians consider the powerful issues of gender oppression that shape the lives of mother and daughter, the relationship between them, and the larger social stories that condition their thoughts and actions. For example, perhaps the daughter struggles against identifying with her mother, who is overworked, undervalued, and depressed about her own life circumstances. Perhaps the mother sees her family as incomplete and herself as an inadequate parent, helpless without the strong voice/authority of a male in the home. How we see and hear affects even the contexts we will create for possible stories to take shape.

In the next section, two "stories," that of the incest victim/survivor and that of the contemporary lesbian, serve to extend the story metaphor and to further examine women's strengths in a context of unequal power.

The Incest Story

Throughout history women have been denied their own experiences in ways that have for many proved destructive to their sanity and their survival, in ways that have been story-silencing. Many of these experiences have to do with violence, as children and as adults, at the hands of men, from sexual harrassment to battering, from rape to murder. Men's violence against women, not only during the rape and pillage of war but in everyday family and community life, has until recently been unspeakable, in the sense of being unable to be spoken. Not only have victimizer and victim alike maintained silence, but so has the world around them, protecting patriarchal definitions and power arrangements in the society and in the family.

The silence and secrecy of these experiences cannot be understood without reference to the larger social contexts and the social discourses or culturally agreed upon sets of meanings that direct interpretations by layperson and professional alike. The story of the battered woman was not only silenced by her husband but could not be heard by her neighbors or the police or the judge, while the raped woman often found that *she* had become the target of social blame and approbation. As Anita Hill showed us recently, even a successful, well-educated African-American attorney did not believe, ten years ago, that she could speak of what she describes as repeated experiences of sexual harassment by her supervisor without endangering her own career. While these kinds of stories are being told today, the Hill-Thomas encounter provides a dramatic example both of the personal costs of breaking silence and of the ways in which one narrative generates multiple meanings, some far from the narrator's own meanings and intentions, all reflecting, among other things, personal and political agendas and ideologies as well as community expectations for moral behavior. Each new "reading" of the text generates new possibilities for meaning. Even so, to break the silence is not necessarily to be "heard." As Senator Kennedy remarked to Anita Hill's corroborating witnesses, "These gentlemen cannot hear you because they do not wish to hear you."

When women do try to fight back, as the Hill-Thomas incident demonstrates, the backlash can be powerful. In a public double-binding process, Professor Hill was excoriated on the one hand for her years of silence, for not leaving the scene of the crime (and no one asks why it is *she* who should do the leaving), for failing to repeat to her friends the graphic language allegedly used by Judge Thomas, and on the other hand for speaking out, for viciously smearing a respected man, for destroying his life and his family, for seeking personal fame and money. Interestingly, the great majority of both men and women seem to have aligned with Thomas, with his story, reflecting the power of prevailing patriarchal discourse concerning, gender, sexuality, and violence. The meta-message was displayed in the context itself, the all-white male Senate Judiciary Committee vividly reinforcing our understandings about who controls the spoken, who makes the rules for social discourse, and demonstrating the precarious future for any woman who does not know when to hold her tongue.

For the victimizer, the offender, the perpetrator (or whatever gender-neutral words are used to describe the violent person, most frequently a male), secrecy is often enforced through threats of retribution. For the victim, denied her story, the pain may be so unspeakable that it can only be repressed, expressed through extreme dissociation and even desecration of her own body. Women who have been battered or whose children have been molested by fathers, stepfathers, brothers, or by more transient men passing through their families help to maintain the silence and to protect the family from outside encroachment. They do this for reasons of fear, shame, and guilt, because they are afraid their families will disintegrate and they will lose the only identity that seems possible, because they have learned to disbelieve in themselves and to be reliant on men, because they do not wish to give up their homes or the only lives for which they have been readied. Many such women are poor already or are dependent on men's incomes, ill-prepared for the poverty and despair that can accompany single parenthood. Some blame themselves. They must have asked for it. They deserved it. They didn't protect their daughters. Why, we rarely ask, should women be in the position of having to defend their daughters from their daughter's fathers?

The abusers not only enforce a code of secrecy and silence but, in Scarry's (1985) sense, they "shatter" the language of pain; that is, like other torturers or killers or men who must kill in war, they detach the pain from its referent. For example, many fathers or stepfathers who abuse their children not only fail to recognize the moral failure of their role as parent or the destruction of the parent-child relationship, but fail to recognize the severe emotional and even physical pain they are inflicting on their own children (Gordon 1989; Herman 1981). In what may be one of the more perverse efforts in modern times to shape a social discourse in order to protect such power injustices, some writers and researchers have greatly minimized the effects of child sexual molestation (e.g., Kinsey et al. 1953), while others have attempted to redefine it as a natural phenomenon pleasurable to the child and positive for her development (Nobile 1977; Pomeroy 1976; Ramey 1979).

The spoken and the unspoken constitute each other. As Linda Gordon (1989) has shown in her fascinating historical study documenting the shaping of social discourse around child sexual abuse, a number of special social categories of language and social institutions to support these social definitions were created to reconstitute the abuse of female children as female sexual delinquency. In a blaming-the-victim solution, father and the privacy and sanctity of home and family were protected from encroachments by the state through the creation of a huge complex for institutionalizing young girls. Also, by constructing the concept of the "town pervert" or the "dirty old man," the occasional deviant, the practice of fathers sexually exploiting their own daughters remained an unspoken part of the social discourse. And for those who were the victims, the lack of language became a lack of consciousness, in extreme cases to the point where young females learned to deny their own experiences, sometimes turning upon their self-hated and "soiled" bodies in self-destructive ways. For others, the more well-meaning and benign among us, it is simply too troubling or too painful to think upon such acts, for they shatter our images of our culture and the institution of family; they imply profound and difficult commitments to change.

But what of the social workers and other mental health professionals, the clinicians who have worked with the victims of male violence? Immersed like everyone else in prevailing larger cultural discourses/"knowledges," professionals have helped to support, indeed to create and define, one of the most hostile of silences in human experience. Here the power of the expert has been used to reinforce the subjugation of the least powerful, women and children. The long conspiracy of silence in Freudian thought about incest and other forms of sexual abuse and its interpretation as female fantasy served to keep generations of therapists focused on children's and women's symptoms (Herman 1981; Masson 1984). This story, this local knowledge, this psychology of women, gained great power over the decades, helping to shape a larger social discourse that defined women as seething with repressed sexual wishes, incompletely developed, and "hysterical." The psychoanalytic interpretation fit neatly with the discourse of patriarchy; in recursive fashion it became such a powerful "truth" that women learned to deny their own experiences or to blame themselves for having been violated by others.

The problem with this storying process is, of course, that it constructs a plot in which the central character is a "sick" woman in need of rescue and help from a "doctor" (sometimes disguised as a social worker). This is not to suggest that victimized women do not need help, but rather to point out that the storying metaphor has great power in redefining the experience and in prescribing the "treatment." Not only are women seen as deficient, defective, and diseased, defined by the effects of their denied experiences as "borderlines," "multiples," or "anorexics," but the very language used serves to divert attention from the social context that allows and indeed promotes such exploitation.

Family therapists, when they wrote about family violence at all, with their language of systems, form, pattern, structure, and game, continued and reinforced the code of silence, ignoring power differentials in the family and in the world, and even shifting major responsibility for the sexual abuse of their children and their own battering by their husbands to the wife-mother or to the marital interaction (see, e.g., Gutheil and Avery 1977; Matchotka, Pittman, and Flomenhaft 1967). Only as the heightened consciousness generated by the women's movement slowly fostered a changing psychology of women and a new sociology of the family did psychodynamic and systemic clinicians begin to scrutinize prevailing clinical models for their gender biases and their blind spots to violence against women.

Recently, women have begun to develop new "local knowledges" and these local knowledges, which begin with the storying of individual experiences, are, in turn, reshaping the larger public discourse. Courageous women from all walks of life are speaking out, from former Miss Americas to leading comedians to mental hospital patients. They are telling and writing, in public forums and in their autobiographies, of their physical and sexual abuse as children and their battering as adults. In the process, they are rewriting their lives, healing themselves through ritual and restorying (Winslow 1990), in self-help movements (Bass and Davis 1988), and in therapy. Some publicly confront their abusers (see, e.g., Randall 1987, 1991). Some see the bearing witness phenomenon as unseemly, a public breaking of a private rule, while others are countering with a powerful backlash that seeks once again to reinforce the norms of patriarchy (Faludi 1991).

But it is unlikely that such women will be easily silenced again. Women have learned that silence, while at times necessary for self-protection and survival, can be costly. The costs of silence, in fact, can be so great that the story one creates to make sense of the world denies the self and validates social interpretations of personhood that are demeaning and distorted. To break the silence, to tell the story, implies a taking charge of one's own herstory, developing a revised story that is congruent with one's lived experience. It means "going public," if only to one other person. It means placing responsibility for unhappiness and shame where it belongs. Sometimes it means confronting the abuser, making the violence *his* shame, not one's own. It means freeing oneself from past stories that are personally debilitating. It means writing a new self-narrative in which the self-definition is revised from that of "victim" to that of "survivor" (Riessman 1989). It means undermining the truth-making power of patriarchy.

As clinicians, captured by the discourse of patriarchy, for a long time we failed to see or to hear what often lay beyond children's and women's symptoms. And thus we failed to create a context in which women's realities might be validated and new, more life-affirming stories, shaped. Some survivors are insisting now that we listen; they are speaking so loudly we cannot not hear. It is incumbent on every practitioner to *always* consider how the larger social context affects our own vision, to always wear our gender lenses, to always create a context in which alternative stories may emerge.

The Lesbian Story

Until relatively recently, the lesbian in this society, with rare exception, has led a life of invisibility and secrecy. Gay men and lesbians, in many cultures and throughout history, have faced everything from execution and murder to more subtle forms of overt and covert hostility and discrimination (Adam 1987; Comstock 1991; D'Emilio 1983). Predominant metaphors and interpretations in public discourse about homosexuality have shifted, over time, from those of evil and sin to those of sexual perversion, mental illness, genetic aberration and, most benignly, arrested psychosexual development.[1] However, sparked by the Stonewall riot of 1969, a spontaneous resistance ignited by a police raid of a gay bar in New York City, and strengthened by the civil rights and women's movements, the gay rights movement gathered momentum throughout the late 1960s and 1970s. A growing number of "out" gays and lesbians today continue to resist oppression in its many guises and are actively restorying the gay and lesbian experience in public discourse. One important marker of progress was, of course, the 1973 removal of homosexuality as an illness or diagnosable condition per se from the American Psychiatric Association's Diagnostic and Statistical Manual of Psychiatric Disorders (DSM II). Many mental health professionals today, however, continue to oppose that move and continue to "treat" homosexuality as an illness or aberration that can be "cured."

While gays and lesbians, by virtue of their sexual orientation, face similar kinds of oppression, lesbians risk double discrimination: they are considered sexually deviant and they are women. If they are women of color, they face multiple prejudices. Lesbian lives, along with incest, have been, perhaps, one of the best kept secrets in American society. The lesbian must be silenced for she represents the most serious challenge possible to patriarchy, to men and to manhood, a living threat to the norm of compulsory hetero-sexuality (Rich 1980). That some women might choose or prefer to love and to spend their emotional and sexual lives with other women is unthinkable in patriarchal discourse. The lesbian's very existence gives testimony to the notion that women do not need men to become complete, to survive, to succeed, to live in families, to raise children. Heilbrun (1988) notes that being single, defined until very recently by society as a pathetic, deviant state, if not a source of mental illness, allowed many women to follow their own muses. Freed from the demands of marriage, homemaking, and childrearing, many famous women leaders over the last two centu-ries have been, at least as far as anyone knows, single women. Some have been mistresses to married men (love and sexuality without responsibility), while for many others, close and intimate friend-ships with other women have been at the center of their emotional lives. While we do not know how many of these intimate connec-tions between women were sexual or would be defined as lesbian in modern times, we do know that many women couples have lived together for most of their adult lives, sharing their dreams and household responsibilities (Faderman 1981, 1991). Less fettered by rigid gender role assignments, such women are freer to pursue their quests and to support each other's visions.

There is space here to focus on only a very small piece of the lesbian story, a social and personal story that is in part about oppres-sion, social approbation, silence, invisibility, shame, isolation, and suffering. But these are not the only parts to this larger story; they are simply the parts that can be and are told. What has not been told, even in the clinical research and practice literature, which has itself undergone profound changes in focus in just a few years, is a story of strength and resilience, a story of private satisfaction and public success.[2]

For a long period of time, the overriding focus in research on homosexuality was a search for "cause." While no one ever asked what "caused" heterosexuality, several generations of researchers attempted to find the sources of homosexuality in genetic or hor-monal aberration, in arrested or incomplete psychosexual develop-ment, in faulty parenting, or sometimes in unfortunate social experi-ences. In the 1970s, after what seems now many years of a futile scholarly journey, researchers began to shift their attention to studying the mental, emotional, and social adjustments of gay men and, to a much lesser extent, lesbians. A number of studies have compared the mental health of gay men and lesbians to their heterosexual counterparts, repeatedly finding few if any links between sexual orientation and mental or emotional health or social adjustment.[3] Furthermore, as society has grudgingly begun to acknowledge that a significant number of lesbians and gay men have children, a phenomenon once considered *by definition* next to impossible, a growing number of researchers have turned their attention to the children of homosexuals (e.g., Golombok, Spencer, and Rutter 1983; Green 1978; Green et al. 1986; Kirkpatrick, Smith, and Roy 1981; Paul 1986). The sexual identity, sex-role behavior, sexual orientation, psychological health, and social adaptation of children of lesbians have been compared to children of heterosexual women.[4] Again, study after study attests to the fact that the sexual orientation of the mother does not seem to have significant influence on the development of children along the dimensions mentioned. If there are any differences of interest, children of lesbians seem more flexible and more comfortably androgynous.

These latter researches are helping to construct a story that in turn may help to correct some of the widespread myths and misconceptions about the experiences of children in gay and lesbian families, myths that have resulted in extensive pain and tragedy. For example, lesbians repeatedly have been judged unfit parents in the courts and social agencies, simply by virtue of their sexual orientation, and it remains extremely difficult for gay men or lesbians to adopt or to serve as foster parents (Ricketts and Achtenberg 1987). Other gay men and lesbians have lost or been denied jobs where they might come into contact with children, victims of various myths that raise the specter of sexual molestation or deviant influence.

Clinicians identified with and/or sympathetic to lesbians and lesbian issues and experienced in clinical work with this population have made important contributions in detailing the impact of social oppression, of homophobia, and familial disapproval on the life experiences of individual lesbians, lesbians in couple and family relationships, and children in lesbian families (see, e.g., Burch

1982, 1985; Crawford 1987; Hall 1978; Krestan and Bepko 1980; Loulan 1986; Roth 1985). Much of this literature, which constitutes the only "ethnography" of lesbian life available to our profession, explores the effects of stress and discrimination on individual and familial adjustment. Much attention is given to internalized homophobia and its insidious effects. Most clinical observers seem to agree that, although there are some issues unique to sexual orientation (for example, attempting to construct a strong, coherent identity and building a satisfying life in a world at worst hostile and at best tolerant of one's sexual orientation; the fact that in couple relationships both partners are women, which affects the nature and quality of the relationship and the kinds of problems that can emerge; the fact that children in lesbian families risk negative peer pressures and social humiliation), the issues that emerge are similar to those faced by all individuals and families (Blumstein and Schwartz 1983).

While these profound shifts in the research and clinical literature represent vital and important progress in documenting lesbian experience, another part of the lesbian story is not yet told. It seems to me that the trends described above fail to capture or communicate that part of the story that tends to appear only in the more radical women's literature, a story of strength, resilience, and astonishing success. Both the research and the clinical literature retain something of a "deficit" or at least defensive stance. Myths must be debunked and troubles linked to oppression. What we do not know enough about and do not hear about are the stories of our lesbian "goddesses" or even the stories of ordinary lesbians, many of whom, in an era of profound dissatisfaction in heterosexual marriage and a tragic degree of male violence against women, lead successful and enormously satisfying and stable lives, in or out of the proverbial closet. Such stories have much to teach us about women's strengths, about resilience, about growth through adversity, and about resistance to an oppressive culture of gender relations.

This is the case even in social work, which has perhaps been more tolerant than some professions. Many of the founding mothers and early leaders in social work, and in other "women's" professions, were single woman or women who spent their entire adult lives in live-in relationships with one or more longtime women companions. Jesse Taft and Virginia Robinson, founders and leaders of the Pennsylvania School of Social Work, lived together for most of their adult lives, adopting and raising two children. Jane Addams, Charlotte Towle, Gordon Hamilton, and Florence Hollis, to mention a few other prominent social work leaders, all remained unmarried, sharing their personal lives and their professional dreams with intimate women companions.[5] We do not know whether or not these women would describe themselves as lesbians in contemporary meanings of the term. What is clear is that they were "women-identified women," living in families with other women. The point I wish to make here is that these essential parts of their life herstories are largely unwritten and undertold; the personal and familial stories of these magnificent women-identified women, who might serve as models of strength for our young, lesbian and other women-identified women students, are largely unavailable to the profession.

One question that needs asking is how is it that lesbians and children of lesbians do so well in all of the comparative studies to date, *in spite of the fact* that they face constant confrontations with homophobia, considerable discrimination, and often alienation from their own families of origin? What can their life stories tell us about resilience? Where do their strengths come from? What can their experiences tell us about how heterosexual women and heterosexual families can resist the debilitating effects of heterosexism and patriarchy?

In my own recent ethnographic interviews with 17 lesbians, one of the patterns that stands out is that, in this sample, almost all of the women seem "exceptional" in their own families. Whether working-class or professional, well-off or marginal economically, urban, suburban, or rural, they dare to be different from family prescriptions, not just in the matter of sexual orientation but in their politics, their academic achievements, their career choices and successes, their life-styles and family values, their selection for health.

For example, one woman, a maintenance worker in an apartment complex, is the only one of her eight siblings who is not actively alcoholic. After several trips to a mental hospital in her teens and young adulthood, provoked by efforts to "cure" her homosexuality and her own excessive alcohol and drug use, she became active in

Alcoholics Anonymous and has been "dry" for many years. She now hopes to attend college. Another woman, from a large and conservative Italian-American family, is the only female member of her sibling group to attend college, itself a violation of family prescriptions for daughters. Now a graduate of a prestigious woman's college, she has won five major academic awards, including Phi Beta Kappa. Her family will not allow her partner in their home and has been unable to participate in this young woman's many successes, a situation that she finds saddening but in many ways personally strengthening.

These women seem unusually thoughtful about their lives and their choices; they bring a remarkable level of "consciousness" not just to the "choice" of lesbianism but to all of their commitments. These successes come in the face of enforced silences, of certain kinds of exclusions from mainstream society.

Perhaps, as Herdt (1992) documents in his collection of essays on gay male culture in America, what we need to be asking about is what is authentic and strong in lesbian experience? "Coming out," in his view, is no longer simply a matter of emerging *from* silence and secrecy to an uncertain reception, a drop into a "well of loneliness," but an active entry *into* a legitimate culture, with its own symbols, language, myths, imagery, art, politics, groups, communities, and so on. Is there a lesbian culture that may be different from gay male culture? What does it look like? How accessible is it to women coming out in the 1990s? What special perspectives might lesbian stories offer us, not just on sexuality but on human nature and the world? Without such knowledge, without such a context, our clinical lenses will have "deficit" distortions. We will tend to see only the pain, only the problems, and we will find it difficult to ask the kinds of questions that will truly affirm the impressive strengths to be found in lesbian women and families.

IMPLICATIONS FOR PRACTICE

Many other examples would suffice to portray how the public storying of women's lives by public mythmakers, our primary purveyors of local knowledges that become writ large upon the screen, serves to define "good" or "healthy" womanliness and femininity and then to label as deficient the very actions women take to live out these stories.

What then, are the implications for us as social workers and particularly as clinical practitioners? The work must begin with a sensitivity both to the ways "stories" are made and the ways in which they shape women's lives, as well as a sensitivity to the ways in which women have been denied their own stories. If clinicians are to help women and their families, they must understand the ways in which the oppression of women has generated secrecy and silence. Otherwise, it is unlikely the clinician can create the conversational spaces or continue the conversation in ways that the unspeakable can be voiced and its multiple meanings explored.

On the broadest level, clinicians can miss no opportunity to bear witness, to insist on public storying of the atrocities women have experienced. This storying process needs to go on in the schools, in agencies, in the media, and in governmental settings.

Furthermore, as a profession largely shaped by women, we must make better efforts to claim our own history, both in terms of its many contributions and for the ways that the lives of our female ancestors may inform and inspire our own. In other words, we need to know our own stories and to take charge of our own storying and mythmaking, essential to the process of developing influential local knowledges, of using the power of discourse for change.

On the clinical level, recent work in the family therapy field offers the potential for radical change in the ways we think about theory, about prevailing notions of the worker-client relationship, and about how change occurs. In relation to theory, the social constructivist movement is deprivileging theories of human behavior in favor of a stance in which there are no certainties, only ideas, meanings, and interpretations of those meanings (Andersen 1987; Anderson and Goolishian 1988, in press; Hoffman 1990). The clinician's interpretations of the meanings of various behaviors or events in the client's life are no more privileged than those of the client herself.

Mirroring the *glasnost* phenomenon, the hierarchical nature of the clinical relationship is shifted. In the process, the clinician as expert is depowered; she begins from a "not-knowing" rather than a "knowing" stance (Anderson and Goolishian (in press); she becomes a respectful facilitator of conversation and a collaborator in a search for new meanings. The clinician's task is to create a conversational space in which the only goal is to continue the conversation long enough for the problems, which are defined as existing "in language," to be redefined or "re-languaged" in a way that loosens their control over the client's life. Laird (1989) describes this restorying process in relation to women's lives and issues as taking charge of one's own narratives, while White and Epston (1990) speak of "narrative means to therapeutic ends." In both of these works, therapy becomes a quest for loosening the control of disaffirming stories and searching for alternative stories that better fit one's "lived" experience. In this kind of work, the therapeutic stance of the clinician is that of the interested stranger/ethnographer whose skill lies in creating a context in which the most fruitful conversations can take place, one that will allow for the voices of the silent and the silenced to be heard.

While I believe that constructivist models have the potential for correcting many of the disempowering aspects of the therapeutic process and for allowing women's stories to surface and to be heard, several cautionary notes must be sounded. First, these theories and models that seem sociopolitically neutral themselves have emerged during an era of political conservatism that has affected the mental health professions. Are constructivist approaches just another way of perpetuating the patriarchal status quo (MacKinnon and Miller 1987)? One possibility is that we could be lulled into thinking that everyone has equal power to shape his or her own story, forgetting that we must always be sensitive to the fact that our individual stories take shape in a powerful sociopolitical context. As social workers we have an obligation to be alert to the larger social stories that constrain individual and family narratives.

In my view, it is not possible to create neutral conversational spaces from a "not knowing" position, as Anderson and Goolishian would have it. Like the ethnographer, we may be successful in bracketing or even abandoning our prior theories with their constraining lenses, but there is never anything "neutral" about the choices we make as therapists about when to speak or when to remain silent. Our own narratives are not neutral. They are, among other things, shaped by gender for, as Goldner (1985) and others have argued, gender is a central organizing category for human experience. Both men and women need special help in connecting their gendered personal silences with their public oppressions. While it may be true, as many constructivist clinicians imply, that the social context is always embedded in the individual narrative, the narratives of both clinician and client alike are shaped and constrained by their own gendered experiences. The clinician who is not particularly sensitive to gendered silences may not be able to create the conversational spaces in which the unsaid may be recognized or spoken, or alternative stories generated.

Clinicians must be alert to the differential ways that men and women story their lives, as well as to the silence and secrecy. Storying is gendered; gender differences may be connected to oppression, to differential exposures to "knowing" or the opportunity to shape "knowledges," to different linguistic styles, to different potentialities in trying to present a coherent self to the self and to others. As clinicians, we must be aware of our own gendered narratives and how they shape and constrain what we hear and what we do not hear, what we ask and what we do not ask.

Finally, it should be noted that, in spite of recent interest in the phenomenon of "disclosure," clinical work takes place in a conversational context in which we as clinicians reveal very little and expect others to reveal a great deal. This inequality in and of itself creates a certain kind of silent power, for the clinician is then always a stranger, always mysterious. If we give up the power in our silence, what then do we have to offer that may be different from the very powerful "story sharing" aspects of the many self-help movements which, if nothing else, have helped so many women to bear witness?

These and other questions must be raised as we search for ways to help women take back their own narratives.

> I musn't feel bad that I haven't done as well as the swordswoman did; after all no bird called me, no wise old people tutored me. I have no magic beads . . . I've looked for the bird . . . But I am useless, one more girl who couldn't be sold. When I visit the family now, I wrap my American successes

around me like a private shawl; I *am* worthy of eating the food. From afar I can believe my family loves me fundamentally. They only say, "When fishing for treasures in the flood, be careful not to pull in girls," because that is what one says about daughters ... and I had to get out of hating range. I once read in an anthropology book that Chinese say: "Girls are necessary too;" I have never heard the Chinese I know make that concession. The swordswoman and I are not so dissimilar. May my people understand the resemblance soon so that I can return to them. (Kingston 1975, 58)

NOTES

1. Browning (1984) reviews and challenges these various understandings of homosexuality. However, what goes around comes around again. At the present time we are seeing a renewed interest in genetic explanations. See, for example, Born or bred 1992.

2. While stories of strength and resilience are rare in the clinical literature, in recent years lesbians have been, sometimes joyously, writing the stories of their lives and telling their lives in music, literature, film and other media. See, for example, Barrett 1990; Hall Carpenter Archives 1989; Lesbian History Group 1989; Penelope and Wolfe 1980/1989.

3. Throughout the 1960s and 1970s, a large number of studies were conducted, using personality assessment measures, to determine if gay men and lesbians were less healthy than their heterosexual counterparts. See Hart et al. (1978) and Mannion (1981) for reviews of these studies, which are methodologically flawed and have contradictory results. Lesbians actually do better than nonlesbian women on many of the measures. Evelyn Hooker (1957) was the first to demonstrate that trained professionals could not differentiate the projective test results on nonpatient homosexual men from those of heterosexual men, a study that was influential in undermining the popularity of "adjustment" research.

4. While most of the mental health research is focused on gay men, most of the research on children of homosexuals has compared lesbian mothers with single-parent heterosexual mothers. Most studies fail to take into account whether a co-parent is involved with child rearing in either type of family. There is much less information in general on gay male parenting, although a recent book by Bozett (1987) helps to correct this deficit. See Patterson (1992) for an excellent and thorough review of the literature on children of lesbian and gay parents.

5. This information comes to me from informal conversations with women social work leaders who knew these women well or, in the case of those long gone, knew other women who knew them well. Rarely are these parts of women's lives "storied" in published accounts of their works or their lives.

REFERENCES

Adam, B. D. (1987). *The rise of a gay and lesbian movement.* Boston: Twayne Publishers.

Andersen, R. (1988). *The power and the word.* London: Paladin Grafton Books.

Andersen, T. (1987). The reflecting team: Dialogue and meta-dialogue in clinical work. *Family Process, 26:* 415-428.

Anderson, H. and H. Goolishian. (1988). Human systems as linguistic systems: Preliminary and evolving ideas about the implications for clinical theory. *Family Process, 27:* 371-393.

_____ (in press). The client is the expert: A not-knowing approach to therapy. In *Inquiries in social construction,* edited by K. Gergen & S. McNamee. Newbury Park, CA: Sage.

Barrett, M. B. (1990). *Invisible lives: The truth about millions of women-loving women.* New York: Harper & Row.

Bass, E. and L. Davis. (1988). *The courage to heal: A guide for women survivors of sexual abuse.* New York: Harper & Row.

Bauman, R. (1986). *Story, performance, and event: Contextual studies of oral narrative.* Cambridge: Cambridge University Press.

Belenky, M.F., B. M. Clinchy, N. R. Goldberger, and J. M. Tarule. (1986). *Women's ways of knowing: The development of self, voice, and mind.* New York: Basic Books.

Blumstein, P. and P. Schwartz. (1983). *American couples: Money, work, sex.* New York: William Morrow.

Born or bred: The origins of homosexuality. (1992). *Newsweek,* February 24: 46-53.

Bozett, F. W., ed. (1987).) *Gay and lesbian parents.* New York: Praeger.

Browning, C. (1984). Changing theories of lesbianism: Challenging the stereotypes. In *Women-identified women,* edited by T. Darty and S. Potter. Palo Alto, CA: Mayfield Publishing Company.

Bruner, E. (1986). Ethnography as narrative. In *The anthropology of experience,* edited by V. Turner and E. Bruner. Chicago: University of Illinois Press.

Burch, B. (1982). Psychological merger in lesbian couples: A joint ego psychological and systems approach. *Family Therapy, 9:* 201-277.

_____ (1985). Another perspective on merger in lesbian relationships. In *Handbook of feminist therapy,* edited by L. B. Rosewater and L. E. A. Walker, 100-109. New York: Springer.

Chesler, P. (1972). *Women and madness.* New York: Avon.

Chodorow, N. (1978). *The reproduction of mothering: Psychoanalysis and the sociology of gender.* Berkeley: University of California Press.

Coates, J. (1986). *Women, men and language: A sociolinguistic account of sex differences in language.* London: Longman.

Comstock, G. D. (1991). *Violence against lesbians and gay men.* New York: Columbia University Press.

Conway, J. (1983). Convention versus self-revelation: Five types of autobiography by women of the Progressive Era. Paper for Project on Women and Social Change, Smith College, Northampton, MA. June 13, 1983.

Crawford, S. (1987). Lesbian families: Psychosocial stress and the family building process. In *Lesbian psychologies: Explorations and challenges*, edited by Boston Lesbian Psychologies Collective, 195-215. Chicago: University of Chicago Press.

D'Emilio, J. (1983). *Sexual politics, sexual communities: The making of a homosexual minority in the United States*. Chicago: University of Chicago Press.

Faderman, L. (1981). *Surpassing the love of men: Romantic friendship and love between women from the Renaissance to the present*. New York: William Morrow.

_____ (1991). *Odd girls and twilight lovers: A history of lesbian life in twentieth-century America*. New York: Columbia University Press.

Faludi, S. (1991). *Backlash: The undeclared war against American women*. New York: Crown Publishers.

Foucault, M. (1980). *Power/knowledge: Selected interviews and other writings*. New York: Pantheon Books.

Geertz, C. (1983). *Local knowledge: Further essays in interpretive anthropology*. New York: Basic Books.

Gergen, K. and M. Gergen. (1983). Narratives of the self. In *Studies in social identity*, edited by T.R. Sarbin and K.E. Scheibe, 254-273. New York: Praeger.

Gilligan, C. (1982). *In a different voice: Psychological theory and women's development*. Cambridge, MA: Harvard University Press.

Goldner, V. (1985). Feminism and family therapy. *Family Process, 24:* 31-47.

Golombok, S., A. Spencer, and M. Rutter. (1983). Children in lesbian and single-parent households: Psychosocial and psychiatric appraisal. *Journal of Child Psychology and Psychiatry, 24:* 552-572.

Goodrich, T. J., ed. (1991). *Women and power: Perspectives for family therapy*. New York: Norton.

Gordon, L. (1989). *Heroes of their own lives: The politics and history of family violence*, New York: Penguin Books.

Graddol, D. and J. Swann. (1989). *Gender voices*. Oxford: Basil Blackwell, Ltd.

Green, R. (1978). Sexual identity of 37 children raised by homosexual or transsexual parents. *American Journal of Orthopsychiatry, 135:* 692-697.

Green, R., J. B. Mandel, M. E. Hotvedt, J. Gray, and L. Smith. (1986). Lesbian mothers and their children: A comparison with solo parent heterosexual mothers and their children. *Archives of Sexual Behavior, 15:* 167-183.

Gutheil, T. and N. Avery. (1977). Multiple overt incest as family defense against loss. *Family Process, 16:* 106-116.

Hall, M. (1978). Lesbian families: Cultural and clinical issues. *Social Work, 23:* 380-385.

Hall Carpenter Archives, Lesbian Oral History Group. (1989). *Inventing ourselves: Lesbian life stories*. London and New York: Routledge.

Hart, M., H. Roback, B. Tittler, L. Weitz, B. Walston, and E. McKee. (1978).

Psychological adjustment of nonpatient homosexuals: Critical review of the research. *Journal of Clinical Psychiatry, 39:* 604-608.

Heilbrun, C. (1988). *Writing a woman's life.* New York: Ballantine Books.

Herdt, G. (1992). *Gay culture in America: Essays from the field.* Boston: Beacon Press.

Herman, J. L. (1981). *Father-daughter incest.* Cambridge: Harvard University Press.

Hoffman, L. (1990). Constructing realities: An art of lenses. *Family Process, 29:* 1-12.

Hooker, E. (1957). The adjustment of the male overt homosexual. *Journal of Projective Techniques, 21:* 18-31.

Imber-Black, E. (1989). Rituals of stabilization and change in women's lives. In *Women in families: A framework for family therapy,* edited by M. McGoldrick, C. Anderson, and F. Walsh, 451-469. New York: Norton.

Kingston, M. (1975). *The woman warrior: Memoirs of a girlhood among ghosts.* New York: Vintage Books.

Kinsey, A. C., W. B. Pomeroy, C. E. Martin, and P. H. Gebhard. (1953). *Sexual behavior in the human female.* Philadelphia: Saunders.

Kirkpatrick, M., C. Smith, and R. Roy. (1981). Lesbian mothers and their children: A comparative study. *American Journal of Orthopsychiatry, 51:* 545-551.

Kirshenblatt-Gimblett, B. (1970). Culture shock and narrative creativity. In *Folklore in the modern world,* edited by R.M. Dorson. The Hague: Mouton Publishers.

_____ (1987). The folk culture of Jewish immigrant communities. In *The Jews of North America,* edited by M. Rischin. Detroit: Wayne State University Press.

Krestan, J. and C. Bepko. (1980). The problem of fusion in the lesbian relationship. *Family Process, 19:* 277-289.

Laird, J. (1986). Women, family therapists, and other mythical beasts. *American Family Therapy Association Newsletter.* No. 25, Fall: 32, 35.

_____ (1988). Women and ritual. In *Rituals in families and family therapy,* edited by E. Imber-Black, J. Roberts, and R. Whiting, 331-362. New York: Norton.

_____ (1989). Women and stories: Restorying women's self- constructions. In *Women in families: A framework for family therapy,* edited by M. McGoldrick, C. Anderson, and F. Walsh, 428-449. New York: Norton.

Lakoff, R. (1975). *Language and woman's place.* New York: Harper & Row.

Lamb, S. (1991). Acts without agents: An analysis of linguistic avoidance in journal articles on men who batter women. *American Journal of Orthopsychiatry, 61:* 250-57.

Lerner, H. (1988). *Women in therapy.* New York: Jason Aronson.

Lesbian History Group. (1989). *Not a passing phase: Reclaiming lesbians in history 1840-1985.* London: The Women's Press.

Loulan, J. (1986). Psychotherapy with lesbian mothers. In *Contemporary per-*

spectives on psychotherapy with lesbians and gay men, edited by T. S. Stein and C. J. Cohen. New York: Plenum Medical Book Company.

Luepnitz, D. A. (1988). *The family interpreted: Feminist theory in clinical practice*. New York: Basic Books.

MacKinnon, L. and D. Miller. (1987). The new epistemology and the Milan approach: Feminist and sociopolitical considerations. *Journal of Marital and Family Therapy, 13:* 139-155.

Mannion, K. (1981). Psychology and the lesbian: A critical review of the research. In *Female psychology*, edited by S. Cox, 256-274. New York: St. Martin's.

Masson, J. (1984). *The assault on truth: Freud's suppression of the seduction theory*. New York: Farrar, Straus, and Giroux.

Matchotka, P., F. Pittman, and K. Flomenhaft. (1967). Incest as a family affair. *Family Process, 6,* 98-116.

Mintz, S., and S. Kellogg. (1988). *Domestic revolutions: A social history of American family life*. New York: The Free Press.

Nobile, P. (1977, Dec.). Incest: The last taboo. *Penthouse:* 117-118, 126, 157-158.

Patterson, C. J. (1992). Children of lesbian and gay parents. *Child Development, 63,* 1025-1042.

Paul, J. (1986). Growing up with a gay, lesbian, or bisexual parent: An exploratory study of experiences and perceptions. Doctoral dissertation, University of California at Berkeley, Berkeley, CA.

Penelope, J. and S. J. Wolfe. (1980/1989). *The original coming out stories*. Freedom, CA: The Crossing Press.

Polkinghorne, D. (1988). *Narrative knowing and the human sciences*. Albany: State University of New York Press.

Pomeroy, W. (1976, Nov.). Incest: A new look. *Forum.*

Ramey, J. (1979, May). Dealing with the last taboo. *SIECUS Report, 7:* 1-2, 6-7.

Randall, M. (1987). *This is about incest*. Ithaca, NY: Firebrand Books.

_____ (1991). Some of you are saying we are both wrong. In *Walking to the edge: Essays of resistance*, edited by M. Randall. Boston: South End Press.

Rich, A. (1976). *Of woman born: Motherhood as experience and institution*. New York: Norton.

_____ (1980). Compulsory heterosexuality and lesbian existence. *Signs, 5:* 631-660.

Ricketts, W. and R. Achtenberg. (1987). The adoptive and foster gay and lesbian parent. In *Gay and lesbian parents*, edited by F.W. Bozett. New York: Praeger.

Riessman, C. K. (1989). From victim to survivor: A woman's narrative reconstruction of marital sexual abuse. *Smith College Studies in Social Work, 59:* 232-251.

Roth, S. (1985). Psychotherapy with lesbian couples: Individual issues, female soocialization, and the social context. *Journal of Marital and Family Therapy, 11:* 273-286.

Scarry, E. (1985). *The body in pain: The making and unmaking of the world*. New York: Oxford University Press.

Spence, D. (1983). *Narrative truth and historical truth: Meaning and interpretation in psychoanalysis*. New York: Norton.

Tomm, K. (1990). Foreword. In *Narrative means to therapeutic ends*, edited by M. White and D. Epston, vii-xi. New York: Norton.

White, M. and D. Epston. (1990). *Narrative means to therapeutic ends*. New York: Norton.

Winslow, S. (1990). The use of ritual in incest healing. *Smith College Studies in Social Work, 61:* 27-41.

Zborowski, M. and E. Herzog. (1952). *Life is with people: The culture of the shtetl*. New York: Schocken Books.

Chapter 9

Overturning Oppression: An Analysis of Emancipatory Change

Ann Weick

INTRODUCTION

In the world of social work, the concept of oppression is hauntingly familiar. Since the origin of the profession, there has been a sometimes stark, sometimes muted awareness of social forces which crush people's life chances and rob them of the dignity and vitality our values claim for them. As with any familiar concept, the word itself can become a substitute for exploring the deeper meaning it holds. If we are to invigorate social work practice for the twenty-first century, it is important to reexamine the nature of oppression so that its dynamics and effects will not flaw our efforts. To fully understand and support women's strengths, we must remember the ways in which that strength is daily drained of its force. Only from that clear-eyed view can we create a path of wisdom into the future.

From its earliest inception, social work has recognized the importance of the social environment in shaping people's lives. Through the course of time, however, the notion of the environment has increasingly been translated into interpersonal dimensions (Weick 1981). The context of people's lives is reduced to personal relationships and attention is paid to the history and quality of those relationships. While attempts have been made to stretch that context beyond close, immediate relationships to include intergenerational patterns, the focus remains narrow and parochial. We are left with the unexamined assumption that an adequate understanding of people's lives rests with a detailed account of their own personal world of meaning. A closer analysis of the concept of oppression is a useful antidote to this unfortunate myopia.

THE GENEALOGY OF OPPRESSION

Foucault's (Gordon 1980) use of the term genealogy is an instructive place to begin the analysis. He uses genealogy to refer to the "painstaking rediscovery" (of) "disqualified, popular knowledge" (83), which has been submerged by dominant systems of knowledge and discourse. Genealogy is an excavation of the cultural history of social practices which have maintained certain forms of knowledge and power in preference to others. The study, then, is not primarily about power itself but about the means by which a particular view retains dominance in the face of other forms of knowledge. The dynamics which create this possibility are the seedbed of oppression.

It is not difficult to describe the dynamics of the dominant model of power. In Kipnis' (1976) terms, it rests on the control of resources defined as scarce. In a capitalist society, money is the major symbol of a scarce resource, but education, physical appearance, and other personal attributes are also treated as resources. In order for power to accrue, it is important that these resources not be seen as widely available.

Those who control scarce resources and those who want or need those resources enter into a collusive relationship. The powerholder (Kipnis 1976) sets the conditions of the relationship and the one needing the resources adapts his or her behavior to meet those conditions. The attendant rewards and penalties, coupled with a continuing level of need, insure that there will be little change in what Baker-Miller (1976) describes as a relationship of permanent inequality.

It is important to note that those in positions of power are not a permanent cast of characters. While historical and social patterns clearly elevate certain groups over others, individual powerholders do not have an unchanging claim to their position. Fame, wealth, and high position can all be lost. At the same time, there are intricately interwoven circles of power, so that powerholders in one arena are themselves lacking some resources held by others. The circles of power and oppression thus establish multiple and overlapping constrictions.

To understand power in this way is only one obvious level of analysis. It is necessary to dig more deeply into the dynamics of power by examining some of the more subtle ways in which dominant patterns of power are connected with the control of knowledge. It is this relationship which brings us more intimately into the world of social work practice and to the resources over which professionals exert control.

The Control of Knowledge

The power of the social work profession rests on two bases: the control of social resources and the control of knowledge. Through its policies and programs, society authorizes social workers within government programs to allocate the money, goods, and services needed by those who cannot obtain these resources with their own income. Social workers are an important conduit for the allocation of these necessities. In this capacity, they have power to give and withhold and thus can, through whim, discretion, or prejudice, affect people's fate.

This obvious form of professional power is linked with a less obvious but equally compelling aspect of professional life, namely, the control of knowledge. Examining the nature of knowledge provides some important insights about how social workers may unwittingly collaborate in knowledge systems which perpetuate oppressive practices. In order to understand how this happens, we need to look at the ways in which knowledge, particularly "legitimate" knowledge, is developed and preserved.

All social institutions can be seen as mechanisms for circumscribing human experience. Over the undifferentiated chaos of stimuli experienced by infants, a certain pattern is woven. The "buzzing, blooming confusion" noted by James (1984) is made coherent through language, customs, and practices which establish a particular shape for human experience (Berger and Luckmann 1967). Infants are literally taught to see and in that seeing, alternative views vanish. A table is no longer a structure to climb on or a place to hide under. It is given a name and a purpose and eventually that is what a table is.

Certain social institutions have exerted powerful influence in shaping the way we see the world. Both science and religion have vied to name reality in particular ways. Both are orthodoxies in the sense that each claims to present a view which is true or right and thus deserves adherence by believers. Both attempt to interpret the "buzzin'" pattern of human experience according to certain rules. The interpretation schemes are not the same but the underlying message of both is.

Both science and religion have established formalized systems of knowledge which purport to interpret reality in a true way. Each has established a class of interpreters, either scientists or priests, who have the power to name reality in particular ways. Each has an elaborate system for insuring orthodoxy, complete with punishment for those who challenge the prevailing views. The scientific world-view, which has been in ascendance since the seventeenth century, significantly shaped the development of human service professions, including social work. The same pattern of establishing a higher authority over human experience prevailed. As professions developed, complete with rituals and elitist practices, the professional practitioner was cloaked with

> powers existing beyond the reach or understanding of ordinary humans. . . . Common sense, ordinary understanding and personal negotiations no longer were the effective means of human communication in society. . . . Clients found themselves compelled to believe on simple faith that a higher rationality called scientific knowledge decided one's fate. (Bledstein 1976, 94)

It is true that human beings seem never to be without systems of interpretation. The prescientific world was no less without its constructions of reality than is the scientific. However, the scientific paradigm has extended its interpretative domain to include virtually all aspects of human behavior. Where medieval religion stopped at the boundaries of moral behavior, social science disciplines and the related helping professions have intruded into the psychological, emotional, social, and physical domains of human life. There is very little about human relations which has not been appropriated by scientific or pseudo-scientific explanation. Under the guise of professional expertise, human needs have become pathological categories, ranging from narcissistic personality to codependence.

The extent of this appropriation of everyday life by experts is staggeringly immense. Its vastness signals the broad outlines of oppression, which are at once more profound and more ordinary than one typically imagines. Creating a monopoly of knowledge, to which only a select few have access, instantaneously establishes a caste system. There will always be some whose knowledge is validated and many others whose knowledge is not credited. Foucault (Gordon 1980) uses the term "subjugated" or "disqualified" knowledges to refer to what is thought of as "naive knowledges, located low down on the hierarchy, beneath the required level of cognition and scienticity" (82). This hierarchical system of knowledge guarantees profound alienation from people's own knowledges and experiences.

Conceptual Straitjackets

The official view of legitimate knowledge is kept in place by a set of guardian concepts. The prevalence and deep adherence to these ideas help insure that the current system of knowledge, with all of its attributes of power, will remain firmly in place. The first concept is that of "normalcy." To be normal is a descriptive category which defines accepted and expected human behavior. Under the gloss of scientific measurement, certain behaviors fit the norm because most people are observed to be doing them. Observing the maturational milestones of a young child, the social behaviors of young adults, and the physical health of elderly persons, we conclude that it is normal to walk, to be married, and to develop osteoporosis within certain age spans.

The application of a statistical approach to human behavior is particularly troublesome. At best, a normal distribution applies to only one trait or characteristic. For any specific behavior, an individual may be above, below, or within the norm. But human beings are not constituted from one characteristic. To give a global judgment of "normal" is a misapplication of a statistical method. But it does accomplish the more subtle goal of insuring that experts can subject any behavior to their tests and their judgment.

The power of the concept of normalcy is best seen in the judgment of abnormality. Since any human behavior can come under scrutiny and be judged abnormal, no one is free from intimidation. The threat of being seen as abnormal strikes a primitive fear in us, a fear of ostracism, of banishment, of rejection from the human community. This threat may account for our deep-seated fear of difference as it manifests itself in racism, sexism, homophobia, and other discriminatory ideologies. Fear of difference is fear of losing our basic grounding in the human community.

Euro-American culture has produced another concept which keeps the knowledge paradigm in place. It is the concept of individualism, which elevates the individual at the expense of the collectivity. As a legacy of the Enlightenment, shaped by American industrial-capitalist ideology, individualism touts people's personal initiative while requiring them to be responsible for their own welfare. At the expense of a view which values mutual cooperation and interdependence, American individualism helps insure that people feel fundamentally estranged from the concept of common goals and shared responsibilities. Making it on one's own is viewed as the highest accomplishment, with no recognition given to the silent partners who made it possible. The result for both winners and losers is a profound alienation and the lack of any communal structure for sharing the real burdens of living in the world.

The scientific view has fostered another belief which supports the dominant paradigm, namely that a solution can be found for every problem. Both the individualistic "bootstraps" mentality and scientific methods have created the belief that problems, over time, are susceptible to solutions. Julian Rappaport (1981) draws on E. F. Schumacher's distinction between convergent and divergent reasoning to make this point. Convergent reasoning assumes that problems in the material world can ultimately yield to the right answer. No problem is unsolvable; the right solution just has not been discovered yet.

Given this type of thinking, there is little impetus to challenge the basic assumptions underlying the approach. Attention is focused solely on methods of discovery and on ways to improve methods to solve problems. Believing that there is a right answer never causes anyone to question the question.

Finally, the predominant knowledge system is supported by two connected concepts of paternalism and patriarchy. The childlike, that is to say, powerless, status of most adults is maintained by the deeply held belief that authority figures should be benevolent parents who will take care of us and solve our problems. Because this belief is embedded in the ideology of patriarchy, the ideal parent is seen as a male and thus a father who will take charge and protect us. Patriarchy maintains the illusion that white, monied men are the most able and most deserving to hold such positions of power.

Each of these concepts forms the boundaries of legitimate knowledge. To accept definitions of normalcy, individualism, problem-solving approaches, and patriarchy insures that monopolistic and hierarchical systems of knowledge and power will remain in place. The beliefs themselves subvert any challenges to the status quo, making the beliefs relatively invulnerable. When challenges occur, it is clearly the challenger whose knowledge, motives, and mental state are suspect.

HIDDEN DYNAMICS OF OPPRESSION

An examination of guardian concepts helps explain the "what" of oppression, that is, the beliefs which hold current systems in place. It is equally important to examine the "how," that is, the personal processes which act like burrs to hold people within the current net of beliefs. The starting point for this examination must be the recognition that the process of socialization is a powerful initiator into a particular worldview. The family is seen as socially useful precisely for that purpose. The dominant beliefs of the culture are imbibed with baby food, long before any possibility of independent thinking or action could occur. The process of socialization, if it is successful by social standards, puts in place two levels of belief: that there is a particular way to interpret reality and that the particular way is the only correct way. The latter level initiates the base for future oppression and subjugation.

Socialization processes work symbiotically with systems of sanctions found in society's institutional structures. Education, religion, politics, economics, and social welfare all serve to reinforce the product of socialization through subtle and coercive means of punishment and reward. Understanding the leviathan power of social institutions to maintain social beliefs is fundamental to an understanding of social oppression.

Within the context of socialization and social structures, there are many subtle ways in which people are kept ignorant of their own power. Women's socialization provides a beginning example. As Chodorow (1978) and others (Gornick and Moran 1971) have found, young girls must contend with a paradox whose resolution sets the stage for their identity throughout life. At the heart of their socialization is a lie. A small girl will, in the normal course of exploring her world, discover that she has certain talents and abilities. Perhaps she is good at climbing fences or running fast or fixing things. Her own experience tells her how good it is to be so capable. But at some point, social gender beliefs will intrude. She will be told that what she thinks is important or good is just the opposite: that only boys are good at or should be allowed to engage in active, physical play, as well as a host of other behaviors. Her dilemma is clear. She can either trust herself and become a very young iconoclast or she can, given the constant chiding from adults and other peers, lie to herself and decide she doesn't want to do it anyway. At the heart of this denial is the important, oppressive message that she cannot trust her own experience.

Socialization sets in motion another preeminent process of disempowerment. It establishes a dynamic in which children are systematically trained to look to external authority figures to interpret their experience. Their world, including their most personal and idiosyncratic ideas and responses, is shaped by the words and actions of powerful others. While it may be easy to rationalize this practice in the interests of their safety and well-being, it sets the stage for the lifelong habit of looking outward. It is rare for children to have the opportunity and support for validating their own experience.

Some researchers (Rotter 1972) have argued that women are especially vexed by an external locus of control. Rather than being able to take charge of their lives based on their own needs and judgments, they tend to look to others to take care of them. Walker (1984) comes at the similar phenomenon of "learned helplessness" by saying that "externalizers" (in contrast to "internalizers") believe that most of the events that occur in their life are caused by factors outside themselves" (48). She used this theory to help explain why many battered women stay with abusive partners even when other options appear to be available.

Because there is a tendency to confuse description and theory, the issue of where one places control deserves some discussion. My thesis thus far is that a significant aspect of socialization is precisely to train people to rely on power outside themselves. Democratic beliefs notwithstanding, the institutional bias is toward claiming and maintaining authority. Given our sexist and racist society, it should not be surprising that women and people of color receive multiple layers of messages about their own inadequacies, making them even more reliant on external sources of authority. But socialization in the broad culture prevents everyone from recognizing her or his own power. Neither women nor men can identify and appreciate their own personal resources, talents, and strengths, although the processes of disguise are different. Males, particularly white men, associate their power with their gender status. Most women attribute power to others. In both cases, the concept of power is externalized, and does not rest on one's own personal worth.

These weighty forces all combine to create a crushing burden in the struggle for personal well-being. Learning to deny one's own experience inserts a duplicity that colors all aspects of life. A basic claim for self-worth is continually denied, resulting in the "wounded dignity" (Sennett and Cobb 1972) which so injures people's image of self. At the heart of oppression is a profound alienation from one's own power which leads to a too ready acceptance of the power of others. The personal costs of oppression are matched by costs to society itself. The overarching cost to society lies in wasted and untapped human resources. Maintaining oppressive beliefs and structures requires a tremendous amount of human energy, spent individually and collectively. Consider the energy required to constantly scan for and react to human differences.

When legitimate behavior is narrowly defined, society becomes hypervigilant in its attempts to search out those whose behavior does not fit. At the same time, those who are thus defined as different must expend precious energy being ever watchful for their own safety and well-being. The upshot is a tremendous loss of human initiative and human talents.

The dynamics of oppression rest on the sands of delusion and myth. To create oppressive human relations, there must be a myth about people's fundamental inadequacy and the corresponding myth that someone else (some individual, some class of people, some institution) has the power to save them. There must also be social processes which insure that the message of inadequacy is reinforced in multiple, daily ways so that the myth itself will not be challenged nor the challengers go unpunished. In this way, the myth persists, even when its basic assumption about human beings is so flagrantly wounding. Why, one could ask, do we continue to sustain a myth whose effects rob us of our energy, our creativity, our very essence?

INTIMATIONS OF EMANCIPATION

It is a tribute to human perspicacity and wisdom that the wounding myth of human inadequacy has not been allowed to go unchallenged. Throughout all of human history there have been prophets and seers who recognized the tremendous potential inherent in all people and whose message, however the language varied, tried to awaken that awareness in others. From the erudite to the ordinary, from the sacred to the secular, they focused on the talents, strengths, and resources so richly evident in people's lives and experiences. One thinks of Jesus, Gandhi, Martin Luther King, Paulo Friere, and Mother Teresa, among many others, as stirring examples of such conviction.

We are living in a time, however, when forces of social change go far beyond the voice of individual prophets. In the past 30 years, we have witnessed a cumulative march toward human liberation, begun in the 1950s with civil rights activism, through the second women's movement, to the current push for human rights for all people of color, for lesbians and gay men, senior citizens, people with physical and mental handicapping conditions, and children. These efforts are mirrored internationally with the long struggle of blacks in South Africa, and the poor in Latin America, the recent shifts in Eastern Europe and failed attempts at democratization in China. Every continent seems to be grappling with its own profound search for freedom.

This global awakening is not confined to the political sphere. In virtually every area of human life, there is collective questioning of the current power paradigm. Health care and ecology stand as two prominent examples of areas where a serious critique has been raised and where the holistic health movement and the green movement offer alternative perspectives. In the academic arena the nature of knowledge itself is being called into question, giving rise to critiques of science (Kuhn 1962), literature (Derrida 1976), psychology (Sampson 1983; Gergen 1982), anthropology (Geertz 1973), biology (Gazzaniga 1985; Ornstein and Sobel 1987), and philosophy (Bernstein 1985; Foucault [Gordon 1980]). Although disparate in content and form, the critiques challenge the monopolistic model of authoritative knowledge which undergirds every discipline and profession. The control of knowledge through narrow definitions of what constitutes legitimate knowledge and its interpretation has come under full-scale attack.

Although a complete discussion of these critiques is beyond the scope of this chapter, it is important to briefly sketch the general design of an alternative way of understanding human knowledge. Sampson (1983), who draws on the work of the philosopher Habermas, is useful in this regard. Central to the work of Habermas (Sampson 1983) and the work of other critical theorists is the notion of emancipatory knowledge, in which knowledge is seen as having a transformative quality. In Sampson's (1983) words, "People can and do reflect on the conditions of their life; the knowledge they obtain about those conditions becomes part of the base of resources which they employ to reproduce or transform those very conditions" (68). This view of knowledge is directed to the larger goal of "return(ing) to the subject the lost or renounced powers of self-reflection and thus (to) restor(ing) real self-direction" (69).

The process of recapturing those powers of self-reflection and self-direction is a powerful and appealing way to reconstitute the notion of human knowledge. In order for knowledge to have emancipatory potential, there must be the assumption that people already have knowledge which is of value. Their ability to recognize and "reflect on the conditions of their life" (Sampson 1983, 68) is a true form of knowledge, not something to be discounted. Such an assumption runs in the face of dominant models of knowledge which assume that only objective, that is, nonpersonal, knowledge can be considered legitimate.

If personal knowledge (Polanyi 1958) is seen to be valid, then emancipation has both personal and political dimensions. On the personal level, it requires processes where one's own experience can be named. To name something is to give it an identity which deserves recognition. Thus, to name one's experience is to call it out of the morass of discounted knowledge. Whether one's experience involves pain or joy, insight or confusion, to claim that knowledge is to honor it as valid.

There is special power in collective sharing of experience. The rapid rise of the self-help movement attests to the validation which comes from hearing others' experiences and sharing stories. Belenky and colleagues (1986) found many ways in which women understood their lives. While they attempted to categorize these processes of knowing within a larger and somewhat rigid framework, their study poignantly shows the range of women's experience in naming, validating, and sharing their stories. Stories are a form of knowledge and, some would say, the only knowledge we have.

But emancipation does not get played out on the personal level alone. If people are able to achieve a radical sense of their own knowledge, they may find that the normative assumptions about knowledge in general become suspect. Borrowing again from E. F. Schumacher via Rappaport (1981), the solutions that seemed so linear and one-sided give way to divergent approaches, which require an appreciation of the paradoxical nature of human situations (6). When a monolithic knowledge structure begins tumbling down, as current challenges would suggest, then an absolutist view of the world crumbles also. In its place is a constructionist perspective which assumes that human perception is always mediated by language, culture, and ideology. There is no unchanging, unequivocal reality "out there." Thus, the act of sharing stories can lead to transformative action. Things can be other than the way we have learned them. The emancipatory potential of human beings, particularly when they act collectively, can truly change the world.

EMANCIPATORY CHANGE IN SOCIAL WORK

Social work is heavily invested in the language of individual and social change. Implicit in its professional orientation is a belief in the possibility of human growth and change. However, this belief has tended to be interlaced with notions of instrumental change, leading to approaches which make people passive recipients of external "intervention." Social workers have traditionally seen themselves as agents who do interventions which can bring about change. The perceived ability to cause change to happen is supported by the dominant power paradigm discussed earlier. Those in power are thought to have power to make change happen.

This traditional notion of change runs counter to a process we are calling emancipatory change. In an emancipatory process of change, growth is seen as an inherent life force which naturally impels people to become more fully who they are. It rests on the assumption that there is a power within each person, as reflected in her unique strength, resilience, capacities, and energy. Emancipatory change is a process of growth which reveals personal and collective power to know and to be who we are. Because oppressive processes and structures disguise this power, emancipation requires a conscious effort to critically challenge and dispel the myth of inadequacy in all its guises.

In order to support a philosophy of emancipation, social work needs to reconsider some of its basic tenets. Just as individuals and communities need to develop a critical stance in understanding their own oppression, professions must be willing to make a critical assessment of the nature of professional practice, particularly its reliance on externalized knowledge and technique and its adherence to models of pathology. Within the past decade, there has been a growing attempt to examine the crisis in the professions (Schon

1983), and social workers have joined this movement (Goldstein 1986; Haworth 1984; Imre 1984; Saleebey 1979; Weick 1987). These efforts are bringing to light the manifold ways in which professional practice can unwittingly add to people's oppressive life conditions or can, when redirected, serve as a resource in people's discovery of their own abilities and strengths.

Feminist critique and practice approaches have been particularly significant in awakening practitioners to the oppression of sexist ideology and behavior. Contributions on the conceptual level (Davis 1985) and in the area of practice (Van Den Bergh and Cooper 1986) have helped heighten awareness about the insidiously pervasive aspects of sexism and the long road of emancipatory change. Feminist critique provides a salutary avenue of redress for the blindness which is so deeply ingrained in our culture.

Efforts to foster emancipatory change as a guiding principle of practice must be moored on more generous conceptions of human behavior than have traditionally existed. To the extent that theories of human behavior are based on rigid schemes of development or focus attention on a concept of normalcy from which all people depart to some degree, those theories will not serve an emancipatory goal. Instead, these theoretical assumptions will add oppressive layers to people's ability to grow and change. The concept of emancipatory change must be lodged in an open-ended, health-oriented view of human behavior which assumes both individual potential for transformative growth and a wide range of ways in which that potential can be expressed throughout a lifetime.

One such approach uses the concept of the lifelong growth tasks of intimacy, nurturance, productivity, creativity, and transcendence to suggest a loose model for human development (Weick 1983). Each of these areas includes challenges which are continually reworked as one engages in life situations. Neither social roles, age, nor stages determine how those challenges will be met or in what ways lessons will be learned. The process of growth for each individual is fundamentally idiosyncratic, even though the larger social structure creates common barriers and opportunities.

Such a view of human behavior provides a resonant foundation for emancipatory practice. It unhinges human behavior from the social imperatives of roles and age-related stages and, in doing so, allows a critical assessment of their impact. Because, in the growth-task scheme, the challenges of intimacy and nurturance are not tied to marriage or motherhood, individuals can more clearly see the limitations those role expectations impose. At the same time, they can explore the liberating goal of understanding within their own life experiences what it means to share themselves in intimate relations or care for others who need nurturing. In this way, a growth-task model demonstrates very vividly that what one assumes at a conceptual level has everything to do with how one practices.

There is, however, an important step between theory and practice. While it is crucial that theoretical assumptions provide the philosophic groundwork for practice, the translation will be very rough unless social workers experience the quality of their own oppression. It is one thing to acknowledge intellectually that a health-oriented model of human behavior provides a good fit for emancipatory practice. It is quite another to "stand under" (understand) the forces which systematically hide our own powers of healing and well-being. For women, people of color, and others who suffer discrimination because of narrow ideas of what is "normal," it is essential to recognize and deeply experience the ways in which social messages and practices have injured us. It is from this experience that both insight and empathy emerge.

Practice begins, then, with the awareness of our own and others' oppression. It becomes emancipatory practice when we work with others to explore ways in which injuring messages and experiences can be replaced by the recognition that we are the source of our own power. Unlike the traditional connotations of power, this type of power is both nutritive and integrative (May 1972, 109), allowing us to explore and use our own wisdom and experience to grow more freely according to our own lights.

Practicing from an emancipatory perspective is closely linked with principles which support people's own power. The first assumption one makes is that each person is an expert on her own life. She knows better than anyone what her experience means to her and what rewards and burdens it presents. Closely allied with this belief in her expertise is the assumption that each person exhibits multiple strengths in living through life's challenges. Because expressions of this personal power may not be fully recognized or acknowledged, emancipatory practice can help in this uncovering process.

Being able to recognize one's own power usually comes as a result of events or circumstances which challenge one to see things in a new way. One of the most profound moments of personal change is often linked to a radical reframing, where some taken-for-granted belief is challenged and changed. For women, these moments may come when they question traditional belief about what it means to be a woman and find that their own experience speaks to them more powerfully and overtly than any external message or meaning.

Knowing that one has the ability to re-image her life is a fundamental aspect of personal power. To see things differently, to name things in new ways, is a source of power that is not given by others. It is a power, however, that can be shared with others, so that the act of seeing differently moves naturally into the realm of collective action. Once it is discovered and possessed, it serves as the seedbed for all other imaginings.

CONCLUDING THOUGHTS

The prelude to the twenty-first century is likely to be fraught with continuing struggles, as a global awakening meets head-on resistance from traditional forces of power and privilege. The degree of challenge to the old order can be measured by the severity of repressive action, whether it is carried out against individuals or the collective. We are likely to see even more attempts to force people into the old molds provided by family, church, and government.

Thus the context of emancipatory practice is not without its snares. To help individuals and communities recognize and value their own power implicitly challenges external power systems. Because these systems rely on the practice of invalidating people's own wisdom and experience, the process of honoring and developing these attributes takes the teeth out of oppressive practices. But all who gain by oppression cannot be expected to willingly give up their teeth.

It is important to recognize, then, that emancipatory practice is not glib or easy. It involves the personal struggle of closely examining our own lives, both for evidence of our own oppression and for signs of how we oppress others. It requires us to relinquish the desire to exercise power over others, even in the name of professional expertise. It calls us to imagine a more generous world, in which human strengths become the focal point for support and action. Finally, it reminds us that liberation has costs. Emancipatory change does not come easily nor are its consequences lightly felt. To see the world differently invites a struggle between the old and the new, a struggle which involves confusion and doubt, as well as joy and hope.

By anchoring our conceptions of practice in the broad themes of oppression and emancipation, social work becomes part of global processes of change. Its purpose and its goals align with our broader vision of what it means to be fully human, bringing to our practice a more vivid appreciation of the values which lie at the heart of social work. It is from the strength of these values that we can redress the injuries of oppression and return to people's lives the dignity and honor which they should rightfully claim.

REFERENCES

Baker-Miller, J. (1976). *Toward a new psychology of women.* Boston: Beacon.

Belenky, M. F., B. M. Clinchy, N. R. Goldberger, and J. M. Tarule. (1986). *Women's ways of knowing.* New York: Basic.

Berger, P. L. and T. Luckmann. (1967). *The social construction of reality.* New York: Anchor.

Bernstein, R. J. (1985). *Beyond objectivism and relativism: Science, hermeneutics and praxis.* Philadelphia: University of Pennsylvania Press.

Bledstein, B. (1976). *The culture of professionalism.* New York: Norton.

Chodorow, N. (1978). *The reproduction of mothering: Psychoanalysis and the sociology of gender.* Berkeley: University of California Press.

Davis, L. (1985). Female and male voices in social work. *Social Work, 30:* 106-115.

Derrida, J. (1976). *Of grammatology.* Baltimore: Johns Hopkins University Press.

Gazzaniga, M. S. (1985). *The social brain.* New York: Basic.

Geertz, C. (1973). *The interpretation of culture.* New York: Basic.

Gergen, K. (1982). *Toward transformation in social knowledge.* New York: Springer-Verlag.

Goldstein, H. (1986). Toward an integration of theory and practice. *Social Work, 31:* 352-357.

Gordon, C., ed. (1980). *Michael Foucault-Power/knowledge*. New York: Pantheon.

Gornick, V. and B. Moran. (1971). *Woman in sexist society*. New York: Basic.

Haworth, G. O. (1984). Socialwork Research, Practice, and Purodigms. *Social Service Review, 58:* 343-357.

Imre, R. (1984). The nature of knowledge in social work. *Social Work, 29:* 41-45.

James, W. (1984). *Psychology: Briefer course*. Cambridge, MA: Harvard University Press.

Kipnis, D. (1976). *The powerholders*. Chicago: University of Chicago Press.

Kuhn, T. (1962). *The structure of scientific revolutions*. Chicago: University of Chicago Press.

May, R. (1972). *Power and Innocence*. New York: Dell.

Ornstein, R. E. and D. S. Sobel. (1987). *The healing brain*. New York: Simon and Schuster.

Polanyi, M. (1958). *Personal knowledge*. Chicago: University of Chicago Press.

Rappaport, J. (1981). In praise of paradox: A social policy of empowerment over prevention. *American Journal of Community Psychology, 9:* 1-23.

Rotter, J. (1972). *Applications of a social learning theory of personality*. New York: Holt, Rinehart & Winston.

Saleebey, D. (1979). The tension between research and practice: Assumptions of the experimental paradigm. *Clinical Social Work Journal, 7:* 267-284.

Sampson, E. E. (1983). *Justice and the critique of pure psychology*. New York: Plenum.

Schon, C. (1983). *The reflective practitioner*. New York : Basic.

Sennett, R. and J. Cobb. (1972). *The hidden injuries of class*. New York: Alfred A. Knopf.

Van Den Bergh, N. and L. B. Cooper, eds. (1986). *Feminist visions for social work*. Silver Spring, MD: National Association Of Social Workers.

Walker, L. E. (1984). *The battered women syndrome*. New York: Springer.

Weick, A. (1981). Reframing the person-in-environment perspective. *Social Work, 26:* 140-143.

Weick, S. (1983). A growth-task model of human development. *Social Casework, 64:* 131- 137.

Weick, A. (1987). Reconceptualizing the philosophical perspective of social work. *Social Service Review, 61:* 218-230.

Chapter 10

Women of the World: The Wonder Class– A Global Perspective on Women and Mental Health

Janice Wood Wetzel

INTRODUCTION

This chapter provides an overview of the reality and stigma of mental illness in women throughout the world. The prevalence of various forms of mental illness is presented, followed by a discussion of the shared profile of women regardless of diagnoses, and the need for gender-specific research relevant to women's problems. Most of the chapter is devoted to the actual prevention of mental illness and the promotion of mental health. The suggestions are based upon international research concerning successful women's projects, a comprehensive model of feminist therapy, and a psychosocial program model for the development of stigma-free therapeutic programs for women. A life span analysis of female and male development and the gender paradoxes that exist throughout the world precedes the final section that recognizes women's strengths and the need to change perceptions of and about women.

Defining Mental Health

The United Nations defines mental health as psychological, physical, social, and spiritual well-being. Quality of life, a social context that includes a loving and competent family, stimulating growth-enhancing early developmental experiences, and "education, jobs, information, and freedom from violence, discrimination, and unjust treatment" later in life is a fundamental prerequisite for mental health (Brody 1990, 3). Vulnerability to mental illness is in direct relation to the absence of such conditions.

At the final United Nations Decade of Women Conference in Nairobi, Kenya in 1985, only three conference presentations out of over 1,400 recognized that mental illness was a problem for women, much less a serious worldwide concern. At that point in recent history, mental health was perceived to be a frill of Western cultures, not to be confused with economic, legal, educational, and health concerns which were deemed to be essential to the social development of women. Any suggestion that there was a direct correlation between social conditions and mental health invited ridicule. The myopic vision of even progressive female leaders was no doubt influenced by the fact that mental illness, as a concept, holds such a stigma in many of the world's societies that denial is rampant. Families who have a mentally ill relative may be shunned long after the demise of the person. So great is the stigma that some cultures do not even have a word for the concept, despite clear evidence of the existence of mental illness (Wetzel 1993).

In contrast to the general attitude at the Decade Conference, two Bangladesh organizations, Women for Women and Concerned Women for Family Planning, wrote *Women and Health* in preparation for the event (Hug, Jahan, and Begum 1985). They were aware of the inextricable link between social conditions and their impact on women's mental health. Society, they point out, in many ways affects the mental health of the family, particularly its most vulnerable members. "Mental health is more than the absence of disease. It implies a feeling of well-being and an ability to function in full capacity, physically, intellectually and emotionally" (Islam 1985, 48). They argue convincingly that it is not enough to be free from a diagnosable mental disorder, psychological symptoms, or grossly maladaptive behavior patterns. In short, to be mentally healthy is more than simply being free from mental illness (Viswanathan and Wetzel 1993). It would not be until the late 1980s, when Dixon's (1980) studies of the failure of social development programs were disseminated, that women began to realize that, no matter what opportunities were open to them, they would not be utilized until women had a sense of their own self-worth. Attention must be given to their fundamental human needs and psychological well-being, as well as to the larger social development issues.

Mental health encompasses a sense of happiness, contentment, satisfaction, security and a positive attitude toward life, based upon one's reality. Further, a woman should have the capacity to function on a daily basis, guided by her own conscience and principles–her internal rather than external values (Islam 1985). Clearly, such a definition of mental health is at the ideal edge of possibility, encompassing qualities that are often ignored in the assessment of mental illness.

Demographics

Throughout the world, it is women who are at highest risk of mental illness. The Bangladeshi research analyzes seven major studies in 14 countries, encompassing over 16,000 people. Their findings corroborate that of the United Nations, which reports higher rates of mental illness among the world's women (World Health Organization 1988). In Bangladesh, as elsewhere, depression and anxiety are the leading diagnostic categories, occurring in women at a 3:1 ratio as compared with men. In the United States, one out of seven women will be hospitalized for depression in her lifetime (Wetzel 1991, 1984/1991). The world either continues to deny the reality, on the one hand, or uses the statistics to label women as weak, on the other. Yet, as far back as 1621, humanist Robert Burton noted that women were most likely to be depressed. His concern about poverty and oppression as the causes of their melancholia (the ancient name for depression) was expressed in five volumes, called *The Anatomy of Melancholy,* the most exceptional literary treatment of depression ever conceived (1621/1927). It would be over 300 years before the insight took hold, and then only with a small number of feminists (Bart 1971; Chesler 1972). As we have seen, even the world's women who are dedicated to the well-being of their sisters have overlooked or downplayed the reality.

Although there are differences between societies, well-executed epidemiological studies indicate that there are no fundamental differences in the prevalence of severe and persistent psychiatric symptoms or in the range of mental disorders. Seriously incapacitating mental illness is likely to affect 1% of the population at any given time, and at least 10% at some time during their lives in all societies (World Health Organization 1988; Law 1985). In the United States, the National Institute of Mental Health (1991) reports that during any six month period about 20% of the population suffers from a diagnosable mental disorder. At some time in their lives, about fifteen million people will suffer from truly severe, long term disability. Of these, 900,000 are institutionalized, with the remainder living in the community, many of them homeless.

Everywhere women's high risk status is reflected in their greater likelihood to suffer from severe depression, panic attacks, and phobic reactions, and to report psychosomatic pains. Men, in contrast, are two to four times more likely to abuse drugs and alcohol, more likely to be diagnosed as an antisocial personality, and commit suicide at a rate five times that of women (Raymond 1991; Viswanathan and Wetzel 1993).

Women's Shared Profile

Summarizing the work of feminist theorists since the 1970s, Kaplan (1983) argues that women's high risk status is really due to biased labeling and masculine-based assumptions that codify healthy behavior as male, and "crazy" behavior as female. Comparative diagnostic research corroborates the fact that behaving in a feminine-stereotyped manner will result in a mental disorder diagnosis. Dependent Personality Disorder and Histrionic Personality Disorder are cases in point (Goleman 1990). The former diagnosis is based upon female socialization to a dependent role, and the latter is founded on the female reproductive system. It is virtually impossible for a man to be so labeled (Wetzel 1991).

Women's shared reality has been fragmented into an array of diagnostic labels. With every generation, new categories are developed to reflect their experience, without recognizing their shared profile within all diagnostic categories. The subservience of females throughout their life course and its devastating ramifications are perceived as a tiresome litany of "women's problems." The implication is that they are complainers, weak, or at best imagine their ills. Highly political experiences are thus hidden from the consciousness of women and men alike. (See Laird, Chapter 8, for a discussion of how the social construction of the incest experience has denied women's reality.)

Yesteryear's neurasthenia, hysteria, melancholia (depression), and dementia praecox (schizophrenia) share common definitions with today's depression, anxiety disorder, borderline and narcissistic personality disorders, and agoraphobia, and so, too, do eating disorders (anorexia and bulimia), Post-Traumatic Stress Disorder (which in women, is usually the result of rape, incest, and battering and is labeled battered women syndrome and self-defeating syndrome), as well as psychosomatic behavior, burn out, teenage pregnancy, alcoholism and other so-called "co-dependencies." Despite minor differences in symptoms, all of these women share the following similar profile:

> They usually are women who are socialized to be dependent, who lack self-confidence and have no self-esteem; they are likely to be women who lack autonomy, living vicariously through others, having no sense of self-worth and identity; they are women who have never been given the opportunity to learn to be authentic; they conform to traditional norms of male superiority and female inferiority, adhering to a strict separation of gender roles; even their traditional work as women is demeaned as **real** work; they blame themselves for their symptoms and maltreatment, believing they deserve punishment (if they even conceive it as such) because they are imperfect according to the norms of society; they are under the control of a significant other [usually a husband or boyfriend (in some cultures a brother or uncle)] and consider their situations hopeless; they receive intermittent or no emotional support to develop their own identities and skills; their anger is often repressed; if they work outside the home, they are likely to be in controlling, often low-level jobs, without peer support; and if they are religious, they are usually associated with conservative religions which interpret scripture literally, viewing women as subservient to men, reflected either overtly in the

spoken word, or covertly in their religious practices. (Wetzel 1991, 18-19)

It is clear that behaviors must be viewed within the context of individual experience, as well as the objective conditions and behavioral consequences of those conditions. Without doing so, women are unjustly labeled, blamed for their oppression, and treated as individual deviants. They either have no knowledge of their shared reality, or they look upon their high at-risk status as a shared shame of their sex.

The Research Gap

In the United States in 1990, the Women's Caucus of the House of Representatives called attention to the lack of research on women's physical and mental health concerns. Their investigation revealed that even breast cancer research samples were primarily male (Schroeder 1990). Appalled by what they had uncovered, the public's attention embarrassed the administration and provided the impetus for new policies in the Alcohol, Drug Abuse and Mental Health Administration (ADAMHA), as well as the National Institute of Mental Health (NIMH), where an Office of Women's Health has been established after much internal controversy concerning discrimination against women. A call for more gender-specific research on women's health and mental health has swept the establishment (Raymond 1991). This need is even greater in many parts of the world where data have never been separated by gender, or in some cases, where the data concerning females are ignored altogether. In the latter societies, neither births nor deaths of females are even recorded (Wetzel 1993a). While gender differences in mental illness may be biologically influenced, societal factors continue to emerge as strong factors, when one cares (or dares) to look.

THE PREVENTION OF MENTAL ILLNESS
AND PROMOTION OF MENTAL HEALTH

The prevention of mental illness and promotion of mental health can best be realized through educational programs, a concept more likely to be accepted throughout the world than either therapy or treatment. The concept is devoid of the stigma that is itself life-threatening in some cultures, and places one at risk of further discrimination, even in some of the most accepting societies. It is imperative, however, that educational programs be based upon therapeutic principles that incorporate both psychological and societal realities.

The Global Zeitgeist: Cross-Cutting Programmatic Components

My study of 70 successful women's programs in 14 countries in Southeast Asia, Africa, Mexico, Central America, South America, Europe, the United Kingdom, and the United States reveals cross-cutting components in their programs for personal and social development. All are directly applicable to mental health, though they are seldom recognized as such. Interestingly, the concepts that are generally accepted are "developing self-esteem" and "overcoming male domination," even though the word "feminism" remains a taboo in many cultures and "mental health or mental illness" is disregarded, denied, or used to "blame the victim."

1. Friere's (1970/1982) model of **conscientization** (raising the consciousness of vulnerable people) is perhaps the most common and the most universally successful model. Even those who do not know his name have adopted his methods. It is as if they have endorsed Friere and Mercado's (1987) assertion that education in the next century will not be a neutral act, remote from the discord of society. Rather, educators must take an ethical stand, openly and without apology standing up for a dream–a perspective or an idea. To ignore dysfunctional cultural reality, whatever one's calling, is to block the development and empowerment of people, perpetuating the condition of their lives.

Conscientization, in programs throughout the developing world in particular, overtly addresses the oppression of girls and women. Women learn that their universal oppression and inequality are grounded in patriarchal systems everywhere in the world; that women do two-thirds of the world's work, yet two-thirds of them live in poverty because their work is unpaid and invisible or underpaid; that there is universal sexual exploitation of girls and women; that women provide more health care, both emotional and physical, than all the world's health services combined, yet have fewer health services themselves; that women are the chief educators of the family, yet outnumber men among the world's illiterates; and that women represent the majority of the world's displaced people, yet continue to remain an underserved population (Wetzel 1993). It is no wonder that women the world over are at risk of being mentally ill.

2. The formation of interdisciplinary professional partnerships with poor women occasionally include men who see themselves as kindred spirits. The work of the partnerships often emerges from participative social action research in which the insights and experience of poor women are elicited and then acted upon.

3. The fundamental right of every female to live without fear and domination, whether in the home or society, to be treated with respect, educated, and paid equitably for her work is a common theme.

4. The sharing of home maintenance and child care with men on an equal basis is a concept that began as a radical idea among nonaligned nations at the start of the Decade of Women. By the end of the Decade, it became a shared demand to be reckoned with in all developing and so-called developed countries. The absence of equitable work load responsibilities results in a universal burden leading to women's exhaustion and other health and mental health problems. (In Africa, for example, exhaustion is the primary physical complaint of all female hospital admissions, with depression the most common emotional symptom [Wetzel 1987].)

5. Most programs educate women about their fundamental rights regarding health needs, both emotional and physical, including the individual and mutual need for nurturance, freedom from exhaustion, and participation in decision making within and outside the home.

6. Women are taught that both personal development and action, and collective social development and action are essential if their lives are going to change for the better. Programs with illiterate, poor women have developed women's credit unions, coupling personal and economic development, ignoring neither end of the spectrum.

7. Throughout the world, women are being educated about their existing rights, how to execute legal and political critical analysis, and how to develop constructive legislation and policies. Extrapolating from their local experience, women are taught to generalize to national and international rights. The connections between the personal and political thus become real (Wetzel 1991, 1992, 1993).

Three-Phase Model of Feminist Therapy

Ballou and Gabalac's (1985) Three-Phase Model of Feminist Therapy, grounded in therapeutic principles and social action, can be adapted to fit the educational program model. The acquisition and maintenance of mental health, they assert, is not possible without addressing the power system. Consistent with Friere's conscientization mandate, before change can occur women must be taught how they have learned to produce self-denying behavior and to accept their devalued status and self-defeating limited options. Ballou and Gabalac's feminist group therapy model is designed to do just that through awareness of what they call **Harmful Adaptation.**

The authors divide Harmful Adaptation, "the process whereby women learn to accept dependency and to practice self-negating behavior," into five stages. They are *humiliation, inculcation, retribution, conversion,* and *conscription.* These stages, representative of the power system's dynamics and their effect on women, are first played out in simulated situations in the group as they experience the uncomfortable, but familiar feelings and behavior associated with each. *Humiliation* evokes doubt, fear, and submission as they experience being overpowered emotionally and even physically. *Inculcation* makes it clear that they must obey the rules of the power system in order to secure their protection. Correct behavior is thus internalized. *Retribution* furthers compliance as they experience anxiety, depression, and helplessness through the threat of loss of rewards and punishment if correct behavior is not practiced. *Conversion* encompasses repression, rejection, and denial of their own values, as the power system's values and goals are accepted as their own. Finally, *conscription* includes ingratiating themselves to superiors, denial of the health needs and worth of all nondependent women, and the self-righteous use of power as they, themselves, serve as spokespersons and "harmful adaptation trainers." Their consciousness raised, the next steps are designed to counter the effects.

The next therapeutic intervention, **Corrective Action,** substitutes a healing quality for each stage of Harmful Adaptation in order to undo and relearn harmful behaviors and feelings. First, humiliation is countered by *separation* through self-discovery, as well as *recognition* and pride in womanhood. Inculcation is offset by the *validation* of their own thoughts and feelings, resulting in the *expression* of their shared experience. Retribution is countered by *association* in the company of women of diverse values and experiences which result in *cooperation* through interdependent working relationships. Conversion becomes *authorization,* the acceptance of responsibility for the self, building on their personal strengths. This in turn leads to *identification,* the acknowledgment of the bond of responsibility between women and the pooling of their strengths. Next, conscription culminates in *negotiation,* whereby women learn to interact with power systems on their own behalf, actively resisting harm, and withdrawing when it is wise to do so. This phase results in *confrontation,* which calls for women to work in alliance with one another toward changing the system and creating alternatives. The end result is **Health Maintenance,** the final phase of therapy, which reinforces the positive changes that have been made in the lives of the participating women. While developed in the United States, the model can be adapted to the realities of women anywhere. It is clearly consistent with Friere's conscientization concepts.

Psychosocial Spectrum Program Model

The Psychosocial Spectrum Model of therapeutic intervention is a stigma-free program model which I have developed, based upon research on the major psychological, social, and spiritual theories of depression, mental health, and human development. A comprehensive analysis resulted in the emergence of four dimensions (common themes) that all of the theories share, underscoring their fundamental importance to human well-being. The positive valence reflects psychological and social catalysts for well-being, while the negative valence reflects psychological and social barriers to well-being. The dimensions are amenable to the development of creative programs for the prevention of mental illness and the promotion of mental health without labeling people as sick, troubled or deviant. The dimensions are *connectedness*, *aloneness*, *action*, and *perception*. Programs should focus on reducing or eliminating negative aspects of each, while increasing positive psychological and social aspects. For example, connectedness that reflects dependence should be decreased, while relational connectedness is increased through social programs.

Note that attention should be directed to culturally appropriate activities in each of these areas, as cultures appropriately emphasize one dimension over another. All societies should not be expected to look alike. Some societies, for example, are much more connectedness- (relationship) oriented, while others emphasize aloneness in the form of independence. As explicated below, mores differ by gender as well. The important point is that one is at personal risk for depression when any dimension is neglected or thwarted. On each dimension, the positive must outweigh the negative in both psychological and environmental aspects of one's life. The end result could almost be thought of as an "inoculation" against mental illness (Wetzel 1984/1991, 1993). A life-span analysis of the different experiences relevant to females and males follows, uncovering myths that have become conventional wisdom. The information should be kept in mind when developing psychosocial programs.

Connectedness

Connectedness on the negative end of the spectrum is reflected in dependence and pathological attachment, considered to be liabilities when developmentally inappropriate. Those who have an over-investment in others, or an extreme psychological need for approval and worth, are subject to depression. They must be sustained externally, for their inner selves are found wanting. Women, research reveals, are more likely than men to fit this description of negative connectedness. What is overlooked is the fact that everyone needs a degree of positive external reinforcement. Women provide it for others, so others need not seek it. Few sustain women.

When looking at the positive end of the connectedness spectrum, we find women excelling. To be relational, to be nurturing, to have the capacity for intimacy and empathy, represents connectedness at its most positive. The problem for women is that so many men do not develop these attributes, so women become nurturers in search of nurturance. They appear to retain their relational attributes as they age, while men in their later years attempt to develop them. Sadly, older men continue to find relationships difficult even when desired. It is a perplexing quality to acquire after years of slighting it.

Aloneness

Aloneness begins at birth when the infant separates from the womb and begins to recognize her uniqueness. Aloneness and the push-pull of human need for connectedness and autonomy plays itself out through life, though infancy, adolescence, and old age are developmental focal points. Alienation represents the flip side of alone-contentedness. The inability to relate may be more allied to premature separation issues than to dependency. Before aloneness as solitude can be experienced, one must experience connectedness. Aloneness that is loneliness is often present in the adult who never had a childhood. While women experience negative aloneness in some societies because of their cultural isolation, or because of their universal reality of living as females in a male world, it is men who are most likely to feel alienated (negative aloneness) in society. They appear to fear intimacy, often choosing to be emotionally alone. Research reveals that males have difficulty being alone all of their lives, in contrast to females who seem better able to be alone contentedly, the mark of an integrated self.

Action

Action is represented on the negative side by concepts of misdirected or dissipated energy in the form of dysfunctional roles and tasks, psychological defenses, and fragmented purposes. Living vicariously through others, in lieu of developing the self, is a typical action of depressed women whose energy is usually exploited and dissipated in maintenance, caretaking, and a multiplicity of low-level supportive roles in and out of the home. Positively speaking, action as mastery, competence, self-development and creative acts, as well as social action on behalf of oneself and others, is indicative of development. Ironically, the very actions that fragment women end up being strengths, for it is women who learn to be survivors, to care for themselves and others, and to be flexible and resourceful.

Perception

Perception is perhaps the most critical of the dimensions and certainly the one most influenced by the interaction of the other variables. Negative cognition is a universal correlate of depression and general emotional dysfunction. Whether theoretically perceived as an internalized self-representation or a negative cognitive set, the end result is low self-esteem and a sense of hopelessness. In tandem with this attitude is the unacceptability of any negative characteristics within the self. Hence, along with negative self-perception goes denial and inauthenticity. Women who think that they must be "superwomen," like "supermen" who must be all-knowing, successful competitors at all times, often find themselves in deep depression. There is no way out of the house of mirrors in which they dwell.

The positive side of perception is no less than exciting. The concrete Western behaviorist, the existential Eastern spiritual healer, and the biochemical laboratory scientist may be strange comrades, but they each are finding that healing is associated with positive perception. Thought, in the form of positive awareness, ideas, affirmation and visual imagery is used as a tool across disciplines. Biochemists find that faith, even that inspired by placebos, releases endorphins, brain substances which relieve pain and produce a sense of well-being. Whatever one's theoretical preference, the same principles hold. For whatever reason, large numbers of women throughout the world who were at high risk for depression as younger adults and suffered from poor self-perception through middle-age, turn 180 degrees in old age, according to naturalistic studies. Conversely, men are likely to become quite negative, dependent, passive, obsessive, withdrawn, and depressed with age (Myerhoff 1980). Although women of all ages attempt suicide more than five times as often as men, it is men who are at high risk of successful suicide throughout the world. The older they are, the more likely they are to succeed. Clearly, the socialization of men is as detrimental in the long run as that of women (Wetzel 1984/1991, 1986).

The Paradox

The Psychosocial Spectrum provides a useful analytic model for the development of educational programs that provide answers to the paradox that has eluded us all: How is it that women throughout the world, thought to be the weaker sex, dependent, inadequate, second rate, second class, marginal to society, and more likely to be alone in the world, in poverty, victims of sexual exploitation and physical violence, end up being healthier and happier in old age is the case for men? How is it that women live longer natural lives than men? How is it that older women are six times less likely to commit suicide than older men? These findings have been reported for years by anthropological researchers of many cultures. Among them is Myerhoff (1980) in her study of Eastern European Jews in the United States, Lewis (1965) in Mexico's Tepotzlan, Simic (1978) in Yugoslavia, and Velez - I (1978) in Central America, to name a few.

Gerontologists, most of whom are not feminists, have posited role reversal and similar theories to explain the universal phenomenon (Hultsch and Deutsch 1981). There is no evidence, however, that women reverse the positive qualities they have developed. More likely, they have learned to transcend the negative perceptions about themselves, taught to them by their societies. When they continue to adhere to cultural norms, they become depressed (d'Epinay 1985). The system does not work for them. But those who turn away from destructive social norms in their later years recognize their own strengths. Men, on the other hand, have been supported by the cultures in which they live, so they are more likely to believe in them. They are taught that they are superior (an idea easier to tolerate, of course) and are reinforced by the women who collude in the fantasy, themselves taught never to "shatter the fragile male ego" by speaking the truth. The tragic result is that men who find themselves facing reality for the first time in old age have a difficult time accepting the fact that they, like women, are only human.

Because men have had to hide their human fragility from the world, even from themselves, their growth is blocked. Many men look to women throughout their lives to provide the ego supports that they need, rather than developing their authentic inner selves. The "fragile male ego" is, in fact, an undeveloped ego-structure that has been hidden behind a facade of superiority. Conversely, women have had to hide their strengths, even from themselves, affecting their self-esteem early in life, and placing them at high risk for mental illness. Their mandated roles, however discriminatory, have necessitated personal development, even when they are not aware of it. No one is there to assuage their bruised egos when they are continually assaulted by negative messages from their world, ranging from the family, the school, the workplace, and their religious institutions, to national and international mass media and governments.

This is not to suggest, in Pollyanna fashion, that the negative conditions in which females live are ultimately worthwhile, the ends justifying the means. The same, or more advanced, development could and should occur without trauma, just as it should for males. That should be the goal of all concerned with the promotion of mental health and the prevention of mental illness for all.

CHANGING PERCEPTIONS: RECOGNIZING WOMEN'S STRENGTHS

If we are to change the perceptions of and about women, it is important to recognize the strengths of women and the reality of their lives. Women are neither weak, lazy, unable to cope or function, inadequate, inept, unskillful, helpless, nor ineffectual. They are almost universally courageous, flexible, and able to handle a multiplicity of responsibilities and problems–not only their own, but those of their families and friends. They are, or have long been, the sole supportive caretakers of children, husbands, elderly parents and others in need. They are the people who are feeding, clothing, and sheltering their kin, despite their long hours, low wages, and poverty. They are the ones who retain the burden of home care and maintenance, even when they take on full marketplace responsibilities. They are the single young women who bravely keep their babies, however foolishly, even though they are poor, alone, and unnurtured themselves. They are the mothers and daughters who boldly go forth in the world, alone or in destructive relationships, unstopped by the violence that threatens and even terrorizes them as women. They are the women who live and work courageously, often without emotional support, and in spite of the fear they feel for both themselves and their children. These are the women who are strangers in new lands, who do not speak the language and have few resources, yet venture forth to meet the challenge. These are the women, often alone, emotionally dependent to be sure, in need of autonomy, yes, but strong, capable, proud, and profound, too. The problems that they cope with daily are often monumental. The fact is that others do not have their mental health problems because women take the problems on themselves, providing support and nurturance to others, while they are themselves denied. It is not the personhood of women that needs to be changed. It is their self-perception. They are already self-reliant, but they do not recognize themselves.

Their story is replicated the world over. Indeed, the strengths of women in some cultures work against them in that they are taught that they do not have the same needs that men do and can work without the rest and nutrition that men receive (Wetzel 1993). Gerontologist Lillian Troll (1981) said it well: "Women are treated like camels. They are expected to cross the desert without nurturance or succorance." Social work researcher David Fanshel (1990), upon completing a longitudinal study of poor Latina mothers and children on the Lower East Side of Manhattan, stresses that what they need to ensure their own mental health and the well-being of their children is a sense of connectedness, reducing their isolation, helping them to act in their own best interests, and changing their negative perceptions so they see themselves as worthy human beings. (It is not difficult to make a conceptual leap to The Psychosocial Spectrum Program Model.) Fanshel's research leads him to conclude that **"these women are not an under class. They are the wonder class!"**

REFERENCES

Ballou, M. and N. W. Gabalac. (1985). *A feminist position on mental health.* Springfield, IL: Charles C. Thomas.

Bart, P. (1971). Depression in middle-aged women. In *Women in sexist society,* edited by V. Gornick and B. Moran, 99-117. New York: Basic Books.

Brody, E. (1990). Mental health and world citizenship: Sociocultural bases for advocacy. In *Mental health of immigrants and refugees,* edited by W. H. Holtzman and T. H. Bornemann, 299-328. Austin, TX: Hogg Foundation.

Burton, R. (1621/1927). *The anatomy of melancholy.* (Oxford: 1621), New York: Dell and Jordan-Smith.

Chesler, P. (1972). *Women and madness.* Garden City, NY: Doubleday.

d'Epinay, C. J. L. (1985). Depressed elderly women in Switzerland: An example of testing and generating theories. *The Gerontologist, 25*: 597-604.

Dixon, R. B. (1980). *Assessing the impact of development projects on women.* Washington, DC: Office of Women in Development and Office of Evaluation, U.S. Agency for International Development.

Fanshel, D. (1990, April). Preventive services for families, children and youth. Keynote Address, Annual Spring Conference for Field Instructors, Adelphi University, School of Social Work, Garden City, NY.

Friere, P. (1970/1982). *Pedagogy of the oppressed.* New York: The Continuum Publishing Corporation.

Friere, P. and D. Mercado. (1987). *Literacy: Reading the word and the world.* Westport, CN: Bergin and Garvey Publishers, Inc.

Goleman, D. (1990, April 10). Stereotypes of the sexes persisting in therapy. *New York Times*: Section C.

Hug, J., R. Jahan, and H. A. Begum. (1985). *Women and health.* Dhaka, Bangladesh: Women for Women.

Hultsch, D. F. and F. Deutsch. (1981). *Adult development and aging: A lifespan perspective.* New York: McGraw-Hill.

Islam, H. (1985). Women's mental health and occupational health hazard. In *Women and Health,* edited by J. Hug, R. Jahan, and H. A. Begum. Dhaka, Bangladesh: Women for Women.

Kaplan, M. (1983). A woman's view of DSM III. *American Psychologist, 38*: 786-792.

Law, M. (1985). Mental health: A shared concern of the international community. *Canadian Psychology, 26*: 275-281.

Lewis, O. (1965). *Tepotzlan: Village in Mexico.* New York: Holt, Rinehart and Winston.

Myerhoff, B. (1980). *Number our days.* New York: Touchstone Press.

National Institute of Mental Health. (1991). *Caring for people with severe mental disorders: A national plan of research to improve services.* DHHS Pub. No. (ADM) 91-1762. Washington, DC: Supt. of Documents, US Government Printing Office.

Raymond, C. (1991, June 12). Recognition of the gender differences in mental illness and its treatment prompts a call for more health research on problems specific to women. *The Chronicle of Higher Education.*

Schroeder, P. (1990). The social agenda for America. Keynote Address, 40th Anniversary Celebration and Conference, Adelphi University School of Social Work, November 9.

Simic, A. (1978). Winners and losers: Aging Yugoslavs in a changing world. In *Life's career–aging: Cultural variations in growing old*, edited by B. G. Myerhoff and A. Simic. Beverly Hills, CA: Sage Publications.

Troll, L. (1981, December). Implications for aging. Presentation for Five-College Gerontology Series, Amherst, MA: University of Massachusetts.

Velez-I, C. (1978). Youth and aging in Central Mexico: One day in the life of four families of migrants. In *Life's career–aging: Cultural variations in growing old*, edited by B. G. Myerhoff and A. Simic. Beverly Hills, CA: Sage Publications.

Viswanathan N. and J. W. Wetzel. (1993). Concepts and trends in mental health: A global overview. In *Mental health: The Indian scenario*, edited by A. Desai. Bombay: Tata Press.

Wetzel, J. W. (1984/1991). *Clinical handbook of depression.* New York: Gardner Press.

_____ (1986). Global issues and perspectives on working with women. *Affilia: Journal of Women and Social Work, 1*: 5-19.

_____ (1987). Mental health and rural women: An international analysis. *International Social Work, 30*: 43-59.

_____ (1991). Universal mental health classification systems: Reclaiming women's experience. *Affilia: Journal of Women and Social Work, 6*: 8-31.

_____ (1992). Profiles on women: A global perspective. *Social Work and Health Care, 16*: 13-27.

_____ (1993). *The world of women: In pursuit of human rights.* London, England: Macmillan Press, Ltd and New York: New York University Press.

World Health Organization. (1988). *Prevention of mental, neurological and psychosocial disorders.* Geneva, Switzerland.

Chapter 11

Building on the Romance of Women's Innate Strengths: Social Feminism and Its Influence at the Henry Street Settlement, 1893-1993

Barbara Levy Simon

I believe that women have something to contribute to the government that men have not, as men have something to contribute that women have not; that their traditions and their experiences combined will make for a more perfect understanding of community needs. (Wald 1914 [quoted in Coss 1989, 74-76])

INTRODUCTION

Nineteenth-century women, according to the belief of many a contemporaneous minister, philanthropist, and agent of charity in the U.S., were endowed by their Creator with a unique ability to soothe, to serve, and to salvage the poor and the vulnerable (Chambers 1986, 4; Hewitt 1984; Sklar 1973). Womanly duties were the

The author wants to express particular appreciation to Dr. Elinor Polansky, Assistant to the Henry Street Settlement's Executive Director, Daniel Kronenfeld, for her generous assistance in providing information about current activities at Henry Street and for her invaluable observations about its present priorities.

sacred duties of mothering, nursing, teaching, and uplifting (Koven and Michel 1990; Rendall 1990). These fundamental functions of womanhood were carried out at home and in volunteer work in religious benevolent societies, two domains unsullied by the contaminating influence of the profane, that is, by wages, competitive market relations, and secular authority.

With consummate artfulness, social feminists in the U.S. from the 1880s to the onset of World War I fought to expand the sphere of the sacred, rather than to transfer women into the realm of the profane. Society, they argued, was in desperate need of good mothering and "civic housekeeping" (Chambers 1986; Cohen and Hanagan 1991). Why not encourage women, social feminists like Jane Addams proposed, to bring the same generosity, empathy, and constancy to urban reform that they had brought historically to their caring for husbands, children, and aging parents? Stepping forward at a historical moment of extreme turbulence, one characterized by massive immigration, migration, industrialization, and urbanization, social feminists claimed that women were suited for two heroic roles at once. Their talents charged them with anchoring and sustaining their families, as they had always done. Now their womanly benevolence was also needed to save a fast-fragmenting society (Cohen and Hanagan 1991; Koven and Michel 1990).

Social feminists exploited and extended the metaphor of mothering in an era in which industrial capitalism was orphaning millions, stripping several continents of their resources, and shortening the lives of members of entire occupations and regions. Their message appealed to many inhabitants of a country nostalgic for a slower, kinder, and more comprehensible social order. The ideal of the nurturant mother who gently but firmly brings order to daily chaos was recognizable and compelling to millions of Americans in the tempestuous period between 1880 and 1920.

Social Feminism

Social feminists, according to historians Miriam Cohen and Michael Hanagan, were:

> those women (and sometimes men) who advocated women's rights as part of a broad agenda of social reform. As women's

rights advocates, they championed the cause of women's suffrage and the expansion of women's rights in the workplace,
but their highest priorities concerned the poor, both adult and
children. (1991, 470)

Social feminists viewed the battle for woman's suffrage and for the
multiplication of women's occupational, educational, professional,
and public roles as a necessary means to the overarching end of
improving the lot of endangered and impoverished women, children, and families, both at home and at work (Cott 1987, 1989).

In mounting their many social reform campaigns, social feminists organized local and state bodies that soon became national
leagues and organizations. In 1874, for example, the Woman's
Christian Temperance Union, whose motto was "Do Everything,"
became the first nationally organized social feminist body (Bordin
1990). Other national organizations soon followed. The General
Federation of Women's Clubs (GFWC) was founded in 1890; the
National Council of Jewish Women in 1893; the National Federation of Day Nurseries in 1895; the National Association of Colored
Women in 1896; the National Congress of Mothers (known in pres-
ent-day terms as the National Congress of Parents and Teachers) in
1897; and the National Federation of Settlements in 1911 (Koven
and Michel 1990; Leiby 1978). These groups organized a wide
variety of projects in the voluntary and public sectors for children,
families, and women throughout the country and actively lobbied at
local and state levels for expanded services for poor and dependent
people. For example, the GFWC, the National Congress of Mothers, and the National Federation of Settlements were central leaders
in state campaigns to win passage of mothers' and widows' pensions, the forerunner of federal Aid for Dependent Children (Abramovitz 1988; Katz 1986; Koven and Michel 1990). They achieved
success in 40 states by 1920, a remarkable accomplishment given
that in 1910 no states had mothers' pension legislation (Katz 1986;
Koven and Michel 1990).

Most social feminists of the Progressive Era held the view that
women were morally superior to men, having been equipped either
by nature, God, or cumulative experience with special capacities for
helping, teaching, and healing others, especially dependent others.

This view, rooted in the much older nineteenth-century ideologies of "the cult of true womanhood" and "republican motherhood" (as historians have characterized them), was held not only by religiously inspired social feminists like Frances Willard, founder of the Woman's Christian Temperance Union, but also by irreligious, politically inspired women like Florence Kelley, the leader of the National Consumer League and a founder of the U.S. Children's Bureau (Kerber 1980; Welter 1966). Kelley, the widely known social reformer who represented the left wing of social feminism, argued as late as 1923 that women had special wisdom in matters of social welfare and social justice (Kelley 1923; Koven and Michel 1990).

Despite their shared belief in woman-as-moral-force and their common commitments to improving the living and working conditions of vulnerable adults and children by means of woman's suffrage and the formal insertion of women into public and professional life, social feminists were a highly divergent group (Cott 1987). Some were militantly pro-union while others were not (Cohen and Hanagan 1991). Some were propelled into feminism and good works by spiritual impulses. Such was the case of Frances Perkins, a Progressive-Era social feminist who became U.S. Secretary of Labor under Franklin Roosevelt. Others were agnostics or atheists, inspired to action by secular and political identification with the disenfranchised. Florence Kelley and Mary van Kleeck, the influential director of industrial studies for the Russell Sage Foundation, embodied this strain. Some became strong advocates of Margaret Sanger's birth control movement; others opposed it or were ambivalent about it (Gordon 1976). For many social feminists, the interests of children came before the rights of women (Gordon 1990). For others, the interests and rights of children were considered inextricably bound to the political, economic, social, and sexual freedom and power of women, especially of poor women. (See Hutchison, Chapter 6, for a discussion of the linkages between women's and children's needs.)

Notwithstanding these internal differences, social feminists found common justification for their heterogeneous visions and activities in "maternalism," a term crafted by historians Koven and Michel (1990) to characterize a cluster of convictions which:

exalted women's capacity to mother and extended to society as a whole the values of care, nurturance, and morality. Maternalism always operated on two levels: it extolled the private virtues of domesticity while simultaneously legitimating women's public relationships to politics and the state, to community, workplace, and marketplace. (1079)

The maternalist views of many social feminists led them to concentrate their energies primarily on issues of maternal and child welfare. Toward that end, reformers like Julia Lathrop, Lillian Wald, and Grace Abbott, all settlement house activists who became nationally recognized architects of maternal and child health policies, helped secure widows' pensions, outlaw child labor, and shape the U.S. Children's Bureau, which mobilized Congress to pass and fund precedent-setting federal maternal and child health legislation in 1921 (Muncy 1991). Other social feminists, such as Frances Perkins, Rose Schneiderman of the National Women's Trade Union League, and Alice Hamilton, who was a founder of the field of industrial medicine, poured their talents into reducing the dangers to women and children's welfare that loomed at work.

Maternalist thinking created an indispensable ideological bridge between women's traditional devotion to family and their emergent leadership in the polity. By invoking their belief that women had special motherly insights and strengths upon which the entire society needed to draw in grappling with its multiple escalating crises, social feminists made citizens out of women by capitalizing on the very essentialism–the belief in the innate moral and temperamental distinctions between the genders–that had, until then, so effectively justified their total exclusion from citizenship and most paid work.

THE HENRY STREET SETTLEMENT

Nowhere were female citizens more eager to apply their "special capacities" to the polity than at the Henry Street Settlement on the Lower East Side of New York City. Lillian Wald founded the Henry Street Settlement in 1893, a year of a severe economic depression. She was a trained nurse who, while pursuing a medical degree, had volunteered to teach a weekly home-nursing class for immigrant women on Manhattan's Lower East Side. Horrified by her first encounters with the misery of tenement life and disillusioned with more traditional forms of nursing which she had encountered in nursing school and in an internship in a juvenile asylum, Wald quit medical school and, with her friend from nursing school, Mary Brewster, decided to "live in the neighborhood as nurses, identify ourselves with it socially, and, in brief, contribute to it our citizenship" (Wald 1915a, 8-9).

And what exactly did citizenship mean to Lillian Wald and Mary Brewster and the dozens of nurses, social workers, educators, union organizers, college student volunteers, social scientists, journalists, and social reformers who were soon drawn into their mushrooming social feminist experiment? How did their devotion to a social feminist version of Progressivism manifest itself in everyday life and work?

Social feminist expressions of citizenship at Henry Street and other similar settlements were direct offsprings of those modes of women's service that had been prized in nineteenth-century middle-class family life and Christian and Jewish benevolent associations (Smith-Rosenberg 1971, 1975). The self-sacrificing altruism, the round-the-clock responsiveness, and the total immersion in the daily rounds of caregiving that had characterized women's domestic lives of the mid-nineteenth century constituted the core characteristics of the role of women "settlers," as they called themselves, at settlement houses like Hull House in Chicago and Henry Street in New York City (Muncy 1991). Settlement houses, the primary incubators of twentieth-century public health care, community-based social services, and social reform, evolved a highly distinctive ethos of social feminist citizenship (Sklar 1985).

It is an ethos which merits detailed scrutiny because of its centrality to Progressive-Era social movements and because of its coevality with the beginnings of the social work profession. To understand the guiding beliefs of social feminist residents of the settlement house movement in the first two decades of the twentieth century is to comprehend one fundamental portion of the bedrock of both past and present feminism and past and present social work. The Henry Street Settlement, which is fast approaching its centennial year, serves as a microcosmic primer in social feminism's meaning and influence.

Social Feminist Citizenship

Service

Sustained service to others was the reason for being of the Henry Street settler in the early twentieth century, as had been true for her predecessor, the nineteenth-century's "Angel in the House." Yet at Henry Street, the service was public and visible rather than domestic and invisible. Headworker Lillian Wald, for example, established the world's first independent public health nursing service between 1893 and 1895 and then used Henry Street as a base to organize a national and international movement of public health nurses (Muncy 1991; Coss 1989).

A long list of other forms of highly visible public service followed. Wald took a leading role in shaping New York City's antituberculosis campaign, serving as a charter member of the first Committee on the Prevention of Tuberculosis of the Charity Organization Society of the City of New York in 1902 (Teller 1988). Together with her settlement colleagues in 1903, she created a milk station at Henry Street, which provided free sanitary milk to poor mothers with small children, maternal and child health workshops, and a system of home health visitation (Wald 1915a). This milk station, and others like it in urban settlement houses, later became the model for the maternal and child health program of the federal Sheppard-Towner Act of 1921 (Combs-Orme 1988).

Henry Street pilot projects at Public School #1 on the Lower East Side of New York and advocacy on the part of Henry Street staff with school system leaders led to numerous reforms in the public school system. The institutionalization of school playgrounds, school nursing, hot lunches, vocational guidance, afterschool recreational programs, classes for children with physical and mental disabilities, and kindergartens throughout New York's school system was a direct outgrowth of Henry Street residents' experimentation and politicking (Coss 1989; Wald 1915a).

This ceaseless devotion to public service and social reform in the first era of Henry Street Settlement's life was fueled, in part, by social feminism's late nineteenth-century essentialist version of womanhood. If one believed that women were endowed from birth with special gifts of charity and compassion and, furthermore, that these inborn gifts carried with them a particular moral charge to serve others, then it followed that one should do all within one's power to make more humane and healthy the housing, neighborhoods, schools, streets, hospitals, and workplaces of the United States.

Social feminism's call to women to save an industrializing society from itself was a message which harmonized gracefully with the teachings of Christian socialism, also known as Social Gospelism, a movement that spread widely within elite Northeastern colleges and universities and liberal Protestant denominations in the U.S. between 1870 and 1920. Leaders of Christian socialism, such as Edward Beecher, Washington Gladden, Richard Ely, and Walter Rauschenbusch, preached that the duty of Christians was not to seek a future place in heaven, but, instead, to create heaven on earth by working toward the immediate enactment in the U.S. of Christ's vision. To accomplish this, they proposed the abolition of poverty and capitalism through the construction of cooperative and collective systems of production and distribution (Cort 1988; Handy 1966).

Middle-class women college students in the 1870s and 1880s received a two-pronged charge. Social feminism taught them that, as women, they had a special vocation to serve a deteriorating social order, while Christian socialism directed them to honor the vision of Jesus by helping to eradicate poverty and injustice. These two allied messages received an especially warm reception among women college students educated in the three decades after the Civil War. They were the first cohort of females to attend the fledgling women's colleges and the handful of coeducational colleges and universities that existed at the time. As the first generation of American women permitted to earn liberal arts degrees equivalent to those of men, they saw themselves as bearing particular responsibilities to employ constructively the higher educations that had been denied to their mothers and grandmothers. However, upon graduating from college, they found that all of the major professions and vocations–the ministry, medicine, law, engineering, government service, diplomacy, architecture, the military, the professoriat, science, and business–were still completely closed to them. Small wonder that these pioneers sought to carve new paths to usefulness, recognition, and citizenship in institutions of their own making, like Hull House, Henry Street, Andover House, University Settlement, and many other settlements.

Knowledge Building

A second attribute of citizenship at Henry Street was the staff's commitment to discovering social scientific knowledge and making it accessible and understandable to their neighbors and key governmental policymakers. Like numerous counterparts in what historian Robyn Muncy has called the "female dominion in American reform," social feminists at the Henry Street Settlement vigorously endorsed the coupling of scientific discovery with popular education and the linking of scholarship with activism (Muncy 1991, 64). "A characteristic service of the settlement to the public grows out of its opportunities for creating and informing public opinion," wrote Lillian Wald (1915a, 310).

With its passion for popularizing knowledge and for yoking research to advocacy, female and male social researchers in the female-led settlement house movement were guided by a markedly different epistemology than was the male-dominated academy. At the very time that Progressive-Era leaders like Lillian Wald, Grace Abbott, and Paul Kellogg, a reporter who became a leading social researcher and advocate for vulnerable groups, were forging the intimate links among good service, good data, and good government, most university-based social scientists, almost all of whom were men, were distancing themselves and their research from social reform movements. They were doing so in consonance with their increasing devotion to positivistic "scientism," Dorothy Ross' (1991) term for an approach to knowledge building that defined science only by its method. Natural scientific method rapidly became the sole standard of excellence in the emergent social sciences. Rather than creating a cluster of research methods that grew out of the particularities of the varied contexts, purposes, and constraints of social scientific discovery, academically based social scientists looked outside their own disciplines to the far older and more prestigious natural sciences (Ross 1991). The carefully controlled conditions and procedural requirements of the chemist's or biologist's laboratory experiment became the model for investigation in social science.

Meanwhile, the women and the minority of men at Henry Street and other leading settlements, the U.S. Children's Bureau, and the emergent schools of social welfare took a decidedly different route to the construction of knowledge. They gathered quantitative and qualitative data about social problems *in situ*, that most uncontrolled of states. From home visits, physical examinations, clinical interviews, historical archives, neighborhood surveys, community studies, and the records of public schools, trade unions, municipal and county offices of vital statistics, immigration centers, and charity organization societies, settlers derived information about the everyday conditions and problems of the urban poor. At Henry Street, as at other major settlement houses, data rapidly were put to use in educational groups and courses with parents and adolescents, in discussions with adults and children during home visits and health examinations, in public health pamphlets, and in a cascade of formal testimonies and reports submitted to local, state, and federal officials, governing bodies, and public interest organizations.

The topics of Henry Street's research were as various as the forms in which the findings were communicated to the public. The conditions of new immigrants, newborns, child laborers, older residents of the Lower East Side, "tuberculars," prostitutes, pregnant women, and juvenile delinquents were subjects of study, testimony, lobbying, and reporting by Henry Street residents. Between 1893 and 1920, Henry Street staff investigated, documented, and publicized the circumstances of mothers who were widows, women workers, the unemployed, workers in the garment trades, unvaccinated and vaccinated children, children with "mental defects," tenements, public schools, recreational sites, street sanitation, night courts, and factories (Chambers 1973, 1986; Coss 1989; Davis 1967; Muncy 1991; Wald 1915a, 1934; Woods and Kennedy 1911, 1922).

Service provision, data collection, reportage, and advocacy were an interlocking quartet of activities that possessed, for the Henry Street staff, an internal integrity that would have been flawed if any of the four functions had been missing. To collect data without providing service or vice versa was unthinkable. Also inconceivable was the prospect of collecting information about pressing social and psychological problems without spreading the word about their findings in the most vigorous manner possible to the public and to relevant governmental and voluntary bodies. It was equally unimaginable for them to testify or advocate without an authoritative data base from which to draw generalizations and recommendations.

This settlement house belief in the indissoluble interdependence of serving, researching, publicizing, and lobbying sprang primarily, in Robyn Muncy's (1991) words, from "a gender-specific need to reconcile their professional goals with Victorian ideals of womanhood" (45). Since altruism had been their justification for moving women's "special virtues" into the public domain, service to others remained their basis for conducting research. As a consequence, a model of inquiry which separated knowledge development from service and politics was incompatible with their conception of womanhood, of female professionalism, of female citizenship, and of social feminism (Furner 1975; Ross 1979).

Cultural Diversity

For Henry Street staff, public service entailed far more than attention to the material necessities of life; it also required attentiveness to the cultural and aesthetic longings of their Lower East Side immigrant neighbors. Those longings, thought Wald and her staff, encompassed the entire spectrum of the music, arts, language, and crafts of neighbors' own countries of origin and of the heritage of Western Europe and the United States. Lillian Wald embedded in Henry Street's structure and repertoire of activities her double-barreled resistance to two movements which she despised: the Americanization movement of the second and third decade of the twentieth century and the effort to stratify the universe of the arts by removing "high" art from arenas of popular culture and from popular access.

"Great is our loss when a shallow Americanism is accepted by the newly arrived immigrant, more particularly by the children, and their national traditions and heroes are ruthlessly pushed aside," wrote Wald (1915a, 303). To help prevent that loss of ethnic heritage, Wald consciously borrowed, from Japan and Paris, the tradition of cultural street fairs, instituting a Fourth-of-July street festival and dance to commemorate the twentieth anniversary of Henry Street in 1913 (Wald 1915a, 1934). Thousands of costumed people, representing dozens of racial and ethnic groups from New York City, took part in the street fair (Coss 1989). It became an annual celebration along with other seasonal Henry Street Festivals in the streets.

Classes for neighborhood children in drama, music, poetry, and dance were introduced in Henry Street's second decade of operation. In 1915, the Neighborhood Playhouse was formed at the Settlement, which became a nationally recognized arena for poetry readings and the production and performance of drama, music, and dance (Wald 1915a). Works created by neighbors of Henry Street; classical and experimental plays by well-known African-American, Jewish, Irish, Italian, and Hindu writers; and the works of Shakespeare, Whitman, Ibsen, Shaw, and Galsworthy were presented, earning, on many occasions, critical acclaim (Wald 1915a; 1934).

That Henry Street's mission encompassed "roses" as well as "bread" was partly an artifact of the continuity between Victorian conceptions and enactments of womanhood and those of Progressive-Era social feminism. One of the few areas of human knowledge to which nineteenth-century middle-class women in the United States had been exposed in a sustained way was that of literature, music, the arts, and the French language. Middle-class mothers were expected to educate their children in the fine arts and literature, as well as the Bible. Genteel womanliness in bourgeois families was demonstrated through women's performance of music, writing of poetry, and recitation of classical literature to family friends. A necessary emblem of social respectability for a husband was a home equipped with a piano or harp, a library, servants, and a wife whom he had freed from wage labor and some aspects of household labor so that she had sufficient time to raise cultured children and ornament the household with her own tasteful gentility (Berg 1978; Sklar 1973; Stansell 1987).

The women who founded and shaped Henry Street Settlement had been raised in middle-class households during the decade following the Civil War. In their childhood and adolescence, literature and the arts had been fundamental sources of nourishment, exposure, and inspiration in an era which offered girls few avenues of exploration and expression. Wald and her Victorian-bred female colleagues carried with them into adult life a firsthand appreciation of the liberating force of the arts. In locating drama, dance, music, crafts, and art at the center of Henry Street's priorities, they merged their own personal knowledge of the freeing powers of cultural activity with a lesson learned from the socialism of Florence Kelley and others, that art is not a class-bound privilege, but is instead a universal resource and entitlement (Chambers 1963; Sklar 1986).

Serving the public by creating a more humane commonwealth, integrating social scientific research with service and advocacy, and melding cultural commitments with campaigns for social justice were the trinity of ambitions that drove Henry Street social feminists. Their underlying belief in the special capacities and responsibilities of women to salvage society constituted the cementing force of the community of believers at Henry Street for four decades.

Social Feminism's Influence at Henry Street: 1933-1993

In 1933, ill health forced 67-year old Lillian Wald to retire as Henry Street's headworker, a position she had held for 40 years. Before resigning, Wald recruited her own successor. She selected Helen Hall, a social worker and social activist who had attended the New York School for Social Work (now the Columbia University School of Social Work), organized a settlement in Westchester County, New York, performed relief work in France, Alsace, the Philippines, and China during World War I, and served as headworker for 11 years at University House, a settlement in Philadelphia (Hall 1971; Trolander 1975).

Wald had managed the nearly impossible–she had found a successor to run Henry Street who would quickly prove to be as much of a social reform visionary, community servant, and national leader as she herself had been. Within the first year of her leadership at Henry Street, Helen Hall became a leading national voice for federal relief programs, testifying and lobbying in Washington, DC for cash relief, federal employment projects and insurance, and for legal protections against evictions for the unemployed (Trolander 1975). From 1935 through 1940, she served as president of the National Federation of Settlements, a body whose vigorous and informed advocacy helped accelerate the onset and expand the scope of New Deal employment and social security programs.

In 1935, Hall married Paul U. Kellogg, the editor, since 1912, of the *Survey,* a widely read publication of the Russell Sage Foundation that explored social welfare and social policy issues, social movements of disenfranchised people, and campaigns for human rights. Hall's predecessor, Lillian Wald, considered Kellogg her "old friend and comrade in numerous adventures" (Wald 1934, *x*). Kellogg moved into Henry Street where his new wife, Headworker Hall, was already in residence. There they resided together for a quarter century until Kellogg's death in 1958.

Throughout their marriage and after, Hall led the Henry Street Settlement through multiple phases of its existence, in which she and her staff pioneered and tested out a variety of community services, social reform strategies, and community arts programs that came to be recognized nationally as prototypical social and cultural experiments. During the years of her leadership, Henry Street conducted numerous studies of housing, unemployment, and gang patterns; created a neighborhood credit union in 1937; a community Mental Hygiene Clinic in 1941; the Predelinquent Gang Project in 1955; the Lower Eastside Neighborhoods Association in 1954; and Mobilization for Youth in 1959, which soon became the model for the next decade's federal antipoverty programs (Hall 1971). Hall's leadership also ensured the continuation of community-based experimental theater at Henry Street and the creation and licensing of Alwin Nikolais' Dance School and the Henry Street Music School, under the direction of Grace Spofford, former dean of the Curtis Institute of Music (Hall 1971).

In her 34 years as headworker, Helen Hall's code of citizenship for herself and her settlement closely resembled that of Lillian Wald. She insisted upon involving the settlement in incessant and multiform public service; in ongoing data collection that served as the basis for the formulation and modification of federal, state, and local legislation and regulations; and in the sustenance and multiplication of the settlement's major cultural projects.

Yet, these three forms of citizenship that were concocted originally by turn-of-the-century social feminists endured long after the core beliefs which had inspired their formation died. Notions of the moral superiority and special strengths of women did not survive in the written discourse or recorded speeches of the post-Wald era at Henry Street. Nor did articulation of the desirability of women's "mothering" society. Helen Hall, in her retrospective account of her work at Henry Street, *Unfinished Business,* described herself from age ten on as a "passionate adherent of women's suffrage." (Hall 1971, 5). Nonetheless, she made no other reference to social feminism or any other form of feminism in a 354-page book that is otherwise replete with references to important social causes, such as the fight against red-baiting, the formation of unemployed councils in the 1930s, and the importance of working toward racial equity and equality (Hall 1971).

Maternalism, social feminism, and, more generally, feminism itself vanished as coherent and explicit ideologies at Henry Street after Wald, just as they did in the public at large during the exigencies of the Great Depression and during the fragmented and attenuated phase of the U.S. women's movement in the 1940s and 1950s (Cott 1987; Ferree and Hess 1985). Belief in women's special ability and responsibility to reform the commonwealth held little appeal to a generation of voting women who were fully engaged, alongside men, in New Deal reforms or socialist or communist activities. Maternalist strains of social feminist thought, especially, had outlived their usefulness and were perceived as relics of a bygone era. Notions of women's particular aptitudes appeared old-fashioned and "unscientific" to reform or revolution-minded women and men of the 1930s, who were busy staffing the burgeoning programs and professions of the expanding welfare state (Koven and Michel 1990).

By the time of Wald's retirement in 1933, widespread unemployment, homelessness, and hunger preoccupied the settlement house staff at Henry Street. Gender-linked rights, disadvantage, suffering, and injustice disappeared as salient categories of professional concern there until the early 1970s, except for the hard and sustained work that Helen Hall and her staff put into the creation of child care centers for working mothers during and after World War II (Hall 1971). Nonetheless, one element of social feminism did endure at Henry Street–the three-tiered version of citizenship that had so passionately consumed the energies of the likes of Lillian Wald, Mary Brewster, and Florence Kelley.

Henry Street During the Past Quarter Century

If Lillian Wald could return to evaluate Henry Street now, would she find her code of citizenship still honored in daily practice by its staff? Is, for example, public service still a principle commitment of Henry Street, and are the data collected in the course of serving neighbors used in campaigns for social reforms? The record suggests clear evidence that this first and second plank of Wald's ethos of citizenship remain intact.

For example, staff members' desire to reduce homelessness and wife battering led them in 1972, to establish Henry Street's Urban Family Center, a model transitional shelter for housing approximately 90 homeless families and battered women in temporary individual apartments in six buildings, each with a live-in social worker who offers vocational, educational, and personal counseling. While at the Center, individuals and families obtain job training, independent living skills, and basic education. For two decades, Henry Street has succeeded in moving 95% of its families in the Urban Family Center into permanent housing (Simpson 1987).

Staff members gather information from residents and from their own experiences in working at the Urban Family Center about the causes and familial consequences of urban homelessness and the range of economic, psychological, and social supports people need to regain their own homes and jobs. With this information, Henry Street staff devised the Shelter Management Training Program, which educates social workers in homeless shelters from other parts of the country to move people from homelessness into stable independence. Data collected from the Urban Family Center are also used in testimony and official reports submitted to city, state, and federal authorities.

Henry Street also took early action in response to the AIDS epidemic. Its Community Consultation Center, a state-certified mental health clinic, is an official provider of AIDS mental health services for the Lower East Side of Manhattan and has pioneered in developing a counseling and bereavement program for children whose parents have AIDS (Henry Street Settlement 1990).

As is true in its work with homeless families and battered women, the staff of Henry Street's Community Consultation Center view adult and children clients as important sources of information about the nature, scope, and effects of the AIDS epidemic. In keeping with Wald's earlier efforts against tuberculosis, influenza, and unsanitary milk for infants, Henry Street staff members rely on their experiences as service deliverers and advocates on the Lower East Side to guide their involvement in international, national, and local health campaigns to slow and stop the spread of AIDS.

Public service, research, and advocacy also go on in relation to other key populations. Mobile and homebound older residents of the Lower East Side, pregnant teens, adolescents who have left school, preschool-aged children, illiterate adults, children in foster care, and unemployed single mothers are a partial listing of the continuum of groups engaged by Henry Street programs, studies, and lobbying.

Finally, Wald would wonder, does Henry Street sustain its commitment to the arts in the neighborhood? In 1991, the Gallery at Henry Street's Louis Abrons Arts Center won its fourth national grant from the Institute of Museum Services. The Gallery has used its four awards to expand its outreach to families, children, and elders (Henry Street Settlement 1991).

Henry Street's Playhouse, Music Program, and Arts Center continue to sponsor classes, workshops, exhibitions, and productions in opera, theater, dance, visual arts, and music. The Master Arts Series promotes the work of little-known but mature artists through its career retrospectives. In 1991, the Settlement's Folk Art Series sponsored an Asian-American Outreach Program, a five-week festival of Chinese-American arts and crafts. Additionally, Henry Street's Arts-in-Education program exposes 15,000 children each year in surrounding community school districts to arts education in their own classrooms (Henry Street Settlement, 1990). It would appear that Wald's requirement concerning a settlement house's cultural responsibility to its surrounding community is being honored in full.

CONCLUSION

In a 1915 address at Vassar College, Lillian Wald declared:

> The roots of public social service and responsibility are deeply planted in the nature of woman and what we are witnessing in our generation are the new manifestations of her unchanged and unchanging interests and devotions.
>
> Her circle of human experience and human feeling has widened. . . . She is capable of doing more, of being more than at any time (Wald, 1915b [reprinted in Coss 1989, 84]).

It was woman's nature, Wald believed, to serve more than her family; the whole of humankind required her attentions and talents. The first third of the 100-year history of the Henry Street Settlement serves as detailed testimony to the catalytic force of gender consciousness among Progressive-Era social feminists. Their shared faith in the romance of women's particular inborn worth inspired them to build enduring institutions of service, reform, and culture against significant odds.

Wald's conception of maternalist feminism has long been abandoned by most feminists and most social workers, even as her version of feminist citizenship continues to form the bedrock of many a contemporary project and agency. Her essentialist premise, that women are innately superior to men in their facility for caring for others, has been discounted in many quarters as an artifact of a Victorian past that was contorted by gender-segregated spheres and roles. Nonetheless, maternalist feminism of a social constructionist variety has grown up in place of essentialist maternalism during the past two decades of resurgent feminism. Not women's genetic makeup, but industrialized cultures' gendered forms of childraising and women's daily rounds of parenting, caregiving, and befriending have developed in them a greater capacity and sense of responsibility for nurturance than most men have developed, claim Jean Baker Miller (1986), Nancy Chodorow (1978, 1989), Carol Gilligan (1982, 1990), Nel Noddings (1984), and many others. The practice of mothering, with its particular activities, aims, and requirements, has created a way of thinking and knowing that is distinctly "maternal," Sara Ruddick (1989) suggests.

Contemporary feminist social workers have cast a wide net throughout the humanities, the social and behavioral sciences, and the multidisciplinary world of women's studies in their search for knowledge that will help them make sense of the marked and sustained differences between the behavioral proclivities and life chances of men and boys as a group and those of women and girls as a group. Whether working with teenaged single mothers on welfare, aged widows, battered women, or incest survivors, social workers who are attempting to assist women and girl clients in restoring and empowering themselves are doing so with the help of multiple "feminist frameworks" of analysis (Bricker-Jenkins, Hooyman, and Gottlieb 1991; Jaggar and Rothenberg, 1984). These varied paradigms through which to view relations between women and men are products of a turbulent contemporary women's movement and an equally turbulent domain of women's studies in the academy, whose participants have come to understand the salience of the intersections of gender, race, age, class, sexuality, religion, and disability in shaping the meanings, constraints, and choices in women's daily lives.

Yet, despite feminist social workers' wide-ranging pursuit of intellectual and political inspirations for their work and despite earnest efforts to draw on the strengths of female clients and colleagues, one major resource is commonly overlooked. Neglected is the rich history of prior social work with women. Neglected is the wealth of example provided by women clients of earlier eras who have sought to overcome abandonment, psychological depression, poverty, sexually transmitted diseases, alcoholism, and a myriad of other difficulties.

To study the history of women is, in part, to excavate the traditions of surviving, healing, resisting, enduring, and transforming that women clients and women social workers have accrued over time in response to every imaginable kind of internal and external challenge. Some of the dreams, visions, and plans of our predecessors are still accessible to those of us who would look. Also retrievable are some of their strategies, interventive approaches, and methods of framing, assessing, and solving problems. The nature, scope, and causes of their major failures as well as their memorable successes as clients and as workers are still available to us, in varying degrees. Some of their assumptions, ideas, and philosophies can be recovered.

However, it is important to ask, why take the trouble to do so? Why, in the midst of the exigencies of responding to clients' escalating crises, stop to look back at the workers and clients of a different era? Why discuss Lillian Wald's perspectives on women, service, knowledge-building, and cultural diversity in a historical moment in which the AIDS epidemic, homelessness, the impoverishment of women, violence, and unemployment preoccupy us and the clients to whom we are accountable?

We look back in order to increase the visibility of women's leadership and of women's paid and unpaid labor. We look back in order to decrease clients' sense of isolation and marginalization by making more available to them the accounts of others who have faced and negotiated similar circumstances in the past. Perhaps most importantly, we look back in order to replenish the reservoir of our imagination, courage, and hopefulness, three elements that undoubtedly will prove to be as indispensable to social work practice in the next century as they were during the nineteenth and twentieth.

REFERENCES

Abramovitz, M. (1988). *Regulating the lives of women.* Boston: South End Press.

Berg, B. J. (1978). *The remembered gate: Origins of American feminism, the woman and the city, 1800-1860.* New York: Oxford University Press.

Bordin, R. (1990). *Women and temperance: The quest for power and liberty.* 2nd ed. New Brunswick, NJ: Rutgers University Press.

Bricker-Jenkins, M., N. Hooyman, and N. Gottlieb, eds. (1991). *Feminist social work practice in clinical settings.* Newbury Park, CA: Sage.

Chambers, C. A. (1963). *Seedtime of reform: American social service and social action, 1918-1933.* Minneapolis: University of Minnesota Press.

————— (1973). *Paul U. Kellogg and the survey: Voices for social welfare and social justice.* Minneapolis: University of Minnesota Press.

_____ (1986). Women in the creation of the profession of social work. *Social Service Review, 60*: 1-33.

Chodorow, N. (1978). *The reproduction of mothering*. Berkeley: University of California Press.

_____ (1989). *Feminism and psychoanalytic theory*. New Haven: Yale University Press.

Cohen, M. and M. Hanagan. (1991). The politics of gender and the making of the welfare state, 1900-1940: A comparative perspective. *Journal of Social History, 24*: 469-484.

Combs-Orme, T. (1988). Infant mortality and social work: Legacy of success. *Social Service Review, 62*: 83-102.

Cort, J. C. (1988). *Christian socialism: An informal history*. Maryknoll, NY: Orbis.

Coss, C., ed. (1989). *Lillian D. Wald: Progressive activist*. New York: Feminist Press at The City University of New York.

Cott, N. F. (1987). *The grounding of modern feminism*. New Haven: Yale University Press.

_____ (1989). What's in a name? The limits of "Social Feminism;" or, Expanding the vocabulary of women's history. *Journal of American History, 76*: 809-929.

Davis, A. F. (1967). *Spearheads for reform: The social settlements and the progressive movement, 1890-1914*. New York: Oxford University Press.

Ferree, M. and B. Hess. (1985). *Controversy and coalition: The new feminist movement*. Boston: Twayne.

Furner, M. O. (1975). *Advocacy and objectivity: A crisis in the professionalization of American social science, 1865-1905*. Lexington, KY: University of Kentucky Press.

Gilligan, C. (1982). *In a different voice: Psychological theory and women's development*. Cambridge, MA: Harvard University Press.

_____ (1990). *Mapping the moral domain*. Cambridge, MA: Harvard University Press.

Gordon, L. (1976). *Woman's body, woman's rights* New York: Penguin.

_____ (1990). Putting children first: U.S. welfarism in the 20th century. Paper presented at Columbia University Institute for Research on Women and Gender, November 9, 1990, Conference on Work and Family Policy.

Hall, H. (1971). *Unfinished business in neighborhood and nation*. New York: Macmillan.

Handy, R. T., ed. (1966). *The social gospel in America, 1870-1920*. New York: Oxford University Press.

Henry Street Settlement. (1990). *Biennial Report*. New York: Henry Street Settlement.

_____ (1991, Spring). *News from Henry Street*. New York: Henry Street Settlement.

Hewitt, N. A. (1984). *Women's activism and social change: Rochester, New York, 1822-1872.* Ithaca, NY: Cornell University Press.

Jaggar, A. and P. Rothenberg. (1984). *Feminist frameworks: Alternative theoretical accounts of the relations between women and men.* 2nd ed. New York: McGraw-Hill.

Katz, M. B. (1986). *In the shadow of the poorhouse.* New York: Basic Books.

Kelley, F. (1923). Should women be treated identically with men by the law? *American Review, 3:* 277.

Kerber, L. (1980). *Women of the Republic: Intellect and ideology in Revolutionary America.* Chapel Hill, NC: University of North Carolina Press.

Koven, S. and S. Michel. (1990). Womanly duties: Maternalist policies and the origins of welfare states in France, Germany, and the United States, 1880-1920. *American Historical Review, 95:* 1076-1108.

Leiby, J. (1978). *A history of social welfare and social work in the United States.* New York: Columbia University Press.

Miller, J. B. (1986). *Toward a new psychology of women.* 2nd ed. Boston: Beacon.

Muncy, R. (1991). *Creating a female dominion in American reform, 1890-1935.* New York: Oxford University Press.

Noddings, N. (1984). *Caring.* Berkeley: University of California Press.

Rendall, J. (1990). *The origins of modern feminism: Women in Britain, France and the United States, 1780-1860.* 2nd ed. Chicago, IL: Lyceum.

Ross, D. (1979). The development of the social sciences. In *The organization of knowledge in Modern America, 1860-1920,* edited by A. Loeson and J. Voss, 107-138. Baltimore: Johns Hopkins University Press.

———— (1991). *The origins of American social science.* New York: Cambridge University Press.

Ruddick, S. (1989). *Maternal thinking.* New York: Ballantine.

Simpson, J. C. (January 23, 1987). Enduring service: A 'Settlement House' has new constituency but same old mission. *The Wall Street Journal, 209,* 16: 1 & 11.

Sklar, K. K. (1973). *Catharine Beecher: A study in American domesticity.* New Haven: Yale University Press.

———— (1985). Hull House in the 1890's: A community of women reformers. *Signs, 10:* 658-677.

———— ed. (1986). Introduction. In *Notes of sixty years: The autobiography of Florence Kelley,* 25-30. Chicago: University of Chicago Press.

Smith-Rosenberg, C. (1971). *Religion and the rise of the American city.* Ithaca: Cornell University Press.

———— (1975). The female world of love and ritual: Relations among women in nineteenth-century America. *Signs, 1:* 1-29.

Stansell, C. (1987). *City of women: Sex and class in New York, 1789-1860.* Urbana, IL: University of Illinois Press.

Teller, M. E. (1988). *The tuberculosis movement.* New York: Greenwood.

Trolander, J. A. (1975). *Settlement houses and the Great Depression.* Detroit: Wayne State University Press.

Wald, L. (1914). Suffrage. Speech of February, 1914. In *Lillian Wald,* edited by C. Coss (1989), 74-76. New York: Feminist Press.

———— (1915a). *The house on Henry Street.* New York: Henry Holt.

———— (1915b). New aspects of old responsibilities. Address to Vassar College students of October 12, 1915. In *Lillian D. Wald, Progressive activist,* edited by C. Coss (1989), 76-84. New York: The Feminist Press at the City University of New York.

———— (1934). *Windows on Henry Street.* Boston: Little, Brown.

Welter, B. (1966). The cult of true womanhood, 1820-1860. *American Quarterly, 18:* 151-174.

Woods, R. A. and A. J. Kennedy, eds. (1911). *Handbook of settlements.* New York: Russell Sage.

———— (1922). *The settlement horizon: A national estimate.* New York: Russell Sage.

Index

Abbott, Grace, 136,251,255
Abortion rights
  choice of, 9
  Roe v. Wade, 10
Abramovitz, M., 47,65,136-140,144,
  249
Achtenberg, R., 198
Addams, Jane, 1, 186,200,248
Administration on Aging, 159-161,
  165
Adoption system, 40-41
African-American women
  Combahee River Collective
    feminist group of, 21
  elderly income statistics and, 161,
    165
  family adjustment process and,
    118,125,128
  National Association of Colored
    Women and, 249
  never-married women of, 38
  reality of, 18
  as single women-headed families,
    35-36,144
  of Women's Employment Network
    (WEN), 90
Aid to Families with Dependent
  Children (AFDC), 37,57
  evaluation of, statistics regarding,
    45-46,61-62,81
  forerunners of, 249
  Job Opportunities and Basic Skills
    Training Program (JOBS), 50-
    51,66-70
  Omnibus Budget Reconciliation
    Act (OBRA) and, 60-61
  original recipients of, 58-59
  Work Incentive Program (WIN)
    and, 59-60

Aid to Families with Dependent
  Children–Unemployed Parent
  (AFDC-UP), 37,59,64-65,145
Alcoff, Linda, 20-21
Alcohol, Drug Abuse and Mental
  Health Administration
  (ADAMHA) , 234
Alimony, 6
Allen, Jeffner, 21
American Association of Retired
  Persons, 159-161,165
American Psychiatric Association,
  196
The Anatomy of Melancholy
  (Burton), 231
Andersen, R., 189
Andersen, T., 202
Anderson, H., 202-203
Anderson, P., 138
Andover House, 255
Antiabortion/antichoice. *See*
  Reproductive rights
Aptheker, B., 18

Baker-Miller, J., 212
Balchen, A., 143
Ballou, M., 237
Bandler, J., 166
Bandura, A., 95,97
Bane, M. J., 62
Bart, P., 231
Bauman, R., 182-183
Beecher, Edward, 254
Beechey, V., 48
Belenky, M. F., 13,181,185,222
Bengston, V., 164
Berg, B. J., 258-259
Berger, P. L., 11-12,213